QUESTIONS AND ANSWERS

Contents

TIGER BOOKS INTERNATIONAL

Part One

ANIMAL QUIZBOOK

Paul Dowswell

Edited by Judy Tatchell

Designed by Ruth Russell

Illustrated by Ian Jackson and Rachel Lockwood

Additional illustrations by Chris Lyon and John Shackell

Consultant: Gillian Standring

Contents

About Part One

There are over two million different kinds of animal in the world. Even baking deserts, the frozen poles, and the deepest oceans have their own unique inhabitants. Part One of the book looks at how animals behave, and how they cope with the different environments in which they live.

How to do the quizzes

Throughout the book, there are quiz questions to answer as you go along, printed in italic type, *like this*. Some of the questions rely on your general knowledge, others have clues elsewhere on the page. Keep a note of your answers and check them against the answers on page 28-31.

The Animal Megaquiz

On pages 26-27 is the Animal Megaquiz – a set of ten quick quizzes to test you on what you have read in Part One. You can check your answers on page 32.

The animal world

There are an extraordinary number of different sizes, shapes and colours in the animal world. These two pages look at the main types of animals and how they fit into their environment.

Scientists have divided the animal world into various groups. Animals in the same group, or class, have similar features, and behave in similar ways. A particular kind of animal, such as a lion or an ostrich, is known as a species. Some of the main groups are shown here.

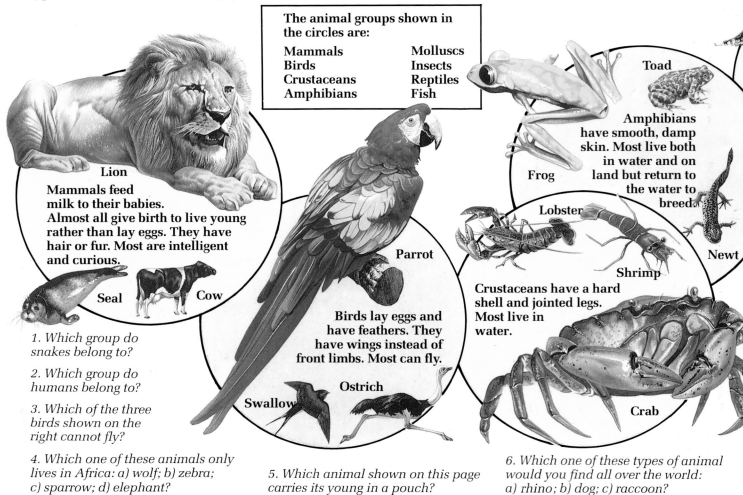

The animal groups shown in the circles are:

Mammals	Molluscs
Birds	Insects
Crustaceans	Reptiles
Amphibians	Fish

Lion
Mammals feed milk to their babies. Almost all give birth to live young rather than lay eggs. They have hair or fur. Most are intelligent and curious.

Seal

Cow

Parrot

Birds lay eggs and have feathers. They have wings instead of front limbs. Most can fly.

Swallow

Ostrich

Toad

Frog

Amphibians have smooth, damp skin. Most live both in water and on land but return to the water to breed.

Newt

Lobster

Shrimp

Crustaceans have a hard shell and jointed legs. Most live in water.

Crab

1. Which group do snakes belong to?

2. Which group do humans belong to?

3. Which of the three birds shown on the right cannot fly?

4. Which one of these animals only lives in Africa: a) wolf; b) zebra; c) sparrow; d) elephant?

5. Which animal shown on this page carries its young in a pouch?

6. Which one of these types of animal would you find all over the world: a) rhino; b) dog; c) raccoon?

Why are some animals only found in certain parts of the world?

Many animals, such as sparrows, beetles and rats, are found in every continent. They can fly, or have been carried on boats. They all eat a variety of foods, and can cope with different climates. Other animals are only found in certain areas. Here are three reasons why.

The three-toed sloth eats cecropia tree leaves, found in South American forests.

The polar bear's thick fur coat suits a cold environment.

The kangaroos of Australia could live elsewhere. The ocean between Australia and the rest of the world prevents them from travelling.

1. They only eat food found in the area they live in.

2. They can only live within a certain range of temperatures.

3. They cannot travel long distances because of barriers like oceans or mountains.

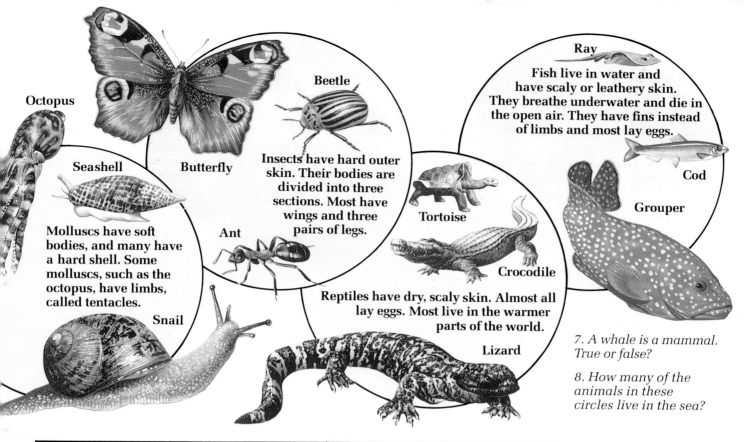

Octopus

Seashell

Butterfly

Beetle

Ant

Insects have hard outer skin. Their bodies are divided into three sections. Most have wings and three pairs of legs.

Molluscs have soft bodies, and many have a hard shell. Some molluscs, such as the octopus, have limbs, called tentacles.

Snail

Tortoise

Crocodile

Reptiles have dry, scaly skin. Almost all lay eggs. Most live in the warmer parts of the world.

Lizard

Ray

Fish live in water and have scaly or leathery skin. They breathe underwater and die in the open air. They have fins instead of limbs and most lay eggs.

Cod

Grouper

7. A whale is a mammal. True or false?

8. How many of the animals in these circles live in the sea?

How do animals fit into their environment?

Animal species can change their appearance and behaviour to fit their environment. This can take thousands of years, and is called evolution. Here you can see how two different sorts of fish have evolved to fit into two completely different kinds of environment.

Tall, narrow bodies help angelfish shelter in coral reefs.

Muscular bodies help barracuda swim huge distances in the ocean.

9. Which one of these is a fish: a) starfish; b) dolphin; c) salmon?

10. Which scientist first suggested the theory of evolution: a) Charles Darwin; b) Galileo; c) Isaac Newton?

Did you know?

Three-quarters of all known animal species are insects. A third of all known insect species are beetles.

11. Which one of these is not an insect: a) moth; b) termite; c) iguana; d) locust?

What are food chains?

All animals need to eat plants or other animals to give them energy to survive. Plant-eating animals, called herbivores, are eaten by meat-eating animals (carnivores). These may be eaten in turn by other carnivores. This sequence is called a food chain. Within the chain, energy from food passes from one living thing to another. An animal that hunts another animal is called a predator. The animal that is hunted is called prey.

Here is a simple food chain, showing who eats who.

Domestic cat

Plant **Greenfly** **Blue tit**

12. Is a lion a carnivore or a herbivore?

13. When one kind of animal dies out this is called: a) extinction; b) exhaustion; c) exhibitionism.

14. The Ancient Egyptians worshipped cats. True or false?

15. Can you put this food chain in the right order? thrush caterpillar fox cabbage

3

Animal families

Apart from staying alive, producing the next generation is an animal's strongest instinct. These two pages look at how animals care for their young.

How many babies do animals have?

The number of eggs or babies that an animal has depends on the type of animal. The giant clam makes millions of eggs every year. Most are eaten by other animals but a few may survive. The sperm whale, though, only has one baby every three or four years.

The clam releases millions of eggs into the water around it.

The clam does nothing to look after its offspring. The whale, on the other hand, provides its calf with milk for at least two years.

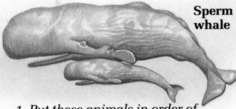

Sperm whale

1. Put these animals in order of size: a) elephant; b) sperm whale; c) giant clam.

How do penguins hatch their eggs?

In order to hatch, birds' eggs need warmth. In Antarctica, the male emperor penguin warms an egg by perching it on its feet under a fold of skin. This keeps it away from the frozen ground. The penguin stays still over the egg for eight weeks waiting for it to hatch.

Emperor penguin

Once hatched, the chick stays next to the warmth of the parent's body.

2. Warming an egg to hatch it is called: a) incineration; b) invitation; c) incubation.

Young penguins too big to shelter under their parents, huddle together to keep warm.

3. What do penguins eat?

4. Penguins fly north for the winter. True or false?

Why do baby animals look different from adults?

Some young animals have different body coverings from the parents. Ducklings, for example, are covered with soft, brown feathers called down. Down keeps them warm and is good camouflage. As they get older, they grow stiffer feathers which help them to fly.

5. Which is bigger, a duck's egg or a hen's egg?

A young emperor angelfish looks very different from an adult. This is to stop an adult mistaking it for a rival for food and mates, and fighting it.

6. Which one of these is not a real fish: a) angelfish; b) butterflyfish; c) flying fish; d) rocket fish?

How does a young gorilla learn gorilla manners?

Gorillas live in large groups. While they are growing up they learn how to get on with their group. They become adults when they are between seven and ten years old.

Pretend fights show who is stronger and who to treat with respect.

8. Are gorillas carnivores or herbivores?

This young gorilla is practising its grooming skills, removing dirt and insects from the other gorilla's fur.

The baby learns by watching everything the mother does.

7. Gorillas beat their chests: a) to make themselves cough; b) to look threatening; c) to crush fleas.

How do animals shelter their young?

Some animals build a nest or den for their young to keep them safe. Many birds, for instance, build nests high up in trees, or on cliff ledges.

9. Which bird lays its egg in another bird's nest?

Polar bears build a den under the snow for their cubs.

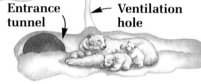

Entrance tunnel ← Ventilation hole

Kangaroos carry their young in a pouch – a sort of built-in nest.

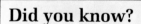

10. Kangaroos are only found in one continent. Which one?

Did you know?

The female praying mantis eats her mate. This provides her with energy to lay eggs.

Where does a crocodile lay its eggs?

Crocodiles lay their eggs in a nest of plants near the river bank and cover them with mud. The mother stands guard over them. The baby crocodiles make squeaking noises to let the mother know they have hatched. She breaks into the nest, and takes them in her mouth to the river, where they are safer from predators.

11. Crocodiles cover their eggs with mud: a) to hide them; b) to keep them warm; c) to stop them breaking.

12. A Korean circus once taught a couple of crocodiles to waltz. True or false?

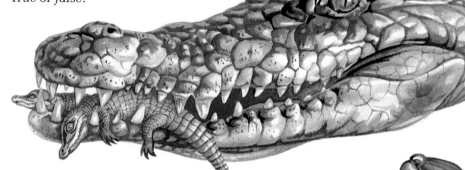

Why might a scorpion eat her young?

Scorpions are very aggressive meat-eaters. If they are hungry they may even eat their young. They can produce another large brood very easily.

13. Baby scorpions sometimes eat each other. True or false?

Scorpions carry their young on their backs.

Are queen bees different from other bees?

Although thousands of bees live together, only one bee, called a queen, lays eggs. Male bees, called drones, mate with the queen. Female bees, called workers, look after the eggs.

14. Honeybees show other bees where to find food by: a) dancing; b) singing; c) buzzing.

15. What are these cells made of?

The queen bee lays eggs in these cells.

Queen

Worker

Staying alive

These two pages look at how some animals hunt, and how other animals avoid being eaten.

What makes a good hunter?

The Indian tiger, like all tigers, has the abilities a good hunter needs. It has speed, strength, sharp senses and a talent for moving silently. Its skills and senses enable it to catch all kinds of animals, from young elephants to birds. Many of its features are found in other meat-eating animals.

Camouflage stripes make the tiger almost invisible in long grass.

Over short distances, the tiger can run as fast as antelope and deer, its swiftest prey.

The body is flexible enough to run, pounce and crawl. The tiger can climb trees to catch birds and monkeys.

Good hearing, sight and smell help find prey.

The strong jaw can kill in a single bite.

Sharp claws come out when the tiger attacks.

1. Tigers can hide in grass as short as 60cm (2ft). True or false?

2. The tiger's favourite food is: a) wild pig; b) potatoes; c) people.

Why do some animals hunt in packs?

Some animals, such as wolves, hunt in packs because it enables them to attack prey bigger and stronger than themselves. They are also likely to catch more food. They have to share their catch with the rest of the pack.

Other animals, such as leopards, hunt alone. They only attack smaller or weaker prey. However, when they do catch anything they do not have to share it with other animals.

3. Where do leopards usually hide their prey after they have killed it?

4. Which of these animals is the wolf's nearest animal relative: a) tiger; b) rat; c) poodle?

5. Which one of these animals hunts in a pack: a) harpy eagle; b) lion; c) giant anteater?

How do animals hunt their prey?

Hunters who are not especially strong or fast have to use special tricks to get close enough to their prey to catch them. Here are some examples.

Some animals, such as moray eels, hide themselves and lie in wait for their prey.

Moray eel

6. A moray eel can grow to:
a) 1m (3.3ft);
b) 3m (10ft);
c) 30m (100ft).

Some animals, like this heron, use bait to attract prey.

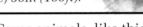

The heron waves a feather which a fish might mistake for a fly.

7. What do you think the angler fish does with this?

Animals that move slower than their prey might use a trap. Many spiders weave a sticky web to catch insects.

8. Spiders eat their webs. True or false?

Some animals have their own weapons. The chameleon has a sticky tongue curled up inside its mouth which shoots out to capture insects.

9. The chameleon can change colour to suit its surroundings. True or false?

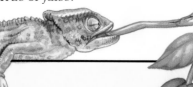

How do animals protect themselves?

Animals only fight to defend themselves as a last resort. Here are some of the ways in which animals try to escape from predators.

Camouflage colouring helps an animal blend in with its environment. Some animals, like the sole, can even change colour to match their surroundings.

10. If a sole is placed on a chess board it will match the squares. True or false?

Some animals try to trick an attacker into thinking they are more dangerous than they really are.

Cats fluff up their fur to look bigger.

The Io moth has a pattern like a frightening face on its wings.

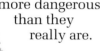

Animals that sting, such as bees and wasps, inject poison into an enemy.

11. Bees die if they sting. True or false?

Some animals offer a part of themselves to eat. They hope this will distract an attacker, and also satisfy its appetite.

12. Which of these animals can break off a part of itself: a) parrot; b) lizard; c) donkey?

If starfish are attacked they can shed an arm. A new one will grow.

How do animals avoid attack?

The size and strength of large animals like elephants make them difficult to kill. Most smaller animals avoid danger by hiding or running away. Healthy animals are seldom caught. It is usually the old, very young, sick or injured who are eaten. They are too slow to escape.

Like many plant-eaters, deer gather in herds. They are safer in groups than on their own.

New-born deer can walk almost immediately. This helps them stay with their herd.

13. What are baby deer called?

Over long distances, the deer can outrun most attackers. The feet can be used to kick if the deer is cornered.

14. Which one of these is not a type of deer: a) caribou; b) elk; c) llama?

Spotted deer are good at defending themselves. They have certain features, found in many plant-eating animals, which help them escape from hunters.

Antlers can jab an attacker.

Good sight and hearing alert the deer to danger.

Male spotted deer

The long neck gives a good view of the surroundings.

Female spotted deer

Spotted camouflage helps hide the deer in grass and forest.

How can bright colours protect an animal?

Some small animals, such as this cinnabar caterpillar, have bright colours to warn hunters that they are poisonous and taste horrible.

15. What do caterpillars turn into?

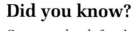

Did you know?

Some crabs defend themselves by placing sea anemones, which have stinging tentacles, on their claws.

Northern forest animals

Much of the land in the far north of the world is covered with forest. These forests, shown in white on the map, almost circle the Earth.

The forest provides animals with a shield from harsh Arctic winds, and a good supply of food – at least in the warmer months. Compared with other parts of the world, though, there are few animals here, especially in the winter.

1. Which three continents contain northern forests?

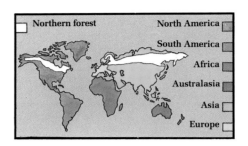

Northern forest — North America — South America — Africa — Australasia — Asia — Europe

How do animals survive the winter?

In the winter the forest is covered with snow and the temperature can drop to −40°C (−40°F). There is little to eat and it is difficult for the animals of the forest to keep themselves warm.

Lynx

In the winter a lynx may have to hunt over an area of 200 square kilometres (80 square miles) to find enough food to stay alive.

2. Why have humans hunted the lynx in the past?

3. Which one of the animals on this page is named after a type of tree found in the northern forest?

Moose

The moose eats as much as it can in the summer. It stores this food as fat on its body, for the harsh winter months.

4. The moose is a type of deer. True or false?

Many of the smaller mammals, like this woodchuck, save their energy by hibernating (sleeping through the winter months).

Woodchuck

To survive without eating, the woodchuck slows its heartbeat from 80 beats a minute to four. Breathing drops from 28 breaths a minute to one.

Pine marten

The pine marten, like most northern forest mammals, has a thick fur coat to keep it warm.

5. Which of these is not a good spot to hibernate in: a) underground; b) hollow tree; c) cave; d) tree top?

What is the forest like in the spring and summer?

Spring brings great changes. Snow melts, trees and flowers bloom, and insect eggs hatch. Lemmings, voles and other small animals come out of hibernation and breed in great numbers.

When summer arrives the forest is like an overflowing larder. There is so much food that birds such as the wood warbler migrate from further south to spend the summer here.

Wood warbler

6. Which one of these animals migrates: a) python; b) thrush; c) dormouse; d) oyster?

7. Which one of these animals is the lemming's greatest enemy: a) owl; b) vole; c) wood warbler?

— **Lemming**

Why do beavers build dams?

Beavers are found throughout the northern forests. They protect themselves from predators by building a large nest called a lodge and flooding the area around it. They do this by building a dam on a stream.

8. In which one of these countries would you find beavers: a) Chile; b) Italy; c) Canada?

9. Beavers build small canals to ferry logs to their dams. True or false?

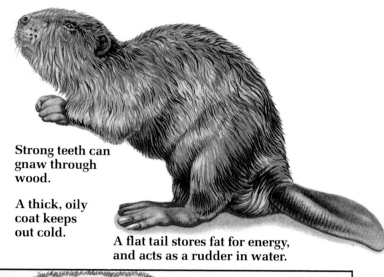

Strong teeth can gnaw through wood.

A thick, oily coat keeps out cold.

A flat tail stores fat for energy, and acts as a rudder in water.

The dam is made of wood, grass and mud. It keeps the entrance to the lodge underwater.

10. What do you think the lodge is made of?

11. Why is the entrance underwater?

A male and female beaver live here with their family.

How do bears bring up their cubs?

Bear cubs stay with their mother for two years. She protects them fiercely and teaches them what to eat. Bears are not normally friendly with each other, but bear mothers sometimes babysit for other bears. They may even adopt another mother bear's cubs if the mother dies.

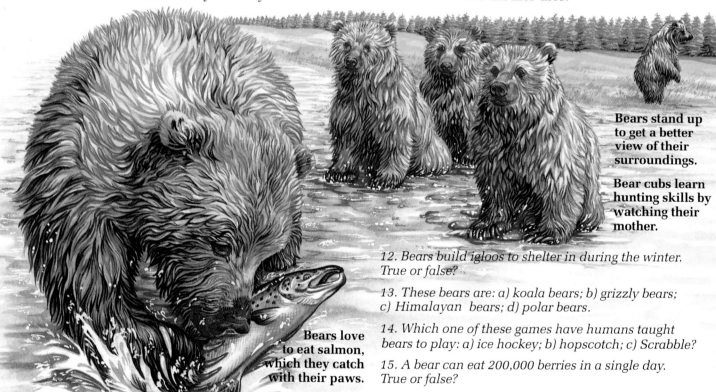

Bears stand up to get a better view of their surroundings.

Bear cubs learn hunting skills by watching their mother.

12. Bears build igloos to shelter in during the winter. True or false?

13. These bears are: a) koala bears; b) grizzly bears; c) Himalayan bears; d) polar bears.

14. Which one of these games have humans taught bears to play: a) ice hockey; b) hopscotch; c) Scrabble?

15. A bear can eat 200,000 berries in a single day. True or false?

Bears love to eat salmon, which they catch with their paws.

Did you know?

In the forests of northern Japan, volcanic springs form pools full of hot water. Macaque monkeys can keep themselves warm in the cold winter by soaking in these pools.

Why is it dangerous to feed bears?

Bears love the food humans eat. Once they have tasted it they may venture into campsites and towns looking for more. Many bears that do this are shot as they can be dangerous.

Rainforest animals

Because most rainforests are hot and damp, the trees and plants that grow in them are the biggest in the world. These forests provide so much food and shelter that far more animals live here than in most other environments.

Most of the animals shown here come from South America, which has the largest single forest in the world. Rainforests are shown in white on the map.

1. Which continent on this map does not have a rainforest?

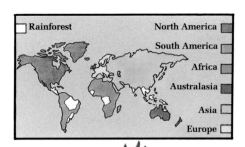

Rainforest
North America
South America
Africa
Australasia
Asia
Europe

What do rainforests look like?

Rainforests have four main layers.

At the top are the tallest trees, called "emergents".

The tops of other trees form a roof, or "canopy", to the forest.

Beneath the canopy is another layer of trees.

The final layer is the forest floor.

Who lives at the top?

Birds and the lightest, most agile climbers live at the top of the forest. Harpy eagles live here. They eat other birds and small mammals. Many animals stay away from this level to avoid them.

2. This harpy eagle could carry off a monkey. True or false?

Are sloths really lazy?

Sloths do everything very slowly. The leaves they eat take a long time to digest and convert into energy, so they need to save their strength. They sleep often and hang motionless for hours when awake.

Sloths come down from the trees once a week to excrete. This is when they are most likely to be attacked and eaten.

3. Jaguars find sleeping sloths by listening for them snoring. True or false?

4. How many hours a day do sloths sleep: a) 3; b) 15 to 18; c) over 24?

Strong claws grip the branches.

Tiny green plants called algae grow over their fur. This helps to camouflage them. Moths often live in the fur.

The fur grows from stomach to back. This lets rain drip off easily.

Who lives at the bottom?

Animals that cannot fly or climb live on the forest floor. Capybaras, tapirs and millions of insects live here.

Jaguars hide in low branches and drop on their prey. They eat tapirs and other plant-eaters.

5. Jaguars don't hunt at the top of trees because they are afraid of: a) heights; b) harpy eagles; c) breaking thinner branches.

The capybara is over 1m (3ft) long. Capybaras are rodents, like rats and squirrels.

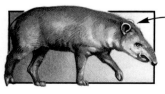

The tapir is a shy plant-eater which only comes out at night. It picks up food with its trunk.

6. The capybara is the largest rodent in the world. True or false?

7. A tapir only comes out at night because it eats bats. True or false?

How are animals suited to life in the trees?

Most animals that live in the forest can either fly or climb.

The spider monkey has a flexible tail which can grasp branches.

The parrot's short, broad wings help it fly through the gaps between trees and branches.

8. What sort of food do parrots eat?

9. Which is not a type of parrot: a) cockatoo; b) parakeet; c) macaw; d) condor?

The marmoset, like all climbers, has long paws to help it grip.

10. Which two rainforest animals on these two pages is the marmoset most similar to?

11. A marmoset is about the size of a kitten. True or false?

How can animals fly without wings?

Some rainforest animals in Africa and Asia have body shapes which help them glide between trees.

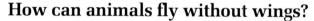

Gliding snakes flatten their bodies in flight.

Flying frogs have large webbed feet for gliding.

Flying squirrels have large skin flaps.

Did you know?

The arrow-poison frog is so venomous that some South American tribes dip arrows into the poison to make them more deadly. A frog 2.5cm (1in) long makes poison for 50 arrows.

Why is the rainforest so noisy?

Many rainforest animals claim an area for themselves. They make a lot of noise to warn others to keep away from their territory.

Howler monkeys make an eerie howling noise every morning and evening.

How big is an army of army ants?

When army ants go out looking for food, up to 200,000 of them march in a column 20m (66ft) wide. They move at about 14m (46ft) per hour capturing spiders, cockroaches, scorpions and ants.

12. Do army ants move quicker than a sloth?

13. Do people live in the rainforest?

14. The sound of a howler monkey's howl travels: a) 1km (0.6 miles); b) 5km (3 miles); c) 16km (10 miles).

15. Which one is the quietest: a) spider monkey; b) tapir; c) parrot?

City wildlife

Ever since towns and cities were first built 8,000 years ago, wild animals have lived in them. The city provides two things that all animals need: plenty of food and shelter.

What sort of animals live in the city?

City animals need to be tough enough to stand noise, pollution and bustle. They have to be able to live close to people and eat a variety of foods. They need to breed easily and make use of all kinds of available space for shelter.

City dustbins provide food for foxes.

Rats and mice live wherever food is stored or left out. Rats can live almost anywhere, even in sewers, but mice prefer warmer places. Rats are tough and can eat many kinds of food, including meat. They can breed at an alarming rate.

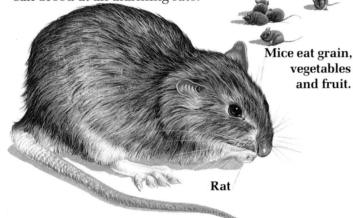

Mice eat grain, vegetables and fruit.

Rat

Bats live in caves in the wild. Attics and towers provide similar shelter in cities.

Pigeon

Pigeons have evolved from seashore birds that nest in cliffs. They feel at home sheltering in the nooks and crannies of tall buildings.

1. Which one of the animals on this page did the legendary Pied Piper drive out of the town of Hamelin?

Insects like silverfish, houseflies and cockroaches compete with each other for food and shelter.

House fly

2. Which one of these is not a real insect: a) clothes moth; b) tile termite; c) furniture beetle?

3. How long does a fly live: a) ten hours; b) ten days; c) ten weeks?

4. Mice grow up to be rats. True or false?

5. A female rat can have twelve babies every: a) twenty minutes; b) eight weeks; c) two years.

6. Which animal shown on this page is seen the most in cities?

Did you know?

Termites that live in the city will eat anything – even plastic-coated wiring which has no food value at all. Nobody knows why they do this.

Why don't more animals live in the city?

Many animals are unsuited to the food and shelter the city provides.

Here are some of the reasons why not all animals can live in the city.

An animal such as the hippopotamus would be too large to find shelter in the city. Foxes are usually the biggest city animals. 	**Some animals cannot find the food that they need in a city. Pandas, for example, can only eat bamboo, which they find in the forests of western China.** 	**Some animals, such as deer, are too timid to live in the crowded, noisy city.**
Animals large and fierce enough to attack and eat humans, like this tiger, would be killed if they came into a city to look for food.	**Some animals cannot live with the noise, smoke, fumes and dirty water of the city. This butterflyfish needs clean, clear water in which to live.** 	*7. How many of these reasons would apply to this crocodile?* 

The night-shift

As day changes to night, most animals retire to their nests and burrows. Night-time (or nocturnal) creatures take their places and share their space and food. Instead of hawks there are owls. Instead of butterflies there are moths.

How do animals see in the dark?

Many nocturnal animals have fine hearing, or large eyes that can see very well in the dark.

Owls are one of the few types of bird which hunt at night. Owl eyes are a hundred times sharper than human eyes. Owls can spot a mouse by candle-light 91m (300ft) away. They also have excellent hearing to help them find prey.

8. Owls cannot move their eyes in their heads. True or false?

Bats are such successful hunters that one in four mammals on Earth is a bat. They hunt with their own unique animal radar system.

Bats make high pitched clicking sounds. Their big ears pick up the echoes these clicks make. The echoes tell the bat what the countryside looks like and where its prey can be found.

How do bats tell the clicks from the echoes?

So they are not confused by too much sound, bats' ears "switch off" when the click is made. They "switch on" a millisecond later to listen to the echo.

9. Do vampire bats really exist?

10. Bats can pick up radio signals. True or false?

How do glow-worms glow?

Glow-worms and fire-flies light up at night. Two chemicals in the tail react together to produce a cold yellow-green light. Despite being so visible they are rarely eaten by predators because they taste horrible.

11. The glow-worm glows to: a) read at night; b) attract a mate; c) light the way for other animals.

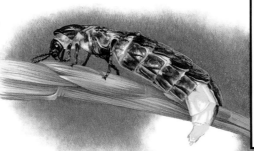

12. Which one of these is not a night-time animal: a) hedgehog; b) mouse; c) eagle; d) potto; e) nightingale?

Why do some animals only come out at night?

Fewer animals are around at night so there is less competition for food. This suits small and timid animals like this African potto.

13. The potto is a type of: a) lion; b) loris; c) lizard.

Most predators hunt during the day. Animals such as this mole, which is almost blind, have less chance of being eaten at night.

14. Where do moles make their homes?

In very hot parts of the world, the heat of the day is tiring. This kangaroo rat comes out at night when it is cooler.

Did you know?

Some frogs and toads do not mind the taste of glow-worms. Sometimes they eat so many they are lit up from inside.

15. In some countries fire-flies are put in lanterns and used for lighting. True or false?

The open ocean

The oceans take up 71% of the world's surface. The Earth's first creatures lived here 3,500 million years ago. Now the oceans are home to a huge variety of animals.

Some areas of the sea are as different from each other as rainforest and desert. Surface winds, light, depth, currents and temperature all affect the amount of life in the sea. This map shows in white which areas of the ocean are the richest in life.

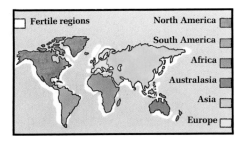

Fertile regions	North America
	South America
	Africa
	Australasia
	Asia
	Europe

1. What do the most fertile regions of the sea have in common?

2. Which is the biggest ocean?

How do fish breathe underwater?

Fish suck water over rows of feather-like gills, at the back of their mouths.

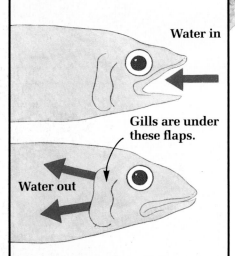

Water in

Gills are under these flaps.

Water out

A fish's gills filter oxygen from the water in a similar way to how our lungs take oxygen from the air.

Who lives in the sea?

Along with fish, animals of almost every type can be found in the sea. On this page are some of the main ones.

Most fish, such as these cod, have bones and shiny scales. The scales overlap and form a flexible, streamlined skin.

Some fish, like the shark, have soft, rubbery skeletons and scales as rough as sandpaper. Fish like these lived in the sea before dinosaurs existed.

Crustaceans like this lobster have hard shells and legs. Shrimps and crabs are also crustaceans.

A few reptiles, like this turtle, live in the sea.

Some birds, like this cormorant, can dive underwater to hunt for fish.

Mammals like this sea lion, and seals and whales, also live in the sea. They cannot breathe underwater but can hold their breath for a long time.

3. A group of birds is called a flock. What is a group of fish called?

4. Fish sleep: a) upside down; b) in a glassy-eyed trance; c) lying on the sea bottom with a pebble as a pillow.

5. Which one of these is a crustacean: a) pangolin; b) piddock; c) prawn; d) pirana?

6. The cormorant is the only bird which has gills. True or false?

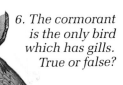

7. Which of these birds is not a good swimmer: a) penguin; b) petrel; c) puffin; d) parrot?

Why do whales leap?

Some whales occasionally leap out of the water, landing with an immense splash. No one knows for certain why they do it. The following reasons have been suggested:

1. To communicate with other whales. The sound of the splash travels far.

2. To let the whale see further than it can at sea level.

3. To shake off little creatures which live on the whale's skin.

Humpback whale

8. Do you know what this sort of leaping is called?

9. What sort of animals live on whales: a) jellyfish; b) barnacles; c) sharks?

10. When whales give birth, how many calves do they usually have?

What is plankton?

Any sea creature that drifts with the tides and currents instead of swimming, is called plankton. Most plankton are microscopic, but some, like jellyfish, can be quite large. There are two main types of plankton, called phytoplankton and zooplankton.

Phytoplankton are tiny plants. They need light to live, so they are found in the top, sunlit layers of the ocean. They provide food for many different animals.

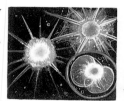 

Zooplankton are animals. They eat each other and phytoplankton. Many are minute crustaceans or newly hatched eggs.

12. Are herring plankton?

Phytoplankton magnified thousands of times.

Zooplankton magnified hundreds of times.

11. A cubic metre (1.3 cubic yards) of seawater can contain 200,000 plankton. True or false?

13. Plankton is a Greek word that means: a) wanderer; b) sea food; c) microscope?

Why do deep sea fish look so extraordinary?

Deeper in the ocean it is very cold and below 600m (1,970ft) it is pitch black. Very little lives here so deep sea fish have to make the most of any chance they get to eat.

Over half the deep sea creatures can light up parts of their body. As well as a lure for prey, these lights are used to attract a mate in the total darkness.

14. What do you think this fish is called: a) a viper fish; b) a gobble fish; c) a fanged blemish?

15. The lights on deep sea fish are solar powered. True or false?

The mouth can be opened very wide by unhinging the bottom jaw. This enables the fish to eat large prey.

Did you know?

Sharks have a row of teeth on a kind of conveyor belt in their bottom jaw. If they bite something tough and their teeth fall out, other teeth move up to replace them.

Luminous spots act as a lure for prey.

Curved, sharp teeth make it difficult for prey to escape.

Life at the edge of the sea

The creatures that live at the edge of the sea are quite different from the animals of the ocean. Instead of open water, they live in mud, rock or coral. For those that live on the shore, the tide comes and goes twice a day, exposing them to both air and water.

Who lives on the beach?

At first glance it is difficult to tell if anything other than seabirds live on the beach. Plants rarely grow here. Only the occasional pattern in the sand gives a clue to the animal life under the surface.

The birds' beaks are various lengths. This lets them search for shells, worms and snails that live at different depths in the sand. They hunt for food right up to the water's edge.

1. Why do you think these birds all have long legs?

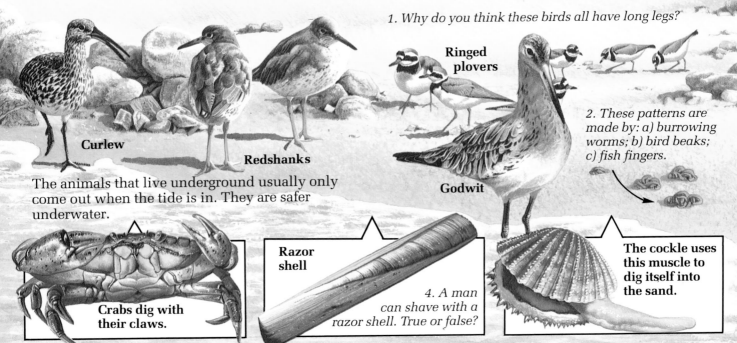

Ringed plovers

Curlew

Redshanks

Godwit

The animals that live underground usually only come out when the tide is in. They are safer underwater.

Crabs dig with their claws.

Razor shell

4. A man can shave with a razor shell. True or false?

2. These patterns are made by: a) burrowing worms; b) bird beaks; c) fish fingers.

The cockle uses this muscle to dig itself into the sand.

3. Which of these causes the tides: a) the moon and the sun; b) the wind; c) earthquakes; d) whales?

5. Which of the animals on this page do people eat?

6. The cockle's digging muscle is called: a) a foot; b) a tongue; c) a toe.

Who lives on the rocks?

Unlike shore animals who can burrow into the wet sand, rock dwellers have to sit out in the open when the tide goes out. They need water in order to breathe, so they will die if they dry out. At low tide, they save a supply of water inside their bodies or shells to prevent this.

The barnacle is protected by a tough shell.

A strong cement binds the barnacle to its perch.

Limpet

In the open air, crabs carry water to breathe inside their shells.

Rock goby

Anemone

Outside the water the anemone can curl itself up. Its outside is tough and leathery to stop it drying out.

A tight seal keeps water in.

The barnacle's tentacles wave in the water, picking up food.

Oyster

7. Barnacles also settle on the underside of: a) aircraft; b) ships; c) windsurfers.

8. Which one of these animals would you not find in a rockpool: a) sea urchin; b) starfish; c) salamander?

What are coral reefs?

Coral reefs are made up of millions of little animals called coral polyps. Their bodies have hard, bone-like cases and they live together in huge colonies. These reefs are the biggest animal-made structures on Earth. The biggest reef, the Great Barrier Reef, stretches for more than 2,000km (1,260 miles).

Coral reefs are the most colourful and crowded underwater environments on Earth. There is a good supply of food and the reef offers many caves and crevices for shelter.

Where are coral reefs found?

Reefs are found in warm, clear, shallow waters off tropical coastlines and islands. Corals need warmth and sunlight to grow.

9. Are there coral reefs in Europe?

10. The Great Barrier Reef is off the coast of which country?

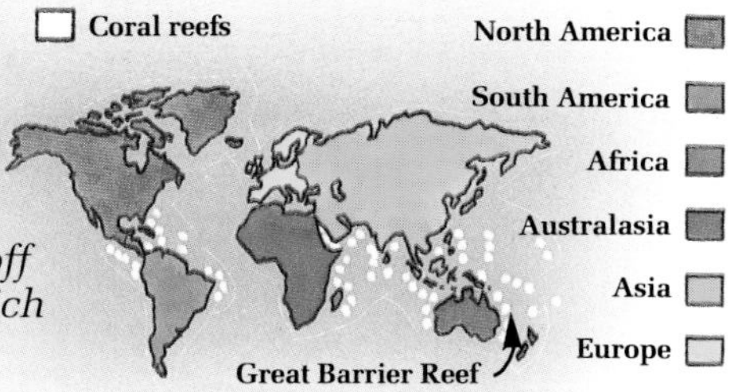

☐ Coral reefs

North America
South America
Africa
Australasia
Asia
Europe ☐

Great Barrier Reef

Who lives on the reef?

An extraordinary number of different sea creatures live on the coral reef. Most of them are brightly coloured to help blend in with their equally colourful environment. This also helps them recognize their own kind from all the other animals which share their environment.

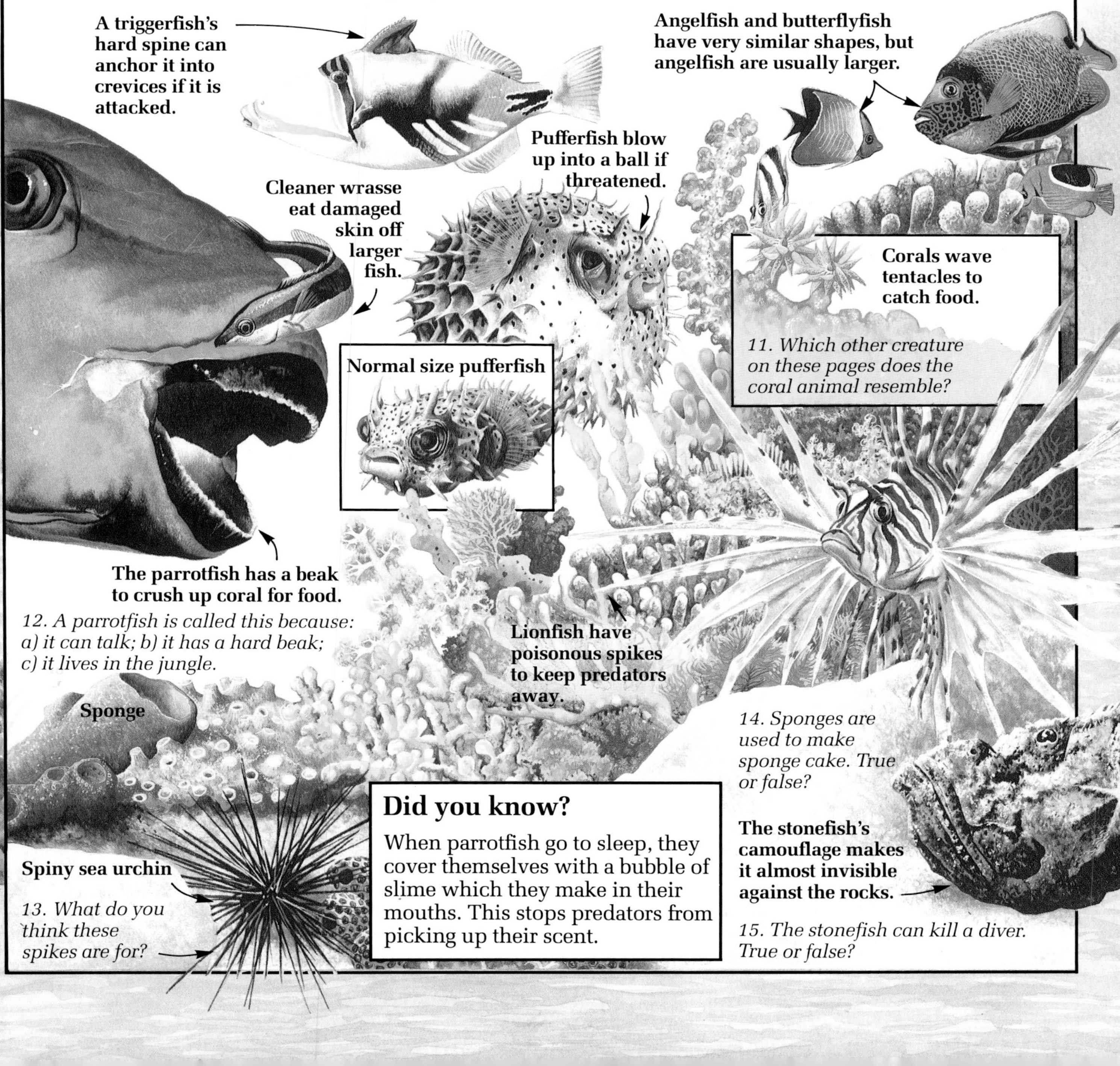

A triggerfish's hard spine can anchor it into crevices if it is attacked.

Angelfish and butterflyfish have very similar shapes, but angelfish are usually larger.

Cleaner wrasse eat damaged skin off larger fish.

Pufferfish blow up into a ball if threatened.

Corals wave tentacles to catch food.

11. Which other creature on these pages does the coral animal resemble?

Normal size pufferfish

The parrotfish has a beak to crush up coral for food.

12. A parrotfish is called this because: a) it can talk; b) it has a hard beak; c) it lives in the jungle.

Sponge

Lionfish have poisonous spikes to keep predators away.

14. Sponges are used to make sponge cake. True or false?

The stonefish's camouflage makes it almost invisible against the rocks.

Spiny sea urchin

13. What do you think these spikes are for?

Did you know?

When parrotfish go to sleep, they cover themselves with a bubble of slime which they make in their mouths. This stops predators from picking up their scent.

15. The stonefish can kill a diver. True or false?

Living without water

The deserts of the world are wastelands of rock, rubble and sand. Scorching hot by day and bitterly cold by night, they have almost no water.

The largest desert is the Sahara, which stretches from northern Africa into Asia. The map on the right shows where deserts are found.

1. Which of these is not a desert: a) Gobi; b) Kalahari; c) Namib; d)Kenya?

2. Which continent on this map does not have a desert?

Deserts

North America
South America
Africa
Australasia
Asia
Europe

Sahara

How do animals survive in the desert?

Desert animals cope with sand and lack of water in a variety of ways. The camel is especially well suited to life in the desert.

In the same way that a large pan of water takes longer to boil than a small one, a large animal like the camel stays cooler in the heat than a small one.

Animals like this gerbil shelter from the sun in burrows.

Animals like this desert hedgehog come out at night when it is cooler.

Many small mammals have big ears, like this fennec fox. These provide a large surface for heat to escape from, in the same way that soup cools quicker on a plate than in a mug.

Hairy ears and eye lashes, and slit nostrils keep out dust and sand.

3. The hump stores: a) water; b) fat; c) fuel.

An insulating wool coat keeps out both the heat of day and the cold of night.

Wide feet stop the camel from sinking into the sand.

4. Camels with one hump are called: a) dormitories; b) doubloons; c) dromedaries.

5. A camel can drink 90l (20gal) in one ten-minute drink. True or false?

How do animals move in the desert?

Sand is very tiring to walk on. It can also be scalding hot. Desert animals cope with this in a variety of ways.

The sidewinder snake winds itself along. Only a very small part of its body touches the sand at any one time.

Jerboas take large leaps over the sand.

Where do animals find water?

Rare streams and springs provide drinking water and create fertile areas of plants and trees. Most animals though find their water in food.

6. What are the fertile parts of the desert called?

The Gila monster reptile finds its water from the animals that it eats.

The addax gets all of its water from the plants and grasses in the desert.

7. The addax never needs to drink. True or false?

8. Which is a desert plant: a) daffodil; b) cactus; c) bamboo?

Living at the ends of the Earth

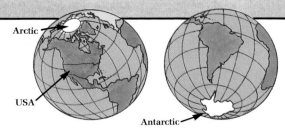

Arctic

USA

Antarctic

The Arctic and the Antarctic are the coldest places on Earth. Very few kinds of animal live here, but those that do can be found in large numbers.

What is the Arctic like?

The most northern part of the world is covered with a great frozen sea – the Arctic Ocean. It is a bleak place. Even in midsummer the temperature rarely rises above 10°C (50°F).

9. What is the central point of the Arctic known as?

Who lives in the Arctic?

The polar bear is the biggest land animal of the Arctic. It is a strong swimmer and hunts seals. The polar bear only lives in this part of the world.

Arctic foxes often follow bears around, eating the food they leave.

Polar bear

Seals leave a breathing hole in the ice.

Fur under the paws gives a good grip on ice and keeps the feet warm.

Did you know?

In severe snow storms, polar bears scoop out shallow hollows in the snow. They sleep in them until the storm is over.

10. Can you name any other type of bear?

Many seabirds come for the summer, when sea food is plentiful.

The walrus is the only animal the polar bear fears. It usually eats fish and shellfish, but it is powerful enough to kill a bear.

What is the Antarctic like?

The Antarctic is a huge island, which is one and a half times the size of the USA. Two thirds of Antarctica has been covered with ice for the last four million years.

11. Is the Antarctic bigger than Africa?

Who lives in the Antarctic?

Most animal life is found around the coast, which is the warmest part of the Antarctic. The sea here is full of life and supports vast colonies of penguins and seals. Inland, only a few insects can survive the intense cold.

12. Ninety five per cent of the world's ice is found in the Antarctic. True or false?

Seals live in seas all over the world, but penguins only live on the coasts of countries in the far south.

The Weddell seal can stay underwater for an hour. When it dives, the heart slows down and oxygen only goes to the most vital body organs.

13. Seals are: a) mammals; b) fish; c) reptiles.

The leopard seal hunts penguins.

Are penguins birds?

Penguins are birds that have lost the ability to fly. Instead they have become superb swimmers.

14. Which one of these birds can fly: a) emu; b) kiwi; c) flamingo; d) penguin?

A layer of fat keeps out cold.

Wings act as flippers.

15. Do polar bears eat penguins?

Grassland wildlife

Grasslands (shown in white on the map) are found inland in some hot, dry countries. The countryside is covered in sturdy, long grasses. All the animals shown on these pages, apart from the South American anteater, are found in the vast, open plains of East Africa.

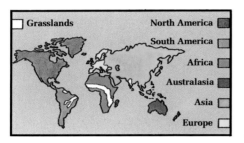

Lions, leopards and cheetahs hunt here, but animals are more likely to die of thirst, hunger or bush fires. They are also in danger from human hunters.

Rhinoceroses, for example, are killed for their horn. Some people believe it has magical powers even though it is made of the same substance as fingernails.

1. A rhino uses its horn to: a) burrow underground; b) scratch its back; c) attack its enemies.

2. The horn of a rhinoceros is made from: a) keratin; b) kerosine; c) korma.

Why do so many wild animals live here?

People have not been able to farm this land because it is too hot and dry for farm animals and crops.

There is usually plenty of suitable food for the wild animals that live here, though.

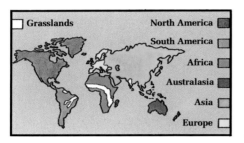

Elephant and giraffe feed on tree leaves.

Wildebeest and zebra graze on the grasses.

The leopard and lion are meat-eaters.

Vultures eat what the hunters leave.

3. Animals that eat plants are called herbivores. What are animals that eat other animals called?

4. How many kinds of animal on this page eat plants?

5. A zebra has black and white stripes because: a) it is a cross between a black horse and a white horse; b) it is camouflage; c) it is blackcurrant and vanilla flavour.

Why do many animals go around in large groups?

Grass-eating animals like the wildebeest and zebra are safest in large groups, or herds. This confuses predators because so many targets make it difficult to decide which one to pick.

Strong animals can shelter weak or very young ones in the herd.

Some animals in the herd can graze while others keep a look out for danger.

Predators such as lions hunt more successfully in groups. They work together to create diversions and ambushes, and share a feast rather than squabble over it.

Herds of up to 10,000 wildebeest travel long distances overland in search of food.

6. Zebra foals can stand and walk within an hour of being born. True or false?

7. Which word is used to describe animals that travel long distances?

8. If lions and tigers mate, their cubs are called tigons or ligers. True or false?

Why do termites build huge mounds?

Termites need a lot of moisture. They cannot survive in the dry heat of the plains so they create a home that suits them better.

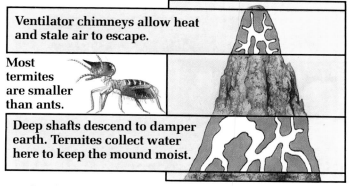

Ventilator chimneys allow heat and stale air to escape.

Most termites are smaller than ants.

Deep shafts descend to damper earth. Termites collect water here to keep the mound moist.

9. What do you think these mounds are made of: a) mushrooms; b) moss; c) mud?

How does an anteater eat?

This South American giant anteater sticks its nose into ants' nests and termite mounds. Its long, sticky tongue shoots out of its mouth at up to 160 times a minute. In this way it can eat up to 30,000 insects a day.

Powerful claws smash a hole in the nest.

10. The giant anteater's greatest enemy is the lion. True or false?

11. An anteater has a large, bushy tail: a) to help it keep warm; b) to sweep its den; c) to hide behind when it is frightened.

Why are elephants and giraffes so big?

An elephant eats twigs, leaves and bark which are difficult to digest. It needs a huge stomach to do this, so its body is big to hold it.

Giraffes' long necks enable them to eat leaves that other sorts of animal cannot reach.

12. Are there any animals in the world which are taller than giraffes?

13. Which one of the animals on this page lives in a termitarium?

When an elephant wants to frighten an enemy it sticks out its ears to make itself look even bigger.

The tusks are used for fighting and finding food. So many elephants have been killed by poachers who can sell the tusks, that these animals may become extinct.

14. Which one of these things does an elephant not do with its trunk: a) suck up water; b) breathe; c) gather food; d) whistle; e) stroke a friend?

15. Some animals keep clean by wallowing in mud. True or false?

Did you know?

Despite being the heaviest land animals, elephants can move around almost silently. They have soft, elastic pads on their feet that muffle their footsteps.

Animal oddities

The shape of an animal's body helps it to survive. It enables it to cope with its environment and compete with other animals for food. The differences between animals help them all fit into their own particular environment.

These two pages look at some of the more unusual looking animals, and how their appearance helps them survive.

Why does the toucan have such a colourful bill?

These colours may help other toucans recognize their own kind among the many brightly coloured birds of the Amazon rainforest.

The bill is useful for reaching into branches for food.

Which animal has eight eyes?

Many spiders have eight eyes but they do not use them all at once. This jumping spider uses different sets of eyes as it stalks prey and then leaps on it.

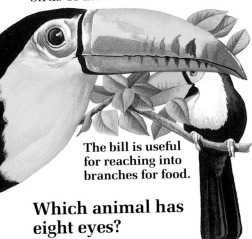

These eyes detect movement from a distance.

These judge how far away insects are.

These eyes are used when the spider is stalking its prey.

1. Why should you be wary of the red back, funnelweb and black widow spider?

2. Some jumping spiders can leap more than 20 times their own body length. True or false?

Which thorns can move?

These African thorn bugs look like thorns on a branch. When they are still, it is difficult for their enemies to see them. Insects have copied many different shapes to stay hidden from predators.

3. Which one of these shapes is not copied by an insect: a) twig; b) bird dropping; c) red berry; d) snake head?

Why does the luminous jellyfish glow?

This jellyfish drifts in the ocean, coming to the surface at night where it glows softly in the dark water.

Jellyfish move very slowly. They cannot chase after food. The glow attracts prey, and other jellyfish to breed with.

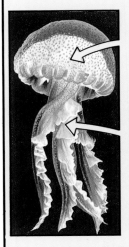

The glow is made by tiny plant-like bacteria, which live in the jellyfish.

The tentacles have stings. They trap prey and discourage animals that may want to eat the jellyfish.

4. What do jellyfish have in common with sea anemones and corals?

5. Which one is not a jellyfish: a) aurelia; b) Portuguese man o' war; c) raspberry; d) purple sail?

Why is the pangolin covered with scales?

The pangolin's body is covered in hard, flat scales made of the same basic substance as your hair and fingernails. If it is attacked it rolls up into an armoured ball.

6. Which other animal in this book has a long sticky tongue and eats ants and termites?

7. Put these animals in order of size: pangolin, jumping spider, platypus, mudskipper.

The pangolin has no teeth. Instead it swallows stones to grind up the ants and termites it eats.

Its long sticky tongue is half the length of its body.

8. South Asian tribesmen make bagpipes out of the hollowed-out bodies of pangolins. True or false?

9. Which is the odd one out: a) rhino horn; b) fingernail; c) pangolin scale; d) elephant tusk?

Why are nudibranchs so colourful?

Gills for breathing.

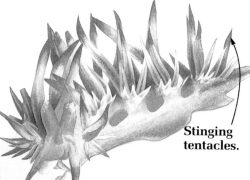

Stinging tentacles.

Many nudibranchs (pronounced new-dee-branks) have amazingly bright colours. This probably warns other sea animals not to eat them as they are poisonous.

10. Which land animal is the nudibranch similar to?

One kind of nudibranch eats jellyfish and corals. It can transfer their stings from its stomach to its own tentacles and use them to defend itself.

What is a platypus?

The Australian platypus is a mammal that lays eggs. It feeds its young on milk (like all mammals) but this oozes out of its skin rather than from the nipples other mammals have.

The beak is covered by sensitive skin. It is used to find worms and shrimps in muddy water.

Webbed toes and a flat tail help it swim.

11. Young platypuses are called platykittens. True or false?

Did you know?

Two platypuses in the Bronx Zoo, New York, ate 25,000 worms a month, along with crayfish, frogs and egg custard. Despite only weighing 1-1.3kg (2-3lb) each, they cost more to feed than the zoo's elephants.

Can a fish survive out of water?

The mudskipper is one of the few fishes that can survive out of water. Like all fish it gets its oxygen from water rather than air. When it comes out of the sea it takes a supply of water along in a chamber inside its body. On land it skips about on muddy shores looking for food.

A chamber full of water, inside here, helps the mudskipper to breathe.

On land, the mudskipper uses these fins as legs.

Which fish shoots insects?

The archer fish of south east Asia shoots drops of water at insects. This knocks them off their perches into the water where they are eaten.

12. Archer fish can also knock birds off their perches. True or false?

13. Would you find the archer fish living in rivers or in oceans?

14. The air tank people use to breathe underwater is called: a) an aqualung; b) an aquarium; c) an aqueduct.

15. Male mudskippers attract females by: a) wh; b) waving their back fin; c) doing somersaults.

24

Extraordinary animals

These pages look at animals who are able to do one particular thing better than any other animal.

These special abilities almost always help them find food or escape from being eaten.

Which animal has the strongest bite?

The great white shark almost certainly has the strongest bite. It attacks whales, dolphins, other sharks, and sometimes humans. It is about 8m (26ft) long. The jaw can bite down with a force equivalent to the weight of four elephants per tooth.

1. All sharks are dangerous to humans. True or false?

The shark's teeth point backwards to make it more difficult for prey to escape.

2. A shark's skin is covered with: a) leather; b) barbed scales; c) bone.

Which animal is the most indestructible?

The sponge is a very simple animal that lives in the sea. It eats by filtering food from the seawater that it sucks through its body. If parts of its body are broken off or eaten it can rebuild them. It is so indestructible that if it was broken up in a food mixer it would still be able to put itself back together again.

Which is the fastest animal in the world?

The fastest of all animals is the spine-tailed swift. It can fly at 170km/h (106mph).

Swifts spend most of their lives in the air, only landing to have their chicks. They can fly 900km (560 miles) in a single day.

The fastest animal in the sea is the sailfish. It can swim at 109km/h (68mph). Its crescent-shaped tail is ideal for pushing it smoothly through the water.

The swift has a very streamlined shape and crescent-shaped wings.

12. What shape does the sailfish have in common with the spine-tailed swift?

Other fast-swimming fish like the tuna and the swordfish also have crescent-shaped tails.

10. Swifts can stay in the air for as long as two years. True or false?

11. What sort of food do you think swifts eat?

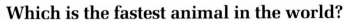

Which is the largest animal that ever lived?

The blue whale is the largest animal that ever lived. It is even bigger than the largest dinosaurs.

It has an average length of 30m (100ft) and weighs 122 tonnes (132 tons). The water supports its huge body.

4. The blue whale sings to other whales when: a) it is having a bath; b) it is happy; c) it wants to let them know where it is.

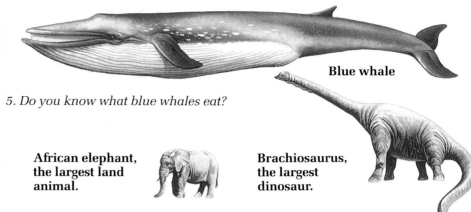

Blue whale

5. Do you know what blue whales eat?

African elephant, the largest land animal.

Brachiosaurus, the largest dinosaur.

Which is the most dangerous animal?

It is thought that mosquitoes have contributed to 50% of all natural human deaths since the beginning of recorded history. They pass on yellow fever and malaria when they feed on human blood.

6. Which of these eats mosquitoes: a) spider; b) snail; c) shark?

7. Which animal on these two pages might you use in your own bathroom?

Which is the greatest traveller?

The Arctic tern makes an annual journey of 38,400km (24,000 miles) from the Arctic to the Antarctic and back. The tern breeds in the Arctic summer. Then it flies far south for the Antarctic summer, which is at the opposite time of the year. It probably does this because the food it eats is plentiful in polar summers.

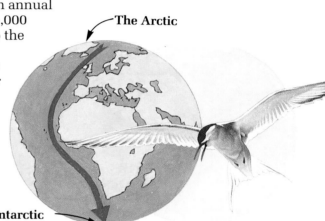

The Arctic

The Antarctic

8. The Arctic tern experiences more daylight than any other animal. True or false?

9. What sort of food does the Arctic tern travel to eat: a) crustaceans; b) polar bears; c) penguins?

---

13. Asian princes once trained cheetahs to catch antelope. True or false?

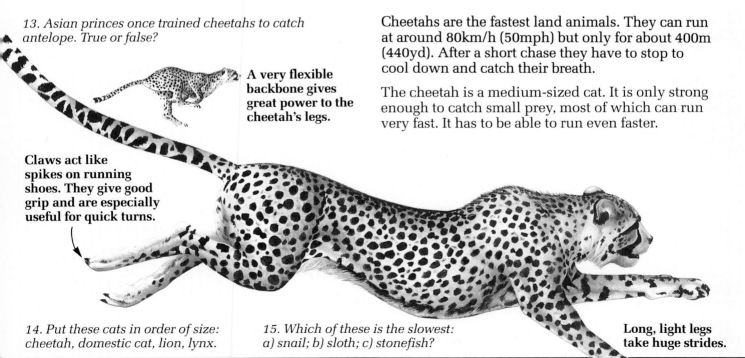

A very flexible backbone gives great power to the cheetah's legs.

Claws act like spikes on running shoes. They give good grip and are especially useful for quick turns.

Cheetahs are the fastest land animals. They can run at around 80km/h (50mph) but only for about 400m (440yd). After a short chase they have to stop to cool down and catch their breath.

The cheetah is a medium-sized cat. It is only strong enough to catch small prey, most of which can run very fast. It has to be able to run even faster.

Long, light legs take huge strides.

14. Put these cats in order of size: cheetah, domestic cat, lion, lynx.

15. Which of these is the slowest: a) snail; b) sloth; c) stonefish?

Animal Megaquiz

All these questions are about animals that have appeared in Part One of this book. You can write your answers on a piece of paper and then check on page 32 to see how many you got right.

What do you know?

1. In which part of the world did life first appear millions of years ago?
2. Which one of these lived on Earth before the dinosaurs: a) shark; b) sheep; c) squirrel?
3. Which one of these birds swims well under water: a) cuckoo; b) crow; c) cormorant?
4. Which kind of animal can weigh 122 tonnes (132 tons)?
5. What does the cleaner wrasse clean?
6. Can you name one of the two main residents in the sloth's fur?
7. Which are tougher – mice or rats?
8. What makes frogs light up from the inside?
9. How do crocodiles know their eggs have hatched in their mud nest?
10. What makes luminous jellyfish glow?

Silhouettes

These silhouettes are all of animals or objects that are in Part One. Can you guess which ones they are?

Which part of the world?

Which part or parts of the world...

1. ...is pitch black all the time?
2. ...are exposed to air and water twice a day?
3. ...is made by animals and stretches for 2,028km (1,260 miles) along the coast?
4. ...shields the lynx from Arctic winds?
5. ...are scorching by day and freezing at night?
6. ...is a frozen ocean?
7. ...have the world's biggest plants and trees?
8. ...are too hot for farm animals but not for antelopes, zebras, termites and anteaters?
9. ...is a whole continent, but inland, only has a few insects living in it?
10. ...have plenty of food and shelter, but also much noise and pollution?

Animal actions

All of these sentences describe a particular kind of animal, or animal behaviour. Can you match them with one of the words from the list below.

1. An animal which hunts other animals.
2. Keeping an egg warm so it will hatch.
3. Animals which drift in the sea.
4. An animal which feeds milk to its young.
5. How animals change to suit their environment over many thousands of years.
6. Sleeping through winter to avoid the cold.
7. Animals which come out at night.
8. An animal which eats plants.
9. An animal which lives on land but returns to the water to breed.
10. A large group of plant-eating animals.

Evolution   Predator   Nocturnal   Herbivore   Amphibian   Herd   Hibernation   Incubation   Plankton   Mammal

Close-ups

These are all parts of animals that have appeared in Part One. Which animals are they?

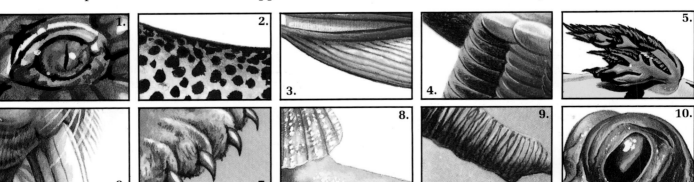

Where in the world?

Can you name these animals and match them with the country, continent or region in which they live?

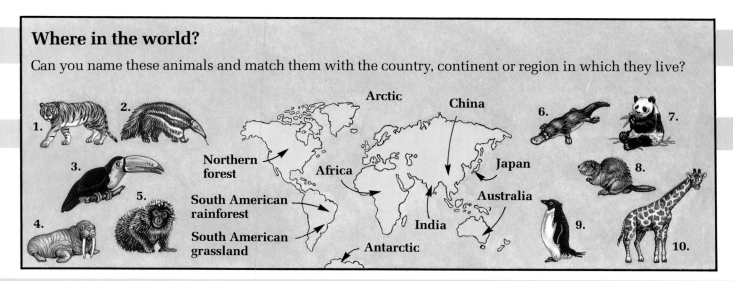

True or false?

1. Lionfish eat zebrafish.
2. Gorillas are vegetarians.
3. Whales cannot breathe underwater.
4. Pigeons have evolved from penguins.
5. Almost three-quarters of the world is covered with water.
6. One in four mammals in the world is a bat.
7. When animals hibernate their blood freezes.
8. Some frogs can fly.
9. The rhino's horn has magical powers.
10. Mudskippers eat mud.

Which animal?

1. Which reptile winds itself along the desert leaving wavy lines in the sand?
2. Which mammal has a tongue half the length of its body?
3. Which insect eats its mate?
4. Which fish sleeps in a bubble of slime?
5. Which mammal's fur grows from its stomach towards its back?
6. Which fish blows itself into a ball if threatened?
7. Which rodents have spread throughout the world on ships?
8. Which bird flies from one end of the world to the other, twice a year?
9. Which insect can eat plastic wiring?
10. Which fish shoots drops of water at insects?

What eats what?

Which of these animals eats the animal or plant in the blue panel below?

Odd one out

1. Which one of these has only one or two babies at a time: rabbit, whale, rat?
2. Which one of these is not a night-time animal: moth, tapir, owl, butterfly?
3. Which one of these is plankton: anglerfish, walrus, jellyfish, lobster?
4. Which one of these cannot survive out of water: mudskipper, crab, anemone, sole?
5. Which one of these northern forest animals does not hibernate: woodchuck, lynx, lemming.
6. Which one of these seashore creatures does not burrow under the sand: cockle, crab, razorshell, barnacle?
7. Which one of these only lives in the Arctic: seal, walrus, Arctic tern?
8. Which one of these animals is not a herd or pack animal: wolf, lion, gorilla, leopard?
9. Which one of these is not a fish: lionfish, butterflyfish, silverfish, pufferfish?
10. Which one of these is a fast mover: army ant, sloth, anemone, tuna?

Quiz answers

The answers to the 12 quizzes from *The animal world* to *Extraordinary animals* are on the next four pages. Give yourself one point for every answer that you get right.

The chart below helps you find out how well you have done in each quiz.

0-5	Read through the answers, then try the quiz again. See how many answers you can remember this time.	11-14	Good score. If you get this score on most of the quizzes, you have done very well.
6-10	Quite good. Think more carefully about the questions and you might get more answers right.	15	Excellent. If you do this well in more than half the quizzes, you are an animal expert!

Your score overall

You can find out your average score over all 12 quizzes like this:

1. Add up your scores on all 12 quizzes.
2. Divide this total by 12. This is your average score. How well did you do?

General knowledge

All the answers to general knowledge questions are marked ★. These questions are probably the hardest in the quizzes. Add up how many of them you got right across all 12 quizzes. There are 40 of them in total. If you got over 25 right, your general knowledge is good.

The animal world

★ 1. Snakes are reptiles.
★ 2. Humans are mammals.
★ 3. The ostrich cannot fly.
★ 4. b) The zebra is only found in Africa.

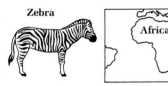

Zebra   Africa

★ 5. The kangaroo carries its young in a pouch. Baby kangaroos are called joeys.
6. b) Dogs are found all over the world.
7. True. The whale is a mammal.
★ 8. Nine. The seal, lobster, shrimp, crab, octopus, seashell, ray, cod and grouper live in the sea. (Crocodiles are found by river banks and swamps.)
9. c) The salmon is a fish.
10. a) Charles Darwin. He suggested the theory of evolution in his book *On the origin of species* published in 1859.
11. c) The iguana is not an insect. It is a reptile.
12. Lions are carnivores.
13. a) When a whole species of animal dies out, this is called extinction.

The dodo became extinct by 1800.

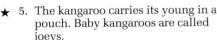

14. True. The Ancient Egyptians worshipped a cat goddess called Bast.
15. The right order for this food chain is cabbage, caterpillar, thrush, fox.

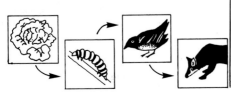

Animal families

1. The correct order is: b) sperm whale; a) elephant; c) giant clam.

b) **14m (46ft) in length.**   a) **5m (16ft) high.**

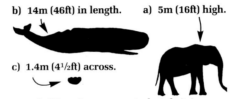

c) **1.4m (4½ft) across.**

2. c) Warming an egg to hatch it is called incubation.
★ 3. Penguins eat fish.
4. False. Penguins cannot fly at all, though they are very good swimmers.
★ 5. Ducks' eggs are bigger than hens' eggs.
6. d) A rocket fish is not a real fish.
7. b) Beating the chest is intended to drive away enemies. Gorillas are really quite gentle, and will rarely attack.
8. Gorillas are herbivores. They eat food such as celery, sugar cane, nettles and thistles.
★ 9. Cuckoos lay their eggs in other birds' nests – leaving them with the task of guarding and feeding their chicks.
★ 10. The kangaroo is only found in Australia, as is the koala bear, emu and duck-billed platypus.

Koala   **Emu**

11. b) Crocodile eggs are covered in mud to keep them warm. Mud keeps heat in like a blanket.
12. False. As far as anyone knows, crocodiles cannot be taught to waltz.
13. True. Baby scorpions will eat each other if there is no other food around.
14. a) Honeybees perform a complex dance to tell other bees in their group where to find food.
★ 15. The cells are made of wax.

Staying alive

1. True. This helps tigers to stalk their prey. They can only run fast over short distances so they need to surprise their prey to catch it.
2. a) Tigers like to eat wild pig.
3. Leopards usually hide their prey in a tree where other carnivores cannot reach it.
4. c) A poodle. The wolf is the largest member of the dog family.

Wolf

Poodle

5. b) Lions hunt in packs.
6. b) Moray eels can grow to be 3m (10ft) long.
7. Angler fish use this lure for bait. It entices other fish, who think the lure is food, within range. Score a point if you got the general idea.
8. True. Most webs only last about a day. They are made of silk, which the spider can eat and use again.
9. True. The chameleon can change its colour to match its environment.
10. True. The sole can match the squares within three or four minutes.
11. True. The sting is shaped like a hook and buries itself into the bee's victim. The bee tears open its tail when it flies off. Although it dies, its action may have saved other bees.
12. b) Many lizards can shed their tails if they are grabbed by them.
★ 13. Baby spotted deer are called fawns.
14. c) The South American llama is not a deer. It is a relative of the camel.

Llama   **Camel**

★ 15. Caterpillars turn into butterflies or moths. Score a point if you got either or both answers.

Northern forest animals

1. The northern forests cover land in the continents of Europe, Asia, and North America.
★ 2. Humans have hunted the lynx for its fur.
3. The pine marten is named after the pine tree, which is common in the northern forests.

Pine trees

4. True. The moose is the biggest member of the deer family.

Southern pudu. The smallest member of the deer family.

Moose

★ 5. d) The tree tops are too cold and too exposed to danger to offer a good place to hibernate.
6. b) The thrush migrates. All the other animals live in one part of the world all year round.
7. a) The lemming's greatest enemy is the owl.
8. c) You would find beavers in Canada.

Canada   USA

Beaver

9. True. Both beaver parents build small canals to help ferry logs to build their dams.
10. The lodge is made of the same material as the dam – wood, grass and mud.
11. The underwater entrance makes the lodge especially safe. Any creature wanting to get in would have to be able to swim and dive underwater.
12. False. The bears of the northern forests hibernate in winter.
13. b) These bears are grizzly bears.
14. a) The Moscow State Circus trained two teams of bears to play ice hockey (complete with skates and sticks).

15. True. In the wild, bears also eat fish, small mammals and fruit.

Rainforest animals

1. There are no rainforests in Europe. It is too cold for rainforests.
2. True. The harpy eagle is strong enough to carry off a monkey. It can also carry off a sloth.

Harpy eagle

3. False. As far as we know, sloths do not snore.
4. b) Sloths sleep for 15 to 18 hours a day.
5. c) Jaguars are too heavy for thinner branches. They are clever hunters though and can stalk their prey on the ground and even in water.
6. True. The capybara is the largest rodent in the world.

Capybara

Mouse

7. False. The tapir is a plant eater. It comes out at night because there are fewer animals around that might catch and eat it.
★ 8. Parrots eat fruit and seeds. Score one point for either or both answers.
9. d) The condor is not a parrot. It is a type of South American vulture. There are 315 different types of parrot in the world.

Condor

★10. The marmoset is a monkey, like the howler and spider monkey.
11. True. A marmoset is about the size of a kitten. It is the smallest monkey in the world.

Marmoset   Kitten

12. No. If it has to, a sloth can move at 1 km/h (0.6mph), considerably faster than army ants.
13. Yes, rainforests do have people living in them. Pygmies and Amazonian Indians are rainforest dwellers.
14. c) Howler monkeys can be heard 16km (10 miles) away.
15. b) The tapir makes the least noise, to avoid being heard by hunting jaguars.

City wildlife *and* The night-shift

★ 1. In the legend, the Pied Piper drove rats out of the German town of Hamelin. When the town council did not pay him his agreed fee, he took all the town's children and they were never seen again!
2. b) The tile termite is not a real insect.
3. c) A fly usually lives for 10 weeks.
4. False. Mice and rats are both rodents, but they are not the same species.
5. b) A female rat can have 12 babies every eight weeks.
★ 6. Pigeons are seen most in any city. They do not need to hide themselves because they live in places that are difficult to reach.

Pigeon

7. Two. Crocodiles are too big to find shelter, and too dangerous to live close by humans. Score a point if you got either of these answers.
8. True. Owls' eyes are too large to move in their heads. They make up for this by being able to turn their heads around almost half a circle.

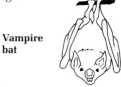

★ 9. Yes, vampire bats do exist. They prefer cattle blood to human blood though.

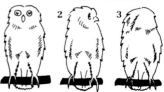

Vampire bat

10. False. Bats cannot pick up radio signals.
11. b) Glow-worms glow to attract a mate.
12. c) The eagle is not a night-time animal.
13. b) The potto is a type of loris. Lorises are forest-dwelling mammals, similar to monkeys.
★14. Moles make their homes in the ground. They are small, burrowing mammals which eat worms and insects.

Entrance to burrow

Mole

15. True. The light of several fire-flies is just bright enough to read by.

The open ocean

1. The most fertile areas of the sea are all off the coast. Score a point if you got the general idea. Shallow seas usually have the most life, and water is always shallow by the coast.

★ 2. The Pacific is the biggest ocean in the world. It contains 52% of the world's sea water.

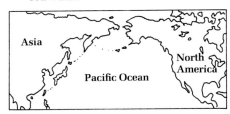

★ 3. Large groups of fish are called shoals or schools. Score a point for either.
4. b) Fish sleep in a trance. They have no eyelids so their eyes stay open when they sleep.
5. c) The prawn is a crustacean.

Prawn

6. False. No birds have gills.
7. d) The parrot is not a good swimmer. Parrots live in trees in rainforests.

★ 8. Whale leaping is called breaching.
9. b) Whales often have barnacles living on them. These are usually found on the head, flippers and tail.

Barnacles on a grey whale.

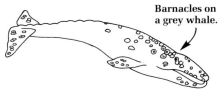

★ 10. Whales usually have one or two calves. These calves are born at sea. Some sea mammals, like seals and walruses, have their calves on land.
11. True. Plankton are so tiny that 200,000 could live in a cubic metre (1.3 cubic yards) of sea water.

★ 12. Herring are not plankton. They can swim independently of the ocean tides and currents.
13. a) The word plankton comes from the Greek word *planktos* which means wanderer.
14. a) This fish is called a viper fish. It is about 30cm (1ft) long.

The hatchet fish is another type of deep sea fish.

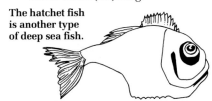

15. False. The light comes from pouches of luminous bacteria on the side of the fish.

Life at the edge of the sea

1. These sea birds have long legs so they can wade in the shallow water at the edge of the beach.
2. a) These patterns are made by burrowing worms.
3. a) Tides are caused by the moon and the sun.
4. False. However, razor shells are called this because they look like old-fashioned razors. This shape helps them move up and down quickly in their burrows.

Old-fashioned razor

★ 5. People eat crabs, oysters and cockles. Score a point if you got two or more of these.
6. a) The digging muscle is called a foot.
7. b) Barnacles settle on ships. In fact they settle on most things in the sea, from driftwood to discarded shoes.
8. c) You would not find a salamander in a rock pool. Salamanders are amphibians which usually live in mountains and caves.
9. There are no coral reefs in Europe. The water is too cold for coral.

★ 10. The Great Barrier Reef is off the coast of Australia.
11. The coral animal looks rather like the sea anemone. They both come from a class of animals called coelenterates (pronounced sel-ent-erates). Their bodies are very similar in structure.

Coral   **Anemone**

12. b) The parrotfish takes its name from its hard, parrot-like beak. The coral that it crushes makes sand for the nearest beach.

| Parrot fish | Parrot |

13. The sea-urchin has spikes like sharp knitting needles, to protect it from being eaten. Some fish can bite off the spikes though, leaving it defenceless.
14. False. Sponges are not used to make sponge cake.
15. True. Stonefish have poisonous spines on their backs which can be fatal to any diver that steps on them.

Poisonous spines

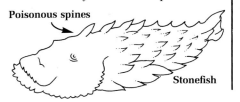

Stonefish

Living without water *and* Living at the ends of the Earth

1. d) Kenya is not a desert. It is a country in eastern Africa.

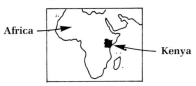

Africa   Kenya

2. Europe is the only continent which does not have a desert.
3. b) The camel's hump stores fat.
4. c) Camels with one hump are called dromedaries. Camels with two humps are called bactrians. You can remember which is which if you think of a D for Dromedary as having one "hump", and a B for Bactrian as having two "humps".

Dromedary

Bactrian

5. True. Camels can drink up to 136l (35gal) in a single day when they get the chance.

★ 6. Fertile areas of the desert are called oases.
7. True. Vegetation can provide all of the addax's water requirements.
8. b) The cactus is a desert plant.
9. The central point of the Arctic is known as the North Pole.

★ 10. Score a point if you got one or more of these: black bear, brown bear, grizzly bear, Himalayan bear, Kodiak bear, sun bear.
11. No, Africa is over twice the size of the Antarctic.

Africa

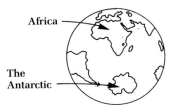

The Antarctic

12. True. The Antarctic is almost entirely covered in ice. In some parts this ice is over 3km (2 miles) thick.
13. a) Seals are mammals, like whales and walruses.
14. c) The flamingo can fly.

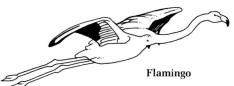

Flamingo

15. Polar bears probably would eat penguins if they lived in the same part of the world. Fortunately for the penguins who live in the Antarctic, polar bears only live in the Arctic.

Grassland wildlife.

1. c) The rhino uses its horn to attack its enemies.

The horn can grow to 1.58m (5ft).

2. a) The horn is made from keratin.
★ 3. Animals that eat other animals are called carnivores (from the Latin *carnis* – flesh, *vorare* – to devour).
4. There are four. The rhino, elephant, zebra and wildebeest are all plant-eaters.
5. b) The stripes are for camouflage. They are especially good at disguising the zebra's shape from a distance.
6. True. New-born zebras are in great danger from predators. Walking with the herd protects them.
★ 7. When animals travel long distances this is called migration. Zebras and antelopes also migrate across the grassland in search of food.
8. This is true, but it only ever happened in zoos, when the two animals were kept together. In the wild, these two animals live in different parts of the world.

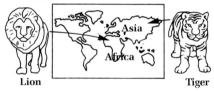

Lion   Asia   Africa   Tiger

9. c) Termite mounds are made of mud. Termites make the mounds by chewing earth and forming it into mud bricks.
10. False. The lion lives in Africa, and the giant anteater lives in South America.
11. a) The anteater's bushy tail helps it keep warm. It curls its tail around itself when it is cold.
12. No. The giraffe is the tallest animal in the world. Some giraffes grow as tall as 6.1m (20ft).

13. Termites live in a termitarium.
14. d) An elephant does not use its trunk to whistle, though it can make a loud trumpeting noise with it.
15. True. Elephants, rhinos and hippos cover themselves in mud to keep clean. When the mud dries it falls off, taking with it irritating ticks and fleas.

Elephant

Animal oddities

★ 1. All three of these spiders have poison powerful enough to make people ill. Score a point if you guessed they were poisonous.

Black widow spider

2. True. Jumping spiders can jump impressive distances. When they stalk their prey their eyes turn from green to brown.
3. c) Insects copy all these shapes apart from the red berry. Red berries are eaten by birds and are very conspicuous.
★ 4. Anemones, corals and jellyfish all have stinging tentacles.
5. c) The raspberry jellyfish is not a real jellyfish. There is one called a sea wasp though, and another called a sea gooseberry.
★ 6. The giant anteater also has a sticky tongue and eats ants and termites.
★ 7. From the biggest to the smallest, the right order is pangolin, platypus, mudskipper, jumping spider.

Pangolin 90cm (36in).
Platypus 70cm (27in).
Mudskipper 15cm (6in).
Jumping spider 1.25cm (½in).

8. False. (Pacific islanders use a shell called a conch as a trumpet though.)
9. d) Elephant tusks are made of ivory. Everything else on the list is made of keratin.
10. The nudibranch is similar to a slug.

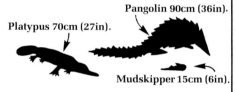

Slug
Nudibranch

11. False. Platypus babies have no special name. There are usually one or two of them in a litter.
12. False. Birds are too big, both to be knocked off, and eaten.
13. Archer fish live in rivers. There are very few insects in oceans.
14. a) The air tank divers use is called an aqualung.

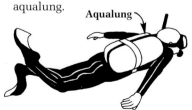

Aqualung

15. b) Male mudskippers attract females by waving their back fins.

Extraordinary animals

1. False. Of 250 types of shark, only 20 are known to eat humans. Most will swim away if they see a human.
2. b) A shark's skin is covered with barbed scales. These cut or bruise any animal that brushes against the shark.
3. a) Mayflies only live for a day as adults. They hatch, lay eggs and die.
4. c) It is thought that whales sing to let other whales know where to find them.
★ 5. Blue whales eat plankton. They have huge brush-like bristles in their mouths, called baleen. These filter the minute plankton out of the water.

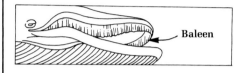

Baleen

6. a) Mosquitoes are eaten by spiders.
★ 7. You may find a sponge in your bathroom. Most bathroom sponges are likely to be artificial ones though.

Artificial sponge   Natural sponge

8. True. Arctic and Antarctic summers have very long days and very short nights. Some terns have lived to be over thirty, and have probably flown a distance similar to the moon and back – over 800,000km (500,000 miles).
9. a) The Arctic tern eats crustaceans.
10. True. Young swifts spend the first two years of their life in the air.
★ 11. Swifts eat insects.
12. The crescent shape. This is ideal for pushing an animal smoothly through air or water.

Crescent shape   Swift   Sailfish

13. True. Cheetahs were used to hunt antelope. They wore hoods until they were unleashed, like trained falcons do today.
★ 14. From largest to smallest the correct order is: lion, cheetah, lynx, domestic cat.

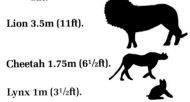

Lion 3.5m (11ft).
Cheetah 1.75m (6½ft).
Lynx 1m (3½ft).
Domestic cat 0.75m (2½ft).

15. a) The snail is the slowest. Garden snails move at 0.05km/h (0.03mph).

Animal Megaquiz answers

There are 100 points in the whole of the Animal Megaquiz. Score a point for each correct answer. If you score over 50 you have done well. Over 75 is excellent. You can find out more about each answer on the page listed after it in brackets.

What do you know?

1. The sea (page 14).
2. a) shark (page 14).
3. c) cormorant (page 14).
4. Blue whale (page 25).
5. Other fish (page 17).
6. Algae, or moths (page 10).
7. Rats (page 12).
8. The glow-worms they have eaten (page 13).
9. The babies squeak (page 5).
10. Luminous bacteria (page 22).

Where in the world?

1. Tiger/India (page 6).
2. Giant anteater/South American grassland (page 21).
3. Toucan/South American rainforest (page 22).
4. Walrus/Arctic (page 19).
5. Macaque monkey/Japan (page 9).
6. Platypus/Australia (page 23).
7. Panda/China (page 12).
8. Beaver/Northern forests (page 9).
9. Penguin/Antarctic (page 19).
10. Giraffe/Africa (page 21).

Silhouettes

1. Jellyfish (page 22).
2. Scorpion (page 5).
3. Pufferfish (page 17).
4. Termite (page 21).
5. Flying squirrel (page 11).
6. Shark (page 24).
7. Termite mound (page 21).
8. Rhinoceros (page 20).
9. Turtle (page 14).
10. Bat (page 13).

True or false?

1. False.
2. True (page 4).
3. True (page 14).
4. False.
5. True (page 14).
6. True (page 13).
7. False.
8. True (page 11).
9. False.
10. False.

Which part of the world?

1. The depths of the ocean (page 15).
2. The seashore (page 16).
3. Great Barrier Reef (page 17).
4. The northern forests (page 8).
5. The desert (page 18).
6. The Arctic (page 19).
7. Tropical rainforest (page 10).
8. Grasslands (page 20).
9. Antarctica (page 19).
10. Cities (page 12).

Which animal?

1. Sidewinder snake (page 18).
2. Pangolin (page 22).
3. Praying mantis (page 5).
4. Parrotfish (page 17).
5. Sloth (page 10).
6. Pufferfish (page 17).
7. *Either* rats *or* mice (page 12).
8. *Either* tern *or* Arctic tern (page 24).
9. Termite (page 12).
10. Archerfish (page 22).

Animal actions

1. Predator (page 6).
2. Incubation (page 4).
3. Plankton (page 15).
4. Mammal (page 2).
5. Evolution (page 3).
6. Hibernation (page 8).
7. Nocturnal (page 13).
8. Herbivore (page 3).
9. Amphibian (page 2).
10. Herd (page 20).

What eats what?

1. (j) Seal (page 19).
2. (d) Zebra (page 20).
3. (i) Greenfly (page 3).
4. (f) Grass (page 20).
5. (h) Tapir (page 8).
6. (b) Mouse (page 13).
7. (a) Coral (page 17).
8. (e) Salmon (page 9).
9. (g) Monkey (page 10).
10. (c) Leaves (page 2) .

Close-ups

1. Crocodile (page 5).
2. Cheetah (page 25).
3. Blue whale (page 25).
4. Spine-tailed swift (page 24).
5. Nudibranch (page 23).
6. Walrus (page 19).
7. Tiger (page 6).
8. Cockle (page 16).
9. Elephant (page 21).
10. Mudskipper (page 23).

Odd one out

1. Whale (page 4).
2. Butterfly (page 13).
3. Jellyfish (page 15).
4. Sole (page 7).
5. Lynx (page 8).
6. Barnacle (page 16).
7. Walrus (page 19).
8. Leopard (page 6).
9. Silverfish (page 12).
10. Tuna (page 24).

Animal index

Below is a list of the animals you can read about in Part One and where to look them up.

Part Two

GEOGRAPHY QUIZBOOK

Marit Claridge and Paul Dowswell

Edited by Judy Tatchell

Designed by Ruth Russell

Illustrated by Chris Lyon

Additional design and illustration by
Richard Johnson and Rachel Lockwood

Consultant: John Brennan

Contents

About Part Two

The Earth's surface is immensely varied. Part Two of the book
looks at our planet, from mountains to rainforests, oceans to
cities. It explains how the planet provides its inhabitants with
air, water and food, and shows why we need to protect the
Earth from the growing threat of pollution.

How to do the quizzes

Throughout the book there are quiz questions to answer as you
go along, printed in italic type, *like this*. Some of the questions
rely on your general knowledge, others have clues elsewhere on
the page. Keep a note of your answers and check them against
the answers on page 60-63.

The Geography Megaquiz

On pages 58-59 is the Geography
Megaquiz – a set of ten quick quizzes to
test you on your general knowledge and
what you have read about in Part Two.

The Earth in space

Planet Earth is a huge ball of rock which spins in space. Earth is one of the smallest of nine planets which circle around a central star, called the Sun. A group of planets circling around a star is called a solar system.

What is a star?

A star is a burning ball of gas which gives off heat and light. The Sun is a star. It is part of a group of millions of stars, called a galaxy. There are about 200,000 million stars in our galaxy which is called the Milky Way. Many stars are bigger than the Sun.

1. A solar system is made up of a star and: a) a Sun; b) a galaxy; c) planets.

The Milky Way

Sun

Mercury

Venus

Moon

Earth

Mars

The farthest that anyone has ever traveled is to the Moon. The first men landed on the Moon on July 20, 1969.

4. Is the Moon a star?

5. The first man on the moon was: a) Christopher Columbus; b) Neil Armstrong; c) Flash Gordon.

6. Which is the coldest planet?

Jupiter

One of Jupiter's 12 moons. A moon circles around a planet, not around the Sun.

Asteroids – rocks circling the Sun.

7. Which planet is named after the Roman goddess of love?

8. Which is bigger, a solar system or the Milky Way?

9. Unscramble these words to find the names of two planets: I STAR JUMPER.

Uranus

Your address in space would look like this:

Name
House
Street
Town
Country
The Earth
The Solar System
The Milky Way
The Universe

What is the Universe?

Four galaxies in the Universe.

Our galaxy, the Milky Way, is part of a group of about thirty galaxies. Beyond this there may be more than 200,000 million other galaxies. Together they make up the Universe. No one knows how big the Universe is.

2. Is the Earth the center of the Universe?

3. Distances between stars are measured in: a) light years; b) string; c) gallons.

Why does it get dark at night?

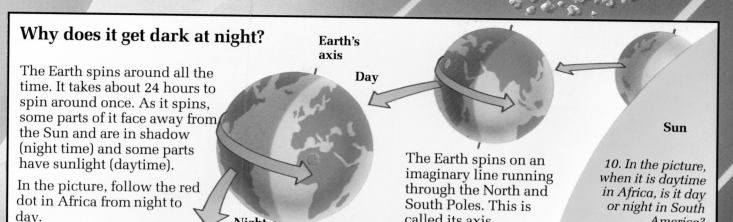

The Earth spins around all the time. It takes about 24 hours to spin around once. As it spins, some parts of it face away from the Sun and are in shadow (night time) and some parts have sunlight (daytime).

In the picture, follow the red dot in Africa from night to day.

Earth's axis

Day

Night

The Earth spins on an imaginary line running through the North and South Poles. This is called its axis.

Sun

10. In the picture, when it is daytime in Africa, is it day or night in South America?

Why do the hours of daylight differ?

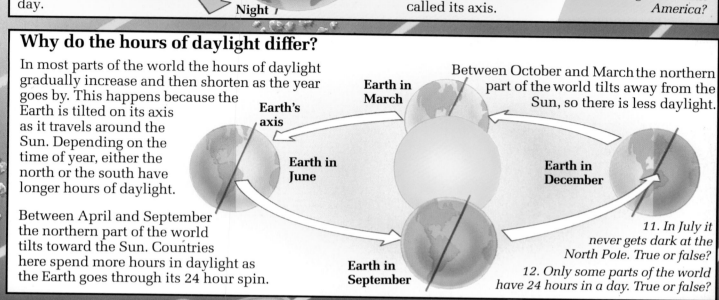

In most parts of the world the hours of daylight gradually increase and then shorten as the year goes by. This happens because the Earth is tilted on its axis as it travels around the Sun. Depending on the time of year, either the north or the south have longer hours of daylight.

Between April and September the northern part of the world tilts toward the Sun. Countries here spend more hours in daylight as the Earth goes through its 24 hour spin.

Earth's axis

Earth in March

Earth in June

Earth in September

Between October and March the northern part of the world tilts away from the Sun, so there is less daylight.

Earth in December

11. In July it never gets dark at the North Pole. True or false?

12. Only some parts of the world have 24 hours in a day. True or false?

Did you know?

The Earth circles the Sun at a speed of 29.8km (18.5 miles) per second. It takes 365¼ days to make one complete circle around the Sun.

We use the 365 days to measure one year. Every fourth year the extra quarters are added together to make a year with 366 days, which is called a leap year.

Saturn

Saturn's rings – these are made of millions of ice-covered rocks.

One of Saturn's moons.

13. Do all planets have moons?

14. Is there life on Neptune?

Neptune

15. Is a New Moon visible?

Pluto

Why does the Moon change shape?

The half of the Moon facing the Sun is always lit up. As the Moon goes around Earth, you see different parts of this half. The Moon takes about a month to go around the Earth.

The bottom part of the picture shows the Moon in five positions which it passes through on its way around Earth. The pink band shows what the Moon looks like from Earth.

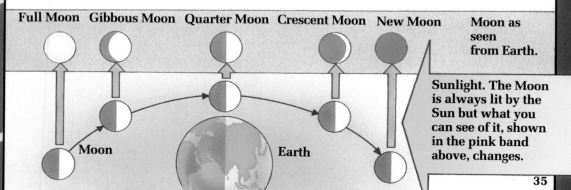

| Full Moon | Gibbous Moon | Quarter Moon | Crescent Moon | New Moon | Moon as seen from Earth. |

Moon

Earth

Sunlight. The Moon is always lit by the Sun but what you can see of it, shown in the pink band above, changes.

35

The surface of the Earth

If you could look at the Earth from space, you would see a browny-green, blue and white planet, half hidden in swirling clouds. The blue oceans make up 71% of the surface of the Earth. The browny-green areas are the land, which is in seven main blocks, called continents.

　　People live on about a third of the land on Earth. Some parts are crowded. Others, such as deserts, are nearly empty.

1. Seen from space, what colour would the Arctic and Antarctic be?

2. Which is the largest continent?

The areas around the North and South Poles are frozen all the time. The North Pole is in the middle of the Arctic Ocean.

3. Do people live at the North Pole?

Mountains cover nearly a quarter of the land on Earth. They are cold places and few people live there.

4. Mountains make good farmland. True or false?

Arctic Ocean

5. In which continent are the Himalayas?

North America

Europe

Asia

Pacific Ocean

Atlantic Ocean

The Pacific Ocean is the largest ocean. It covers nearly one third of the surface of the Earth.

Africa

Indian Ocean

South America

The South Pole is in the continent of Antarctica.

6. Are there more people or penguins in Antarctica?

Australia

There are volcanoes, valleys, plains and mountains on the ocean floor, just as there are on land.

Southern Ocean

Antarctica

Deserts have almost no water. The Sahara is the largest desert in the world.

7. The Sahara covers almost one third of Africa. True or false?

Most people live on flat land in places that are neither too hot nor too cold. Many people live along rivers where there is rich farmland.
8. The River Nile flows through: a) Ecuador; b) Egypt; c) England.

Very few people live in the hot, wet rainforests around the middle of the Earth.

9. Brazil has the largest rainforest. True or false?

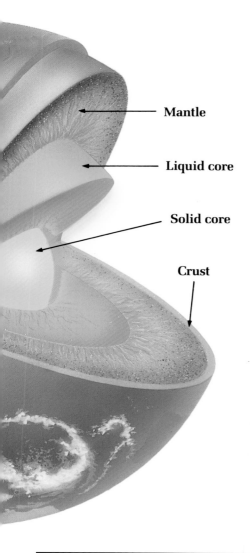

Mantle

Liquid core

Solid core

Crust

Is the Earth solid?

The Earth is made up of layers. The continents and oceans are part of an outer layer of solid rock called the crust. This rests on hot, toffee-like rock called the mantle.

The centre of the Earth, the core, is made of very hot, heavy rock. Scientists think that the core is liquid on the outside and solid in the middle.

Do the continents move?

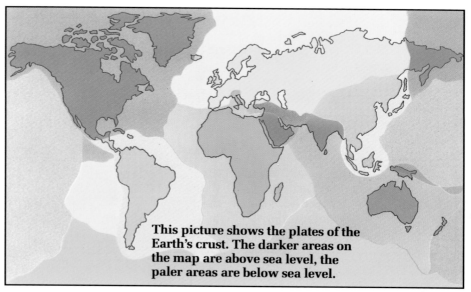

This picture shows the plates of the Earth's crust. The darker areas on the map are above sea level, the paler areas are below sea level.

The continents are part of the Earth's crust which is made up of several huge pieces, like a big jigsaw puzzle. These pieces, or plates, are shown on the map. The mantle underneath the crust is heated by the liquid rocks around the Earth's core. This sets up currents in the mantle, in the same way that boiling water swirls around in a saucepan. These currents move some of the plates together while other plates move apart. The main mountain ranges, volcanoes and earthquake zones all run along the edges of the plates.

10. Is it hotter at the centre of the Earth or in the Sahara desert?

11. Africa was once joined to America. True or false?

Did you know?

The Earth's crust is about 64km (40 miles) thick. If the Earth was the size of a soccer ball, the crust would be the thickness of a postage stamp.

What happens when the Earth's crust moves?

When plates move together, the crust is slowly pushed up into folds. These are mountains. The highest mountains in the world, the Himalayas, were formed when India bumped into Asia.

12. The lowest places on Earth are at the bottom of: a) the sea; b) lakes; c) mineshafts.

Pressure builds up as plates push or slide against each other. If the pressure becomes too great the rocks suddenly snap and move, shaking the ground. This is called an earthquake.

13. Which of these cities is famous for its earthquakes: a) Paris; b) San Francisco; c) Sydney?

Volcanoes occur along the edges of plates as these are the weakest spots in the Earth's crust. The hot, liquid rock under the crust forces its way through the surface as a volcano.

14. Can volcanoes erupt under the sea?

15. What is the name of the world's highest mountain?

Volcano

Plates pressing together. ➙

Folds of rock

Mapping the world

A map is a picture of any part of the Earth. A map can be of a very small area, such as a museum, or of a whole country, a continent or the whole world.

Maps can show different things, such as roads or what sort of food is grown in an area. They help you to find out where places are on the Earth and how to get there.

How are flat maps made of the Earth?

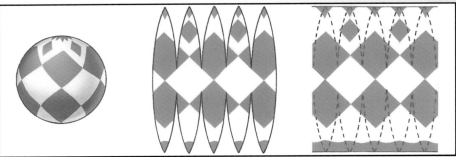

It is difficult to draw a flat map of the Earth because the Earth is ball-shaped. The picture above shows how a map-maker might draw a map of a ball. The ball is divided into segments which are then spread out flat. Parts of the ball have to be stretched on the map to fill the gaps between the segments.

In the same way, map-makers have to change the shape of countries slightly to make flat maps of the Earth. There are several ways of stretching out a ball-shape to fit on a flat surface. These are called projections. The maps above show how two different projections make Australia appear to be two different shapes.

1. Which is more accurate, a globe or a flat map?

2. Which continent is missing from this list: Australia, Europe, Africa, North America, Antarctica, South America?

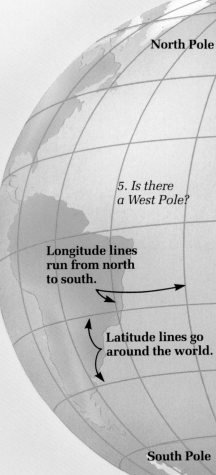

North Pole

5. Is there a West Pole?

Longitude lines run from north to south.

Latitude lines go around the world.

South Pole

Which way up?

The four main directions used on maps are north, south, east and west.

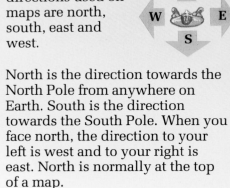

North is the direction towards the North Pole from anywhere on Earth. South is the direction towards the South Pole. When you face north, the direction to your left is west and to your right is east. North is normally at the top of a map.

6. What is the direction half way between north and east?

How do you find North?

You can use a compass to find out which way you are facing. The needle of a compass always points north.

Turn the compass until the needle points to letter N. You can then see which way is west, east or south.

7. Which direction is at the bottom of most maps?

What is a political map?

A political map shows how the Earth is divided up into countries. A country is an area which is usually run by its own government. This political map shows the countries in South America.

3. Would you use a political map to find a country's borders, or to find where mountains are?

4. How many countries are there in South America?

Longitude 0° runs through Greenwich in England.

Latitude 0° is called the Equator. It is half way between the North and South Poles.

8. Can space travelers see latitude and longitude lines on the Earth?

9. Greenwich is in: a) Madrid; b) Paris; c) London.

Why are there lines on a map?

Lines are drawn on maps to divide them into sections. The lines help you to find places on a map. On continental and world maps, the distances between the lines are measured in degrees (°).

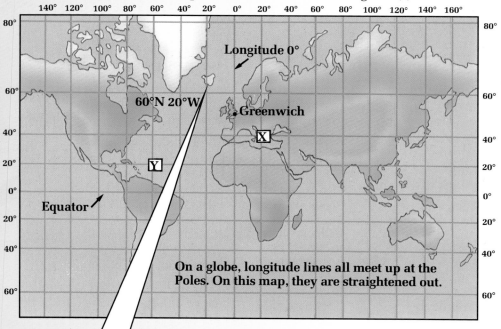

Longitude 0°

60°N 20°W

Greenwich

X

Y

Equator

On a globe, longitude lines all meet up at the Poles. On this map, they are straightened out.

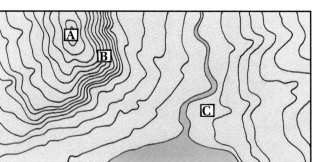

Imagine two ships colliding at sea. They radio for help and tell the rescue services that their position is 60°N and 20°W. This means 60° north of the Equator and 20° west of longitude 0° (the north-south line running through Greenwich). The rescue service can pinpoint their position at once and direct any nearby ship to their aid.

10. Are the ships nearer North America or Europe?

11. If a volcano erupted at point X on the map, what would its position be?

12. If a hurricane was approaching Central America from point Y, what would its position be?

Did you know?

You can use the stars to find your direction. In the northern half of the world (called the northern hemisphere), look for a group of stars called Ursa Major*. A line through the end of Ursa Major points to the North Star. This is directly above the North Pole.

In the southern hemisphere, look for the Southern Cross to find which way is south.

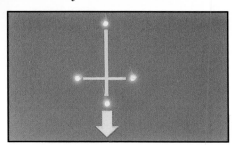

*Also known as the Big Dipper.

What is a physical map?

A physical map shows the Earth's natural features – such as rivers, mountains and valleys. Lines on some maps, called contour lines, indicate the height of the land in regular intervals. The closer together these lines are, the steeper the slope. This map shows the coastline at the bottom of the page.

A
B
C

13. Is there flat land on the map at A, B or C?

14. Is it very steep at A, B or C?

15. Is A, B or C at the top of a hill?

The Earth's atmosphere

The Earth is wrapped in a layer of air, called the atmosphere. The air acts like a blanket around the Earth. During the day it protects the Earth from the Sun's harmful rays. At night it stops heat from leaving the Earth.

Air is a mixture of gases. The main gas is nitrogen. Most of the rest, about 20% of air, is oxygen.

1. Which gas do you need to breathe in order to stay alive?

How high is the sky?

The Earth's atmosphere is about 32km (20 miles) thick. Beyond this is space and the other planets and stars in the Universe. The picture below shows what happens at different levels of the atmosphere.

32km (20 miles) **Scientists send research balloons up to 30km (18 miles) high.**

18km (11 miles) **There may be clouds in the sky up to here.**

16km (10 miles) **The weather affects the atmosphere up to about this level.**

15km (9.3 miles) **Jets cruise at about this level.**

8.8km (5.5 miles) **Mount Everest**

2. Are jets affected by storms?

3. At 0km (0 miles) it is: a) ground level; b) sea level; c) sky level.

Did you know?

Although you cannot feel the air around you, it does have a weight. Altogether the air in the Earth's atmosphere weighs about 5,000 million tonnes (tons). The weight of air is called air pressure.

4. Air pressure is less at the top of a mountain than at sea level. True or false?

What causes the wind?

The air around the Earth is always moving. You feel this moving air as wind.

At the Equator the land heats the air. Warm air is lighter than cold air so it rises. Warm air rising makes an area of low air pressure. Cold air is sucked in from elsewhere to take the place of the warm air.

At the Poles, air presses down on the Earth and makes an area of high air pressure. The wind is caused by air moving from areas of high pressure to low pressure areas.

5. Is it hot or cold at the Equator?

6. Which of these tells which way the wind is blowing: a) weather vane; b) compass; c) barometer?

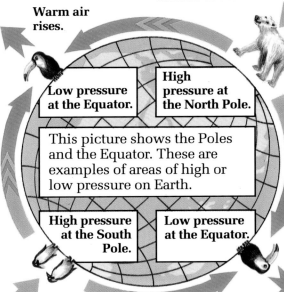

Warm air rises.

Cold air presses heavily on the surface of the Earth.

Low pressure at the Equator.

High pressure at the North Pole.

This picture shows the Poles and the Equator. These are examples of areas of high or low pressure on Earth.

High pressure at the South Pole.

Low pressure at the Equator.

Cold air, as wind, flows to take the place of rising warm air.

What are weather and climate?

Weather is sunshine, wind, rain, snow and so on. In some parts of the world, the weather is much the same day after day. In other places, the weather changes all the time.

A place's climate is the average amount of sunshine, wind and rainfall that it has, year after year.

7. It is warmer on a mountain top, which is nearer the Sun, than at sea level. True or false?

You see rainbows when sunlight shines through raindrops.

Snowflakes are made of tiny ice crystals. Each one is different.

8. Which has more changeable weather, the Sahara desert or Great Britain?

9. Are weather and climate the same thing?

What are clouds?

Clouds are patches of air which contain millions of tiny drops of water. Clouds have different shapes and are at different heights. Some are shown below.

Cirrus clouds are very high and are made of tiny ice crystals. They usually mean rain is coming.

Cirrocumulus clouds are a sign of unsettled weather.

Cumulonimbus clouds often bring thunderstorms with rain, snow or hail.

Cumulus clouds appear in sunny, summer skies.

Stratus cloud is a low blanket of cloud which often brings drizzle.

Fog is cloud at ground level.

10. Which are the highest clouds in the sky?

11. Smog is a mixture of smoke and: a) rain; b) smelly dog; c) fog.

What are thunder and lightning?

Lightning makes the air it goes through very hot. The air expands violently, like an explosion, and makes a clap of thunder. Below, you can see what causes lightning.

Inside cumulonimbus clouds, particles of water and ice move up and down in air currents.

As the water and ice rub against each other, there is a build-up of static electricity.

The electricity builds up until there is a giant spark. You see this as a flash of lightning.

You can tell how far away a thunderstorm is by counting the time between the lightning and the first clap of thunder. The distance is about 2km (about a mile) for every five seconds.

12. If you hear thunder ten seconds after seeing lightning, how far away is the storm?

13. Are there more thunderstorms at the Equator or at the Poles?

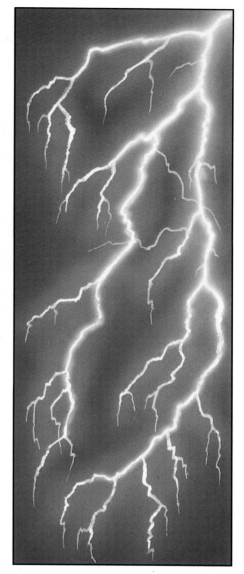

What are hurricanes and tornadoes?

A hurricane is a violent storm with strong winds and rain. Areas of extremely low pressure build up over warm oceans. Warm, wet air spins into the middle of the low pressure area causing the strong winds. The warm air rises and the water vapour in it becomes clouds and heavy rain.

14. Hurricanes have eyes. True or false?

A tornado is like a very small hurricane. It is a whirling funnel of upward-spinning air. Winds in a tornado reach up to 500kmph (300mph). They suck up anything in their path, sometimes even people, animals and cars.

15. Tornadoes can pick up trains. True or false?

Rivers and rain

Plants and animals need water to stay alive. Your body is about 75% water. Without water, your body would not work.

Only 3% of the water on Earth is fresh water. The rest is salty. Two thirds of the Earth's fresh water is frozen in ice sheets and glaciers. The remaining third is in rivers, lakes and water underground.

1. Camels can survive without water for: a) 21; b) 7; c) 2 days.

Where does water come from?

There is always the same amount of water on Earth. It moves from place to place. When a puddle dries up, the water does not disappear. Tiny particles of water rise from the puddle. They become a gas called water vapor. This is called evaporation.

When water vapor rises into cooler air, it turns back into tiny water droplets and becomes clouds and rain. The movement of water from the land to the air and back to the land is called the water cycle.

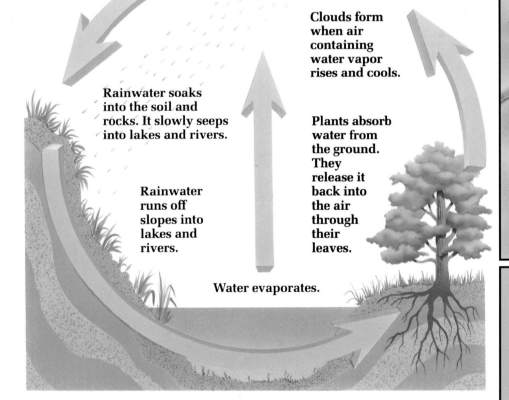

Clouds form when air containing water vapor rises and cools.

Rainwater soaks into the soil and rocks. It slowly seeps into lakes and rivers.

Rainwater runs off slopes into lakes and rivers.

Plants absorb water from the ground. They release it back into the air through their leaves.

Water evaporates.

2. When washing dries, the water in it: a) disappears; b) becomes water vapor; c) becomes air.

3. What are clouds made of?

4. In big cities, each glass of water someone drinks has already been drunk by someone else. True or false?

5. Is there water vapor in your breath?

Where do rivers begin?

Rivers begin in hills and mountains as small streams. They carry rainwater from the land to the sea. A river gets bigger as it collects more and more water on its way.

6. Which of these rivers is the shortest: a) Thames; b) Nile; c) Amazon?

As the water flows downhill it sweeps away small pieces of rock. These rub at the bottom and sides of the stream and make it wider and deeper.

Rivers flood when there is more rain than usual on the land which drains into the river.

7. Some rivers flow uphill. True or false?

Did you know?

You need to drink about 1.7 litres (3 pints) of water a day. Where there is plenty of water, each person uses about 20 times as much as this a day, for washing, cooking, etc.

8. What happens to water at 0°C (32°F)?

9. You can live without water for: a) a day; b) four days; c) a month.

What is hydroelectricity?

The power in falling water can be used to make electricity, which is then called hydroelectricity. The water is trapped by a dam. It is then piped to a power station where it flows over big water wheels, called turbines. These turn generators which make electricity.

River water also has enormous power. It wears away rocks and shapes the land into hills and valleys.

10. Hydroelectric power stations are only found in flat areas. True or false?

11. What do hydroelectric, tidal and wave power have in common?

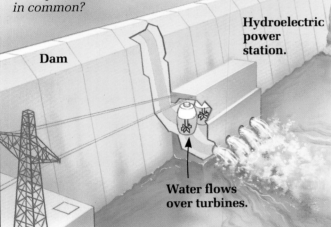

Dam

Hydroelectric power station.

Water flows over turbines.

How is a waterfall made?

When a river flows from hard to softer rock, the softer rock wears away more quickly and makes a small step. The water falls over the step on to the soft rock below, wearing it away even more. Gradually the step and the waterfall get bigger.

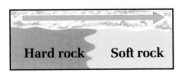

Hard rock **Soft rock**

Waterfall

The highest waterfall in the world is Angel Falls in Venezuela. The river drops 979m (3,214ft).

12. Which of these is not a famous waterfall: a) Niagara; b) Grand Canyon; c) Victoria?

What is water pollution?

Many towns and factories are built near rivers so that they can use the water. Sometimes towns and factories pour dirty water back into the rivers. The rivers become dirty, or "polluted". Pollution can make rivers smell and can kill water plants and animals. Polluted rivers drain into the sea and pollute the seas as well. (See pages 56-57 for more about pollution.)

13. Fish caught in polluted rivers can be poisonous. True or false?

Farmers spray chemicals on fields to make crops grow better. The chemicals may drain into streams and rivers and pollute them.

People sometimes dump garbage in rivers. As garbage rots, it uses up oxygen in the water. Fish may die due to lack of oxygen.

Some harmful cleaning chemicals in waste water from homes remain harmful even after treatment in a sewage treatment plant.

Garbage from towns is often buried in huge holes in the ground. Chemicals in garbage can drain through the ground into rivers.

What is a glacier?

Glaciers are rivers of ice. They occur in very cold areas and on high mountains. When snow falls here it crushes snow beneath it to ice. The snow and ice slide slowly down the mountain.

14. Glaciers are found in: a) Mexico; b) Great Britain; c) Scandinavia.

Glacier

U-shaped valley

Glaciers wear away the sides and bottoms of valleys. They leave behind deep U-shaped valleys.

15. Which flows faster, a river or a glacier?

Oceans and coasts

Nearly three quarters of the Earth's surface is covered by oceans. There are five oceans (see page 36) and they contain smaller areas called seas. The coast is where the land meets the sea.

The shape of the coasts is always changing. Waves pound at beaches and cliffs, slowly wearing them away. The sea also drops sand and mud in sheltered areas. This builds up and becomes new land.

1. Are all the oceans joined together?

2. Which of these is a sea, not an ocean: a) Atlantic; b) Pacific; c) Mediterranean; d) Indian?

Why is the sea salty?

Water dissolves salt in rocks on the ocean floor. On land, streams and rivers carry salt from rocks to the sea. Also, water evaporates from the sea leaving the salt behind.

River water does not taste salty because a river is continually filled with fresh water from rain or thawing snow. There is only a small amount of salt in it at any one time.

3. Can salt be collected from the sea?

4. There is gold in seawater. True or false?

How are cliffs formed?

Cliffs are formed where a hard band of rock meets the sea. Waves carrying small pebbles break against the rock just above sea level. They erode, or eat into it, and a small cliff is made. The sea continues to eat away at the rock and makes an overhang. In time the overhang breaks off, leaving a bigger cliff for the sea to beat against.

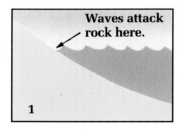
Waves attack rock here.
1

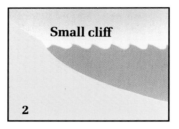
Small cliff
2

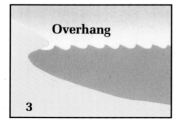
Overhang
3

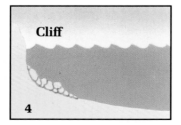
Cliff
4

5. Cliffs can form overnight. True or false?

6. Cliffs are only found on the coast. True or false?

How are beaches made?

Waves wash sand along the coast. When they reach a sheltered area they slow down, and drop the sand. In time, the sand builds up into beaches. Beaches are often found in sheltered bays.

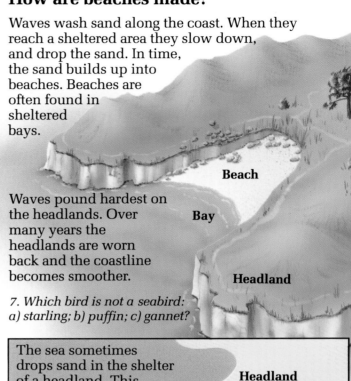
Beach
Bay
Headland

Waves pound hardest on the headlands. Over many years the headlands are worn back and the coastline becomes smoother.

7. Which bird is not a seabird: a) starling; b) puffin; c) gannet?

> The sea sometimes drops sand in the shelter of a headland. This makes a ridge of sand, called a spit.
>
> Headland
> Bay
> Spit

What is sand?

Sand is tiny particles of rock. It is washed into the sea by rivers and made when waves grind down rocky cliffs. Sand is also made from broken down shells, and coral which is washed ashore from nearby reefs. Few plants can grow in the sand on the beach, but many tiny creatures live in it.

8. Do you find sand dunes on beaches or on cliff tops?

Did you know?

The icebergs that float in the oceans of the far north and far south of the world come from glaciers (see page 43). Some glaciers flow down from mountains into the sea, and huge chunks of ice break off them and float away. Icebergs also break off from the thick sheet of ice that covers most of Antarctica. Frozen water does not contain salt, so all icebergs are made up of fresh water.

9. How much of an iceberg can you see above water: a) one half; b) one quarter; c) one eighth?

10. Which famous British cruise liner was sunk on its first voyage in 1912, by an iceberg in the Atlantic?

How do people use the sea?

The picture below shows how people use the oceans and coasts for energy, transport, food and pleasure. Careless use of the sea has damaged this environment, though. Look for the red boxes which describe some of the ways in which people have polluted the sea.

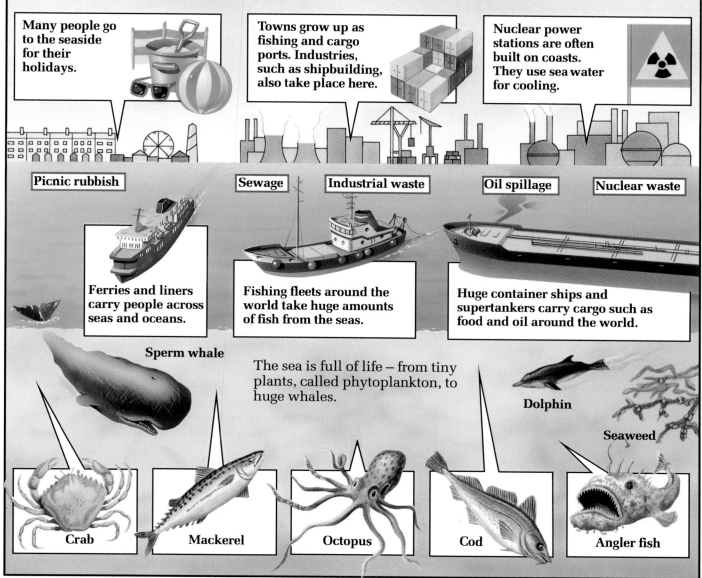

Many people go to the seaside for their holidays.

Towns grow up as fishing and cargo ports. Industries, such as shipbuilding, also take place here.

Nuclear power stations are often built on coasts. They use sea water for cooling.

Picnic rubbish

Sewage

Industrial waste

Oil spillage

Nuclear waste

Ferries and liners carry people across seas and oceans.

Fishing fleets around the world take huge amounts of fish from the seas.

Huge container ships and supertankers carry cargo such as food and oil around the world.

Sperm whale

The sea is full of life – from tiny plants, called phytoplankton, to huge whales.

Dolphin

Seaweed

Crab

Mackerel

Octopus

Cod

Angler fish

11. If attacked, an octopus will try to escape: a) in a cloud of black ink; b) on roller-skates; c) in the sand.

12. Can you eat seaweed?

13. How many of the sea animals in the picture are fish?

14. Fish living 3,000m (10,000ft) down in dark ocean waters can switch on lights. True or false?

Why do fish need protection?

When too many fish are taken from the sea, fewer fish are available to breed and numbers drop rapidly. Some countries are trying to make international laws to control the numbers of fish caught and to make fishing methods less cruel. Many sea creatures die unnecessarily in nets used to trap other fish. Thousands of dolphins, for instance, have been killed in huge nets called purse seines, used to catch tuna fish.

15. Dolphins are small whales. True or false?

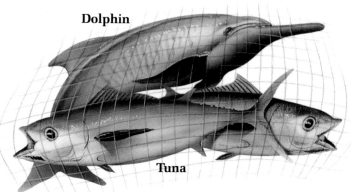

Dolphin

Tuna

People around the world

There are over 5,000 million people in the world. The world's population is now so large that there are more people alive today than have ever lived before. Most live where it is neither too hot nor too cold and there is a good supply of food.

Differences in skin color and face shape developed many thousands of years ago to help people to survive in one particular climate. For example, dark skin protected people in very hot countries from the sun. These differences are not so important today because modern clothes, houses and heating enable people of any physical type to live almost anywhere. Below are three of the most common types, or races, of people.

Negro people originally came from Africa.

1. Which race are Japanese people?

Caucasian people originally came from Europe and Asia.

Mongolian people originally came from Asia.

2. Which race are Scandinavian people?

Where did the first people come from?

People have not always lived all over the world. Scientists believe that the first people came from Africa. They could make tools to hunt with, and fire to keep themselves warm. When their numbers grew these skills enabled them to travel to cooler areas in search of fresh food supplies. The map below shows how people spread to the rest of the world from Africa.

3. The first humans might have hunted: a) camels; b) koalas; c) antelope.

4. No one lives in Antarctica because: a) there are only penguins to eat; b) it is too cold; c) the nightlife is dull.

5. One fifth of the world population today is Chinese. True or false?

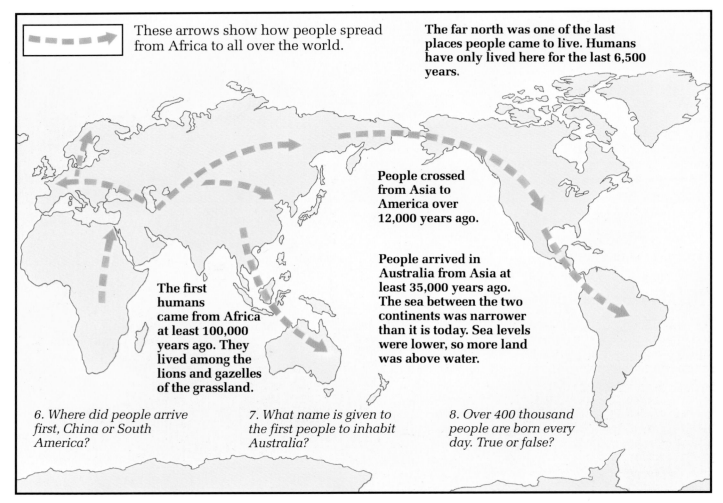

These arrows show how people spread from Africa to all over the world.

The far north was one of the last places people came to live. Humans have only lived here for the last 6,500 years.

People crossed from Asia to America over 12,000 years ago.

The first humans came from Africa at least 100,000 years ago. They lived among the lions and gazelles of the grassland.

People arrived in Australia from Asia at least 35,000 years ago. The sea between the two continents was narrower than it is today. Sea levels were lower, so more land was above water.

6. Where did people arrive first, China or South America?

7. What name is given to the first people to inhabit Australia?

8. Over 400 thousand people are born every day. True or false?

Why do people's lives vary so much?

People live very different lives across the world. Whether a country is rich or poor makes the greatest difference to the quality of everyday life. Religion, language and traditions also influence the way people live.

Families vary in size around the world. In rich countries like the USA, families have an average of two children. Many parents can afford to buy their children expensive clothes and possessions. Many children are encouraged to stay at school and are educated to a high standard.

9. Which of these items do not need electricity?

In poor countries like India, families usually have over six children. In some areas half these children die before they are five. Women have several children to make sure that some survive. Diseases carried in dirty water and sewage are the cause of most childhood deaths. Children cost their parents very little and by the age of 11 or 12 they can work and bring money into the home.

10. Throughout the world an average family has: a) one child; b) four children; c) ten children.

11. Which one of these is essential for any family: a) money; b) food and water; c) television; d) a home?

Did you know?

People in North America and Europe use about forty times as much energy, and eat three times as much food, as people in poor countries in Asia and Africa.

Which country has the most people?

China has the most people. There are over a thousand million Chinese. Two-thirds of them work on farms, which grow enough to feed this huge population. The government encourages couples to have only one child, to stop the population from getting so big it would be impossible to feed.

Rice is the main crop. It grows easily, but needs a lot of water.

A wide hat protects against the hot sun.

Almost all farming is done by hand, rather than with machinery.

12. Which one of these is not a Chinese dish: a) Chow mein; b) Dim sum; c) Shanghai?

How long do people live?

Throughout the world the average lifetime is around 64 years. People currently live the longest in Japan – the world's richest country. Men can expect to live to around 76 and women to around 82.

In Japan people eat a healthy diet. They eat more fish than any other country, and very little fat. Fish is often eaten raw, like this dish on the right, called *sushi*. Health services are good. Most people's lives are stable and comfortable.

Afghanistan is one country where people have much shorter lives. Few people live beyond forty. War, famine and disease are common and health services are poor.

Chopsticks

13. Which continent is Afghanistan in?

How many languages are there?

There are over 5,000 languages in daily use in the world. Mandarin is the most spoken one. It is used by two thirds of the Chinese population – 770 million people. Over 330 million people grow up speaking English, but around 1,000 million people learn it as an additional language. This pie chart represents all the people in the world. It shows how many speak Mandarin, and how many speak English as a first (dark blue) or second (light blue) language.

14. A mandarin is also a type of: a) lemon; b) orange; c) banana; d) grape.

15. The Romans spread the English language around the world. True or false?

Speakers of other languages

Mandarin speakers

English speakers

Cities and towns

The first people on Earth moved from place to place hunting animals and gathering wild fruits and seeds to eat. There were no villages, towns or cities.

About 10,000 years ago, people in some places began to keep animals and grow crops. This enabled them to stay and make homes in one place. These homes were the beginnings of villages, towns and cities. Today, about one third of the world's people live in towns and cities.

1. Which lived on Earth first, dinosaurs or people?

2. Which of these cities was built first: a) Rome; b) Los Angeles; c) Hong Kong?

Tall buildings make the best use of land, which can be expensive in city centres.

What is a city?

A city is a large or important town, where many people live. Thousands more will travel in and out of a big city every day. Some come to work, others to shop or visit professional people such as hospital doctors. Cities are busy, bustling places and city roads are often jammed with traffic – especially when people are travelling to and from work or school. Here are some of the things you might find in a city.

3. Village people might need to visit a town or city to buy: a) bread; b) a newspaper; c) a compact disc.

4. Would cities be cleaner and quieter if everyone came into them on buses and trains, or in their own cars?

5. Put these forms of transport in order of their invention: motorbike, aircraft, train.

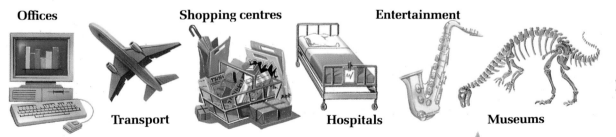

Offices Transport Shopping centres Hospitals Entertainment Museums Factories

What goes in and out of a city?

A huge amount of food, water and fuel is taken into cities every day. Cities also send out a huge amount of sewage and rubbish as well as dirt into the air. The picture on the right shows roughly how much goes into and out of an American city of about a million people each day.

Water 625,000 tonnes (tons).

Food 2,000 tonnes (tons).

Fuel for heating, cooking and cars 9,500 tonnes (tons).

Sewage 500,000 tonnes (tons).

Refuse 2,000 tonnes (tons).

Air pollutants 950 tonnes (tons).

6. Chicago in the USA has nearly three million people. How much food will it need every day?

7. Air pollution is mostly caused by sewage works. True or false?

Where are cities built?

There is always a good reason why a town or city grows up where it does. The picture below shows what some of these reasons might be.

Towns grew up in good farming areas where there was plenty to eat.

Towns were built near forests so that the wood could be used for heating and cooking.

Towns on a hill or cliff were easy to defend against enemies.

Towns were built near building materials such as stone, wood or clay.

Towns often grew up where routes crossed.

Capital cities are where a country's government meets. They usually began as ports or trading centres which grew successful and powerful.

Towns were built near a source of fresh water.

Industrial towns are usually near mines or ports.

Some towns grow up where people go for holidays. These are called holiday resorts.

8. Which one of these is not a capital city: a) Rome; b) Paris; c) New York; d) Wellington?

9. Capital cities are always found in the middle of a country. True or false?

10. Does a new town nowadays need to be built near farms and rivers for food and water?

11. Which one of the towns above would have had most difficulty finding fresh water?

What is a shanty town?

Shanty towns are areas in some cities where the poorest people live. Homes are made from scrap materials like cardboard boxes and corrugated iron. These homes will probably have no gas, drains, electricity or clean water supply. Six or more people may share two small rooms and diseases spread quickly. In Lima, the capital of Peru, one in six people live in a shanty town.

People come to cities such as Lima when they cannot find work in the countryside. They live in shanty towns if they are unable to find a job and a home.

12. Another name for a shanty town is: a) a barriada; b) a boom town; c) a new town.

13. Which continent is Peru in?

Lima has expensive homes too. There is a great difference in the lives of the rich and poor.

14. In some cities homeless children live in sewers. True or false?

Did you know?

The underground trains in Tokyo are so crowded that special "pushers" are employed to squeeze people into the carriages.

15. Tokyo is the capital city of: a) Mexico; b) Australia; c) Japan.

Spaces and wild places

The empty areas of the Earth are almost always hot, cold or high. Very few people live in these places but those that do have learned how to cope with the extreme conditions.

Many of these people have lived in the same way for thousands of years. This is changing, though. Today, large companies are moving into these areas to look for minerals such as oil, gas and coal. Many wild places can also be turned into farmland.

Who lives in the mountains?

As you go up a mountain, the air gets colder. Fewer plants can grow and only a few types of animal, such as sheep and llamas, can survive.

There is less oxygen the higher up you go. The Quecha Indians live 3,650m (12,000ft) up in the South American Andes. They have bigger hearts and lungs than people living at sea level. These can carry more blood and therefore more oxygen.

1. What are these flat sections cut into the mountainside used for?

2. The Quecha Indians use llamas for: a) transportation; b) pets; c) bed warmers.

Llamas

3. Quecha Indians can walk barefoot over icy rocks without feeling cold. True or false?

Beans and potatoes are tough enough to grow in cold places.

Where are the coldest places?

The coldest places on Earth are the areas within the Arctic and Antarctic Circles round the North and South Poles.

Who lives in the Antarctic?

The continent of Antarctica is covered by a layer of ice three or four kilometres (about two miles) thick. It is too cold for anyone to live a normal life here. Scientists come to study the wildlife or carry out experiments on the air, which is very pure. They live in homes built under the snow, away from the fierce winds and cold.

Outside, the average temperature is –50°C(–58°F).

Entrance

Inside it is 20°C (68°F).

Double door with airlock.

4. Palm trees grow on the coast of Antarctica. True or false?

5. Are polar bears a danger to Antarctic scientists?

Who lives in the Arctic?

Some people live just inside the Arctic circle. The Inuit, for instance, live in northern Canada, Alaska and Greenland. It is warmer here than in Antarctica because inside most of the Arctic Circle is ocean, which is warmer than land. Near the North Pole, though, the Arctic Ocean is frozen solid.

6. Which one of these countries does not have land inside the Arctic Circle: a) Greenland; b) Canada; c) Scotland?

7. Do the Inuit all live in igloos?

These traditional Inuit clothes are made of animal skins. Many Inuit now wear clothing made from man-made materials.

Thick skin jacket.

Thick sealskin or reindeer skin trousers.

Strong sealskin boots stuffed with dry grass.

The Inuit are mostly short and stocky. This helps them to keep warm as there is less body area exposed to the cold than in tall, long-limbed people. Many Inuit now work in the local oil and gas industries instead of making a living by hunting and fishing in the traditional way.

Who lives in deserts?

Deserts are areas with little or no rain. People who live in them have to be able to survive when there is very little food or water. The San of the Kalahari desert live by hunting animals and gathering plants.

The San live in small groups of 20 people or less. They camp for only a few weeks in one place. From each camp they hunt and gather over an area of 600 sq km (230 sq miles). Today, much of the San's richer land has been taken over by wealthy cattle ranchers.

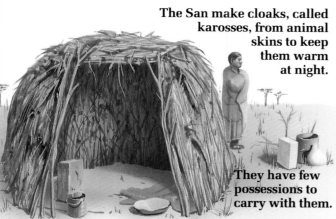

The San make cloaks, called karosses, from animal skins to keep them warm at night.

They have few possessions to carry with them.

8. Is it hot or cold at night in the desert?

The San search for water-filled plants such as tsama melons. These may be the only source of water for up to nine months of the year. San women's bodies adapt themselves so that they do not get pregnant when there is a drought.

Tsama melons

The San eat every scrap of meat killed in a hunt. They can store more fat on their bodies than most people.

The San hunt with bows and arrows.

9. In droughts, San only hunt male animals. True or false?

Did you know?

The San store water in ostrich eggshells. They sometimes bury the shells, so that they can use the water when rivers and water holes dry up. The eggshells are around 1cm (1/2in) thick, so they are quite tough.

10. Which are bigger, ostrich eggs or hen eggs?

What is a tropical rainforest?

Tropical rainforests grow near the Equator where it is very hot and wet. They are the home of nearly half the world's different kinds of plants and animals.

The soil in a rainforest is kept rich by dead leaves and rotting wood from the trees. If the forest is cut down the soil loses its goodness and can no longer be used for growing crops. People who live in the forest survive by looking after it.

11. About two million different kinds of plants and animals live in rainforests. True or false?

Who lives in the rainforest?

The Mbuti pygmies of Central Africa live by hunting wild animals and gathering edible plants. They move from place to place in search of food. They do no damage to the forest.

12. Are pygmies short or tall people?

13. Which people have a bigger choice of food, the San or the Mbuti?

Women and girls build houses. They cover a stick framework with a layer of large leaves.

Honey   **Nuts**

Yam

14. A yam is a vegetable which tastes like: a) a potato; b) a carrot; c) a cabbage.

15. It takes about: a) a week; b) a day; c) five minutes to build a pygmy house.

Today, the forest is being cleared for farmland and timber. This is taking away land from the pygmies. Many now work as farm laborers in villages at the edge of the forest.

Using the land

Two out of three people on Earth live and work on farms. They grow food, or crops such as rubber and cotton. The land is farmed in many different ways. Some people only grow enough to feed themselves and their families. Others have huge areas of land where crops such as wheat are grown. These crops are sold to large companies who then sell them all over the world.

1. Which two of the following are made from wheat: a) corn flakes; b) bread; c) spaghetti; d) rice pudding?

2. Which one of the following foods is not farmed: a) beef; b) trout; c) apples; d) tuna; e) rice?

Who are the small farmers?

Most farms in poor countries are small. Many people only have enough land to grow food for themselves. Some farmers also keep farms small to protect the soil. In tropical rainforests, for example, the soil would be destroyed if large areas of forest were cut to make fields.

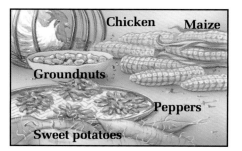
Chicken Maize
Groundnuts
Peppers
Sweet potatoes

The Yanomami of South America clear small gardens in the tropical rainforest. Some trees are left to protect the soil. After two or three years the garden is left to return to forest and a new area is cleared.

3. Sometimes a Yanomamo person is eaten by monkeys. True or false?

The Tuareg of the Sahara keep herds of camels and goats, to provide them with milk and meat. They need to travel from place to place to find enough food to feed their animals.

4. The Sahara is a huge desert in South America. True or false?

On some small farms, the farmers grow more than they need to feed themselves. They sell the extra at local markets. The picture shows the kinds of food you could buy in a Nigerian market.

5. In which continent is Nigeria?

Why are some farms so big?

In richer countries, where most people work in towns and cities, farmland is likely to be owned by only a few farmers. Most of these farms cover large areas of land. Some farms grow a single type of crop, or keep just one breed of animal. In the USA, grain is grown in huge fields. Expensive machines do most of the work and very few people work on the farm.

Wheat farm in central USA.

Merino sheep. These are reared for their fine wool, on huge sheep farms in Australia.

6. The farm machine shown above is: a) a combine harvester; b) a plough; c) a crop sprayer.

7. Are there more sheep-farmers or sheep-shearers in Australia?

Some Australian sheep farms are so huge that farmers travel around their farms in small planes.

8. Which of these countries is also well-known for its sheep: a) Peru; b) New Zealand; c) Finland?

What is a plantation?

Plantations are large estates where one crop, such as coffee, cocoa, tea or rubber, is grown. Most plantation crops need to be picked by hand, and many people work on plantations for low wages.

More than one third of the farmland in poor countries is used for plantations. They produce crops to be sold to other countries. Many plantation workers have their own plot of land to grow food for themselves.

9. Bananas grow underground. True or false?

10. Which of these countries is not a major tea producer: a) China; b) India; c) Belgium?

Cocoa beans are used to make chocolate.

Tea leaves are picked by hand.

Coffee beans are inside coffee berries.

Where does your food come from?

The food you eat comes from all over the world. Different kinds of food need different kinds of climate. Coffee grows well in Brazil and Kenya, for example. These countries usually have a very hot climate and a lot of rain. Apples, though, like a warm climate, as in France, and medium amounts of rain. The map below shows some examples of where your food might come from.

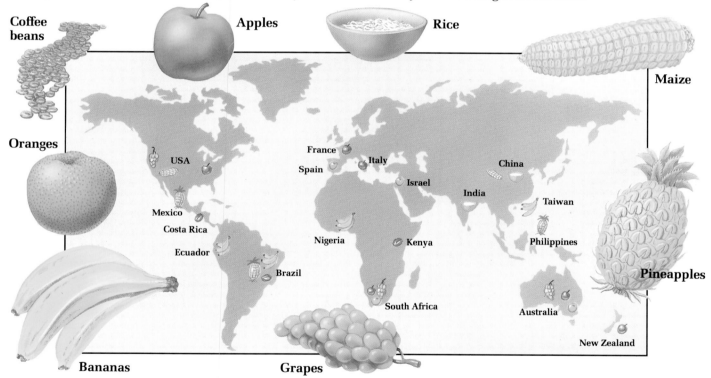

Coffee beans · Apples · Rice · Maize · Oranges · USA · France · Spain · Italy · Israel · China · India · Taiwan · Mexico · Costa Rica · Ecuador · Nigeria · Kenya · Philippines · Brazil · Pineapples · South Africa · Australia · New Zealand · Bananas · Grapes

11. Can bananas be farmed in parts of Europe?

12. Are there farms in all seven continents?

13. Do dates grow best in warm or cold countries?

Did you know?

Potatoes and many other common foods were unknown in Europe until the sixteenth century. Explorers brought them back from the mountains in the northern Andes, in South America. Explorers also brought tobacco, tomatoes and chillies from America to Europe.

14. South American Indians worshipped the potato. True or false?

15. Which one of these is not needed in a balanced diet: a) carbohydrate; b) protein; c) meat; d) vitamins; e) minerals?

Fuel and energy

Anything that lives or moves needs energy. A car needs fuel to drive its engine. You need food to give your body energy.

Energy in fuels such as coal, oil and gas can be converted into electricity by burning and processing them in power stations. You can use this electricity for lighting, heating, cooking and many other things. Most ways of producing electricity cause pollution*, and new ways are being developed that are cleaner and safer.

How was coal made?

About 300 million years ago large areas of the Earth were covered in hot, wet, tropical swamps.

As plants died, they collected in the bottom of the swamps.

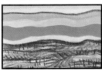

Over millions of years, layers of sand and clay settled on top. They pressed down and hardened into rocks.

The pressure from the rocks gradually changed the plants into peat and then into coal.

When coal is burned, it produces gases which make the air dirty. This is called air pollution (see pages 56-57).

1. Is coal found only underground?

2. Do trees contain energy?

What are fossil fuels?

Fossil fuels are fuels such as coal and oil which are found buried below the land and sea. They are made from the remains of animals and plants which lived millions of years ago. They contain energy which was stored by the animals and plants when they were alive.

3. Which of these is not a fossil fuel: a) oil; b) wood; c) coal?

When will fossil fuels run out?

Fossil fuels will not last forever. The world's coal supplies will probably run out in about 400 years. Oil and gas supplies will probably run out by the middle of the next century. There are plenty of energy sources on Earth besides fossil fuels. Some of them are shown below.

You can see how the energy is released from these sources on the next page. This sort of energy is called renewable or free energy because it will never run out.

4. Where is natural gas found?

5. Oil is found underground in: a) oil mines; b) oil wells; c) oil barrels.

What is nuclear energy?

You, and everything in the world, are made from atoms. Atoms are so tiny that there are more atoms in an ant than there are people in the world. Nuclear energy is made from splitting the atoms of a metal called uranium. When the center, or nucleus, is split, heat is given off. This can be used to make electricity.

6. A piece of uranium the size of a pin contains as much energy as 5,500 tons of coal. True or false?

7. Put these in order of discovery: a) steam power; b) nuclear power; c) electricity.

This picture shows how an atom is split.

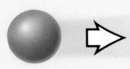

A tiny particle, called a neutron, is fired at the uranium nucleus.

Uranium nucleus

What is the energy of the future?

The pictures below show several ways of supplying energy which do not depend on fossil fuels.

Solar panel

Windmill

Windmill blades turn turbines to make electricity. One hundred windmills could provide enough electricity for 400,000 people.

Solar panels trap the Sun's heat. This heats water to make steam to run turbines in power stations. Solar power can also be used to heat houses.

*8. It costs nothing to convert free energy into electricity.
True or false?*

Tidal power dam

The movement of the tide can be used to turn turbines and make electricity, by building a tidal power dam across an estuary.

9. Is tidal power made inland or by the sea?

10. Do bicycles, skateboards and horse-drawn carts need fuel to make them move?

11. Which is the best source of energy for hot desert countries?

12. Which one of these uses energy from water: a) steam train; b) yacht; c) aircraft?

13. Which is the best source of energy for flat, windy countries?

Are there other energy sources?

These sources of energy are also being developed.

 Biogas is a gas made from rotting animal, plant and human waste. A small farm can provide itself with enough biogas to cook with.

 There is a lot of heat energy inside the Earth. In Iceland and New Zealand, hot springs heat homes and make electricity.

 Chains of rafts around a coastline absorb the energy of waves and turn it into electricity.

 The power in falling water can be used to make electricity.

14. What is electricity made from the power in falling water called?

 Many kinds of household and industrial garbage, which is usually buried, can be burned, and the heat used to make electricity. This also gets rid of the garbage. However, burning garbage does cause air pollution.

More neutrons are given off. These in turn split other atoms.

The nucleus is split and heat is given off.

Neutrons

When an atom is split, it sends harmful, invisible rays into the air. This is called radiation. It can cause burns and cancer. The waste from nuclear fuel is also radioactive (it gives off harmful radiation). No one has yet found a completely safe way to get rid of this waste.

Did you know?

It is possible to run a car on alcohol. In Brazil, an alcohol called ethanol is made from sugar cane. Ethanol burns easily and can be used for fuel in cars with modified engines. In 1990 a third of all cars in Brazil ran on ethanol.

*15. Cars can also run on cow dung.
True or false?*

Pollution

When air, water or land is made dirty or poisonous it is described as polluted. A polluted environment can be very harmful to the people, animals and plants within it.

1. Which of these cause pollution: a) planes; b) bicycles; c) cars; d) sailing dinghies?

What is acid rain?

Acid rain is made when poisonous gases and smoke in the air mix with water droplets in the clouds. This makes weak acids which fall to the ground as acid rain. This is sour, like vinegar, and it can kill plants and fish. The pictures below show where most of the poisonous gases that make acid rain come from.

Burning fossil fuels in power stations.

Burning fuel in factories, to drive machinery.

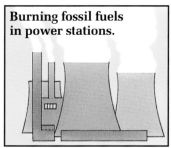

Exhaust fumes from cars, trucks and buses.

Burning fuel for cooking and heating in homes.

2. Is there such a thing as acid snow?

3. Can you name two ways of producing electrical energy which do not pollute the air?

What is the ozone layer?

Ozone is a gas which occurs 20-50km (10-30 miles) above the ground and forms a protective layer around the Earth.

6. Is the ozone layer above or below where the weather happens?

Ozone protects the Earth from dangerous light rays, called ultra-violet light, in sunlight. Too much ultra-violet light can cause skin cancer and eye diseases as well as damaging food crops, fish and other sea life.

7. Ultra-violet light can turn your skin purple. True or false?

The ozone layer is being damaged by gases called CFCs (short for chlorofluorocarbons, pronounced kloro-floro-carbons). These are used in things like foam boxes for take-away food, and in refrigerators and air-conditioning units. When these things break down or are destroyed, CFCs are released into the atmosphere.

Ozone layer wraps around the Earth.

Hole in ozone layer

Ultra-violet rays

Scientists have discovered two huge holes in the ozone layer – one over the Antarctic as big as the USA and another over the Arctic as big as Greenland.

8. Which of these might contain CFCs: a) cereal packet; b) hamburger carton; c) paper bag?

What harm does acid rain do?

Clouds containing acid rain may be carried more than 1,000km (over 600 miles) by the wind. The acid rain then falls a long way from the city, factory or power station which caused it. Acid rain can affect the environment in several ways, as shown in the pictures below.

Acid rain damages plants and crops. It removes the richness from the soil so crops cannot grow well.

Acid rain attacks leaves on trees. Half of western Germany's forests are dying due to acid rain.

Acid rain pollutes water. About 4,000 lakes in Sweden now have no fish due to poisoning by acid rain.

Acid rain eats away at buildings. It is a particularly damaging type of air pollution. An Ancient Greek temple called the Parthenon has been worn down more in the last 30 years than in the last 2,000.

4. The Parthenon is in: a) Rome; b) Athens; c) Cairo.

5. The Parthenon is made of concrete. True or false?

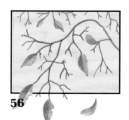

Acid rain eats into buildings.

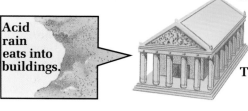

The Parthenon

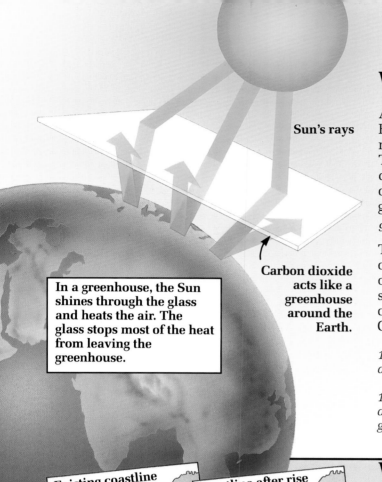

Sun's rays

Carbon dioxide acts like a greenhouse around the Earth.

In a greenhouse, the Sun shines through the glass and heats the air. The glass stops most of the heat from leaving the greenhouse.

What is the greenhouse effect?

A certain kind of air pollution is making the Earth's atmosphere act like a greenhouse. It is making the Earth's temperature rise very slowly. The Sun warms up the Earth but the atmosphere does not let the heat escape into space. This is called the greenhouse effect. It is also called global warming.

9. Only green plants grow in greenhouses. True or false?

The main cause of global warming is too much carbon dioxide in the atmosphere. Fossil fuels give off carbon dioxide when they are burned. Power stations which use coal are big producers of carbon dioxide. Fumes from car exhausts and CFCs also add to global warming.

10. Carbon dioxide in the atmosphere acts like the: a) glass; b) plants; c) air in a greenhouse.

11. Which one of these can help stop global warming: a) planting forests; b) burning fossil fuels; c) building greenhouses?

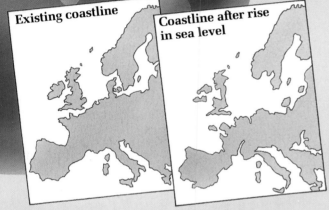

Existing coastline

Coastline after rise in sea level

12. Would you use a physical or a political map to work out how a rise in sea level would affect the land?

Why is global warming a problem?

If the world heats up by just a few degrees, some of the ice around the North and South Poles will melt. The extra water in the oceans will make sea levels slowly rise all over the world. Cities such as London and New York could disappear under the sea. Low-lying countries like Holland and Bangladesh could disappear completely.

The pictures on the left show how the map of Western Europe would change if all the ice at the poles were to melt. The sea would rise by 61m (200 ft).

13. Which two of these could cause flooding in a country: a) tidal waves; b) monsoon rain; c) severe drought; d) overflowing baths?

Did you know?

If a plastic bottle is dumped in the countryside, it will stay there for ever. Sunlight will decompose the plastic a little but once the bottle is buried in the ground it will not rot any more.

14. Which one of these everyday items cannot be made out of plastic: a) reading glasses; b) raincoat; c) ham sandwich; d) carpet; e) carrier bag?

15. Which of these words means "to use again": a) recycle; b) reset; c) reserve?

How can pollution be reduced?

Here are some of the ways you can help to reduce pollution.

Use less electricity. Switch off lights and heaters when you do not need them. **If you have a short journey, walk instead of travelling by car.**	**These will help reduce gases which cause acid rain and global warming.**
Use washing powders which do not contain phosphate cleaning chemicals. **Use smaller amounts of washing-up liquid and lavatory cleaner.**	**All these cleaners pollute water.**
Make sure that all your rubbish goes in the bin, not in the street or countryside. If you can, buy glass or tin containers rather than plastic, and recycle them.	**Glass and tin can be broken down and used again. Many plastics are indestructible.**

Geography Megaquiz

These ten quizzes test you on what you have read in Part Two of this book and also on your general knowledge of geography.

You can write your answers on a piece of paper and then check on page 64 to see how many you got right.

Capitals and countries

Can you match the capital cities in the blue strip to the countries in the mauve strip?

Canada	New Zealand	India	Denmark	Argentina	USA	Australia	China	Spain	Peru

Delhi	Copenhagen	Buenos Aires	Ottawa	Wellington	Beijing	Madrid	Lima	Washington DC	Canberra

Earth facts

1. Which is the largest ocean?
2. Which is the most southern continent?
3. Latitude and longitude lines are found:
   a) on the sides of mountains; b) on maps;
   c) on fishing boats.
4. Which is the thinnest layer of the Earth:
   a) the crust; b) the mantle; c) the core?
5. How long does it take for the Earth to spin around once on its axis?
6. Glaciers are frozen: a) lakes; b) waterfalls;
   c) rivers.
7. Are tropical rainforests getting larger or smaller?
8. Is more of the Earth covered by sea or by land?
9. Where might you find phytoplankton:
   a) in the sea; b) under the ground; c) in the atmosphere?
10. What is the name of latitude 0°?

Seas and oceans

Can you match the seas and oceans in the list below with the areas marked a – j on the map?

Atlantic Ocean
Antarctic Ocean
Indian Ocean
Pacific Ocean
Black Sea

North Sea
Arctic Ocean
South China Sea
Arabian Sea
Mediterranean Sea

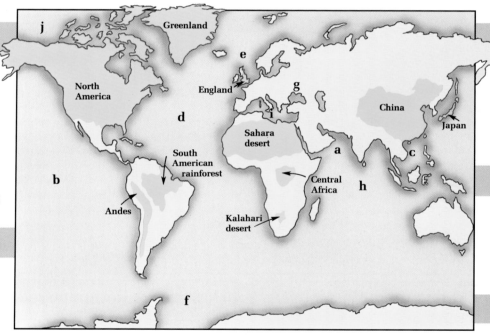

People and places

Can you match the people described below to the shaded places on the map?

1. The first people on Earth probably lived here, according to scientists.
2. People here currently have the longest lives.
3. The Tuareg live in this desert.
4. The Inuit live here.
5. The San live in this desert.
6. The Yanomami live in this rainforest.
7. The Quecha Indians live in these mountains.
8. People in this country form the largest population.
9. People crossed from Asia to this continent 12,000 years ago.
10. Over a fifth of the world can speak the language of the people from this country.

Close-ups

These are all close-ups of pictures in Part Two. Can you recognize what they are?

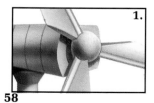
1.

2.

3.

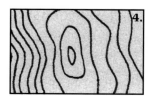
4.

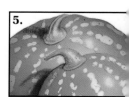
5.

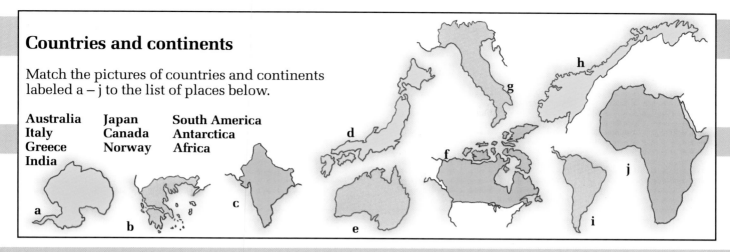

Countries and continents

Match the pictures of countries and continents labeled a – j to the list of places below.

Australia   Japan   South America
Italy   Canada   Antarctica
Greece   Norway   Africa
India

The sky and beyond

1. The first person landed on the Moon in:
   a) 1928; b) 1969; c) 1989.
2. The Moon takes about: a) a day; b) a week;
   c) a month to circle the Earth.
3. Which part of the environment do CFCs harm:
   a) the ozone layer; b) the sea; c) the soil?
4. Which planet is closest to the Sun?
5. Does lightning make the air it goes through hot
   or cold?
6. Is the Sun; a) a planet; b) a star; c) an
   asteroid?
7. Which is bigger, the Universe or our solar
   system?
8. Which of these is not usually found in the air:
   a) oxygen; b) nitrogen; c) plutonium?
9. What is a mixture of falling ice and rain called?
10. Which is bigger, a hurricane or a tornado?

Misfits

In each set of three below, there is one misfit. Can you spot which it is?

1. Jupiter; Saturn; the Moon.
2. Brazil; Tokyo; Sweden.
3. Mediterranean; Pacific; Atlantic.
4. Tornado; hurricane; lightning.
5. Quecha; San; Merino.
6. Wood; coal; oil.
7. Wave power; wind power; nuclear power.
8. Cirrus; axis; stratus.
9. Alabama; Andes; Alps.
10. Sahara; Kalahari; Nairobi.

Silhouettes

How many can you recognize?

True or false?

1. The Moon circles around the Earth.
2. Some mountain people have bigger hearts and lungs
   than people living at sea level.
3. Saturn's rings are made of gold.
4. Scientists have traveled to the center of the Earth.
5. Most of the people in the world live or work on
   farms.
6. A country is a small continent.
7. Thunder is caused by two clouds bumping into each
   other.
8. The Earth is traveling through space at nearly
   30km (18.6 miles) per second.
9. Some cars can run on sugar.
10. Asteroids are a drug for fattening cattle.

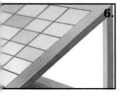    

Quiz answers

The answers to the 12 quizzes from *The Earth in Space* to *Pollution* are on the next four pages. Give yourself one point for every right answer. The chart below helps you find out how well you have done in each quiz.

0-5	Read through the answers, then try the quiz again. See how many answers you can remember second time around.
6-10	Quite good. Think more carefully about the questions and you might get more answers right.

11-14	Good score. If you get this score on most of the quizzes, you have done very well.
15	Excellent. If you do this well in more than half the quizzes, you are a geography genius!

Your score overall

You can find out your average score over all 12 quizzes like this:

1. Add up your scores on all 12 quizzes.
2. Divide this total by 12. This is your average score. How well did you do?

General knowledge

All the answers to general knowledge questions are marked★. These questions are probably the hardest in the quizzes. Add up how many of them you got right across all 12 quizzes. There are 50 of them in total. If you got over 30 right, your geography general knowledge is good.

The Earth's atmosphere

1. c) A solar system is made up of a star and circling planets.
★ 2. No. The Earth is just one tiny planet in one of millions of galaxies.
★ 3. a) light years. A light year is the distance a ray of light would travel in a year – 9,460 thousand million km (5,878 thousand million miles).
4. No. Stars give off light and heat. The Moon only reflects sunlight.
★ 5. b) Neil Armstrong was the first man on the Moon, in July 1969.

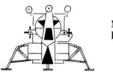

Neil Armstrong's landing craft.

6. Pluto is the coldest planet, as it is the furthest (5,900 million km or 3,700 million miles) from the Sun.
★ 7. Venus is named after the Roman goddess of love.
8. The Milky Way is much bigger than a solar sytem.
9. JUPITER and MARS.
10. In the picture when it is day in Africa it is night in South America.
11. True. In July the top of the Earth is tilting towards the Sun. The North Pole never moves into the area of shadow.

Earth's axis — North Pole — Sun's rays

12. False. All parts of the world have 24 hours in a day.
13. No. In our solar system, Mercury and Venus do not have moons.
14. No. Neptune is a very cold planet with a poisonous, frozen atmosphere. Nothing could survive there.
15. No. You cannot see a New Moon because the side of it that is lit up is facing away from the Earth.

The surface of the Earth

1. The Arctic and Antarctic would be white or bluey-white. They are both covered with ice and snow.
★ 2. The largest continent is Asia.

Asia

Australia is the smallest continent.

3. No. Nobody lives at the North Pole. It is in the frozen Arctic Ocean.
4. False. Cold weather and steep slopes make mountains difficult to farm.
★ 5. The Himalayas are in Asia.
6. There are many more penguins than people at the Antarctic.
7. True. The Sahara desert covers almost all of northern Africa.
8. b) The River Nile flows through Egypt.
9. True. Around two-thirds of Brazil is covered by the Amazon rainforest.

Amazon rainforest

★ 10. The centre of the Earth is much hotter than the Sahara desert. It is probably about 6,000°C (11,000°F) at the centre of the Earth – over one hundred times hotter than any temperature recorded on land.
★ 11. True. Africa and South America used to be joined together. They began to separate about 135 million years ago.
12. a) The lowest places on Earth are at the bottom of the sea. The lowest place known is the Marianas Trench which is more than 11,000m (36,000ft) below sea level.
13. b) San Francisco is famous for its earthquakes.
★ 14. Yes. Volcanoes can erupt under the sea as well as on land.
★ 15. Mount Everest. It is 8,848m (29,028ft) high.

Mapping the world

1. A globe is more accurate than a flat map of the Earth. Map-makers do not need to change the shapes of the land and sea to make a globe.

Globe

★ 2. Asia is the missing continent.
3. You would use a political map to find a country's borders. Political maps usually also show the position of major cities.
4. There are 13 countries in South America. These are: Argentina; Bolivia; Brazil; Chile; Columbia; Ecuador; French Guiana; Guyana; Paraguay; Peru; Surinam; Uraguay and Venezuela.
5. No. There is not a West Pole (or an East Pole).
★ 6. The direction half way between north and east is north-east.
★ 7. South is the direction at the bottom of most maps.
8. No. Latitude and longitude lines are only found on maps.
9. c) London. Longitude 0° runs through an astronomy museum, called the Royal Observatory, and is marked on the floor with an iron bar.

Greenwich Royal Observatory

10. The ships are nearer to Europe.
11. The volcano's position is 40°N, 20°E.
12. The hurricane's position is 20°N 60°W.
13. There is flat land on the map at C.
14. It is very steep at B.
15. A is at the top of a hill.

The Earth's atmosphere

★ 1. You need to breathe oxygen.
2. Yes. Jets cruise above most weather, but still have to fly through bad weather when they take off and land.
★ 3. b) At 0km (0 miles) it is sea level. This is the same everywhere, unlike land with its mountains and valleys.
4. True. There is less air above you on top of a mountain than there is at sea level, so air pressure is less.
★ 5. It is hot at the Equator. The Sun's rays are most concentrated here.

★ 6. a) A weather vane tells you which way the wind is blowing.

Weather vane

7. False. It is warmer at sea level than on the top of a mountain. This is because the Sun's rays have more land surface area to heat in mountainous areas than in flat ground and sea. Also, air holds heat, and the higher you go, the less air there is to hold it.

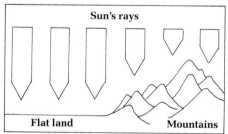

8. Great Britain has more changeable weather than the Sahara desert, which is hot and dry all through the year.
9. No. Climate is the kind of weather a place has on average year after year. Weather is what a place has from day to day.
10. Cirrus clouds are the highest clouds. They are found at around 18km (11 miles) up in the sky.
★ 11. c) Smog is a mixture of smoke and fog.
12. The storm is about 4km (2 miles) away if you hear thunder ten seconds after seeing lightning.
13. There are more thunderstorms at the Equator. Weather here is far more changeable, with plenty of the hot air currents thunderstorms need.
14. True. The centre of a hurricane is called the eye. The eye is a calm area with no wind.
15. False. Tornadoes have never been known to lift trains right off the ground. They can, however, turn over trains and grounded aircraft.

Rivers and rain

1. a) Camels can survive without a drink for 21 days (three weeks) if they only eat dry food. If they eat succulent desert plants which contain water, they never need to drink.

Desert plant

2. b) The water in wet washing becomes water vapour when it dries.
3. Clouds are made of water. Most clouds are made of tiny water droplets, but high cirrus clouds have tiny ice crystals in them.
4. True. In fact all the water in the world is constantly being re-cycled.
5. Yes. Your breath contains water vapour. You can see the water in your breath when you breathe out on a cold day.
★ 6. a) The Thames (346km/215 miles) is much shorter than either the Nile (6670km/4145 miles) or Amazon (6448 km/4007 miles). The Nile is the longest river in the world.

Relative length of rivers:

Thames ▬

Amazon ▬▬▬▬▬▬▬▬▬▬▬▬▬

Nile ▬▬▬▬▬▬▬▬▬▬▬▬▬▬

7. False. Rivers can only flow downhill.
★ 8. Water freezes at 0°C (32°F).
9. b) You can live without water for four days.
10. False. Hydroelectric power stations are often found in mountainous regions where fast flowing water drives the power station turbines.
11. Hydroelectric, tidal and wave power are all forms of water power.
★ 12. b) The Grand Canyon is not a famous waterfall. It is a deep, steep-sided valley, cut by the Colorado River in the USA.

The Grand Canyon

13. True. Fish caught from polluted rivers and eaten can cause stomach upsets or more serious poisoning.
14. c) Glaciers are found in Scandinavia. Glaciers are also found in many other parts of the world, such as India, where there are high mountains.
15. Rivers flow a lot quicker than glaciers. Glaciers only move a few centimetres (an inch or two) a day, so slowly that you cannot see them move.

Oceans and coasts

1. Yes. The Earth's oceans are all joined together.
2. c) The Mediterranean is a sea.

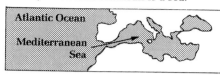

★ 3. Yes. Seawater evaporates in shallow pools and salt is left behind.
4. True. Seawater contains a tiny amount of gold.
5. True. In big storms cliffs can form overnight. In 1953 at Covehithe in England the coast was cut back 27m (90ft) in a day.
6. False. Cliffs can also be found along river banks where the river has worn away the valley in its path.
★ 7. a) A starling is not a seabird.
8. Sand dunes are found on beaches. They occur when the wind usually blows in the direction of the shore and sand is blown up the beach.

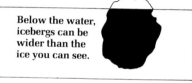

9. c) You can see about one eighth of an iceberg above the water.

Below the water, icebergs can be wider than the ice you can see.

★ 10. The Titanic. This luxury passenger liner was travelling from England to the USA. When the Titanic sank, over 1,500 people drowned.
11. a) An octopus will try to escape from an enemy in a cloud of black ink. The octopus carries this ink, called sepia, in a special sac in its body. Artists have used sepia in paintings since Roman times.
12. Yes, seaweed such as laver, dulse, and sea lettuce can be eaten.

Edible seaweed

★ 13. Three of these animals are fish – the mackerel, cod and angler fish.
14. True. Many deep sea fish have parts of their bodies which light up. The light comes from luminous bacteria, which live in the fish. These lights attract prey to eat, and also other deep sea fish to mate with.
15. True. Dolphins are small streamlined whales.

People around the world

1. Japanese people are of the Mongolian race.
2. Scandinavian people are of the Caucasian race.
3. c) The first humans might have hunted antelope in the African grassland.
4. b) No one lives permanently in Antarctica because it is too cold.

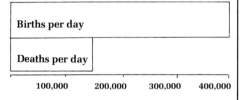
Antarctica

5. True. About one in five people on Earth are Chinese.
6. People arrived in China first. There have been people in China for at least 70,000 years. Scientists think that people only reached South America around 11,000 years ago.
★ 7. The original inhabitants of Australia are called Aborigines.
8. True. Around 400,000 babies are born every day. Around 150,000 people die every day too, so each day there are 250,000 more people on Earth.

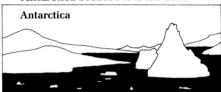

Births per day	
Deaths per day	
100,000 200,000 300,000 400,000	

9. The tennis racket and the books do not need electricity. Electrical power has only been widely available since the beginning of this century.
10. b) Throughout the world the average number of children in a family is four.
11. b) Food and water are essential for survival.
★ 12. c) Shanghai is not a Chinese dish, it is a city in China. Beijing is China's capital city, but Shanghai is its biggest city, and largest port.

CHINA Beijing• Shanghai•

★ 13. Afghanistan is in the continent of Asia.

EUROPE Afghanistan ASIA AFRICA

★ 14. b) orange.
15. False. The Romans spoke Latin.

Cities and towns

★ 1. Dinosaurs lived on Earth first. They died out about 65 million years ago. The first people lived on Earth less than one million years ago.

Dinosaur

2. a) Rome was built first, over 2,500 years ago.
3. c) Village people might need to visit a town or city to buy a compact disc.
4. Cities would be cleaner and quieter if everyone came into them on buses and trains.
★ 5. The right order is train, motorbike, aircraft.

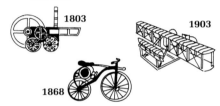
1803   1903   1868

6. Chicago would need about 6,600 tons of food every day.
7. False. Air pollution is mostly caused by industry, power stations burning fossil fuels, and cars.
8. c) New York. The capital of the USA is Washington DC.
9. False. Capital cities may be anywhere in a country. For example, Madrid, the capital of Spain, is in the center of the country, but Washington DC is on the east coast of the USA.

Madrid    Washington• DC

10. No. Water can be piped and food transported over huge distances, so new towns can be built almost anywhere.
11. The town that has been built upon a hill to defend itself from enemies would have had the most difficulty finding fresh water.
12. a) A barriada is another name for a shanty town.
★ 13. Peru is in the continent of South America.

Pacific Ocean   Atlantic Ocean   Peru   SOUTH AMERICA

14. True. For example, in Brazil in South America, there are homeless children who live in sewers.
15. c) Tokyo is the capital city of Japan.

Spaces and wild places

★ 1. The flat sections cut into the mountainside are used for growing food. They are called terraces and they stop soil from being washed away.
2. a) The Quecha Indians use llamas for transport.
3. True. The Quechas' feet become toughened so they do not feel cold.
4. False. Palm trees only grow in warm climates.

Palm trees

★ 5. No. Polar bears do not live in the Antarctic. Like walruses, they are only found in the Arctic.
★ 6. c) Scotland does not have land within the Arctic Circle.
7. No. Very few Inuit still live in igloos, although some Inuit build them on winter hunting trips.

Igloo

8. It is cold at night in deserts. The temperature can drop below freezing.
9. True. In a drought the San take care not to hurt female and young animals so that some animals will survive for another time.
★ 10. Ostrich eggs are much bigger than hen eggs. An ostrich egg can be 20cm (8in) long and 15cm (6in) around.

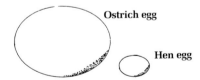
Ostrich egg   Hen egg

11. True. There are more varieties of plants and animals in tropical rainforests than anywhere else on Earth.
★ 12. Pygmies are short people. Men in pygmy tribes are usually less than 150cm (5ft) tall.
13. The Mbuti have a bigger choice of food than the San. The rainforest provides the Mbuti with nuts, roots, vegetables and fungi, as well as termites, freshwater crabs and animals like antelope.
★ 14. a) A yam is a vegetable which tastes like a potato.

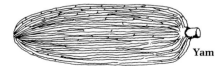
Yam

15. b) It takes about a day to make a pygmy house.

62

Using the land

1. b) and c). Bread and spaghetti are made from wheat.

Wheat

2. d) Tuna are not farmed. Tuna are fished from the open ocean, using large nets.
3. False. However, the Yanomami do sometimes eat monkeys.
4. False. The Sahara desert is a huge desert in Africa. It is about as big as the USA.
★ 5. Nigeria is in the continent of Africa.

6. a) The farm machine shown in the picture is a combine harvester. Combine harvesters are used to cut wheat and other crops. They cut the straw and separate it from the grain. The grain is stored in the machine and the straw is dropped out of the back of the machine.
7. There are more shearers than sheep farmers in Australia. Each sheep is sheared by hand and shearers travel from farm to farm.
★ 8. b) New Zealand is also well-known for its sheep.
9. False. Bananas grow on huge herb plants which look like trees.

Banana plant

10. c) Belgium is not a major tea producer. Belgium is too cold for growing tea.
11. No. Bananas need a hot, wet, tropical climate to grow well.
12. No. There are no farms in Antarctica.
13. Dates grow best in warm countries.

Dates

14. False. South American Indians grew potatoes for food.
★ 15. c) Meat is not needed in a balanced diet. However, meat is a good source of protein, vitamins and minerals.

Fuel and energy

★ 1. No. Coal is not found only underground. Layers, or seams, of coal can be found on the surface and on the sides of hills. Collecting coal from these seams is called "open-cast mining".

Digger used in open-cast mining.

2. Yes. The energy in trees is released when they are burned for heating or cooking.
3. b) Wood is not a fossil fuel.
★ 4. Natural gas is found underground. It is often found with or near oil.

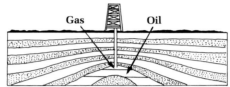

★ 5. b) Oil is found underground in oil wells.
6. True.
★ 7. Beginning with the earliest, the order is: a) steam power (early 18th century); c) electric power (late 19th century); b) nuclear power (mid-20th century).

Light bulb 1879

8. False. It is expensive to build power stations and turbines to convert free energy to electricity. Once completed, however, they are inexpensive to run.
9. Tidal power is made by the sea. A dam is usually built across a tidal river estuary.
★ 10. Yes. Even though skateboards, horse-drawn carts and bicycles do not use fuel, they still need energy. This comes from the food that the cyclist, skateboarder and horse eat.
11. The best source of energy for desert countries is solar energy, as the Sun shines nearly all the time.
12. a) Steam trains convert water to steam, which powers their wheels.
13. Wind to drive windmills is the best source of energy for flat, windy countries.

Wind farm in California.
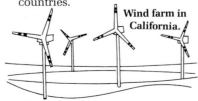

★ 14. This kind of electricity is called hydroelectricity.
15. False. Dried cow dung can be used, however, as a fuel for heating and cooking.

Pollution

1. a) and c). Plane and car engines burn fossil fuels, which cause pollution.
2. Yes. Acid snow is made in a similar way as acid rain.
★ 3. Give yourself a point if you got two of the following: hydroelectric power, wave power, tidal power, wind power, solar power, underground heat.
★ 4. b) The Parthenon is in Athens.

5. False. The Parthenon was built of white marble, nearly two and a half thousand years ago.
6. The ozone layer is above where weather happens. (See page 40.)
7. False. Ultra-violet light will tend to make fair-skinned people browner.
8. b) A hamburger carton might contain CFCs.

Hamburger carton

9. False. Many kinds of different plants are grown in greenhouses.
10. a) Carbon dioxide in the atmosphere acts like the glass in a greenhouse.

Greenhouse

11. a) Planting forests can help to stop global warming. Trees, and other plants, take carbon dioxide from the air to give themselves energy, in a process called photosynthesis. They give off oxygen. Forests are very important on Earth as they help to keep the correct balance of oxygen and carbon dioxide in the atmosphere.

Carbon dioxide **Oxygen**

12. You would use a physical map to work out how a rise in sea level would affect the land.
13. a) and b) could cause flooding in a country.
14. c) A ham sandwich cannot be made out of plastic. Food is just about the only thing which cannot be made from plastic. Plastics can be used for almost everything else – from beach balls to aircraft fuselages.
★ 15. a) Recycle means "to use again".

Geography Megaquiz answers

There are 100 points in the Geography Megaquiz. If you score over 50 you have done well. Over 75 is excellent. You can find out more about the answers on the pages listed after them.

Capitals and countries

1. Canada/Ottawa.
2. New Zealand/Wellington.
3. India/Delhi.
4. Denmark/Copenhagen.
5. Argentina/Buenos Aires.
6. USA/Washington DC.
7. Australia/Canberra.
8. China/Beijing.
9. Spain/Madrid.
10. Peru/Lima.

Earth facts

1. The Pacific Ocean (page 36).
2. Antarctica (page 36).
3. b) on the maps (pages 38-39).
4. a) the crust (page 37).
5. A day – 24 hours (page 35).
6. c) rivers (page 43).
7. Smaller (page 51).
8. Sea (page 44).
9. a) in the sea (page 45).
10. The Equator (page 39).

Seas and oceans

1. Atlantic Ocean (d).
2. Southern Ocean (f).
3. Indian Ocean (h).
4. Pacific Ocean (b).
5. Black Sea (g).
6. North Sea (e).
7. Arctic Ocean (j).
8. South China Sea (c).
9. Arabian Sea (a).
10. Mediterranean Sea (i).

People and places

1. Central Africa (page 46).
2. Japan (page 47).
3. Sahara desert (page 52).
4. Greenland (page 50).
5. Kalahari desert (page 51).
6. South American rainforest (page 52).
7. Andes (page 50).
8. China (page 47).
9. North America (page 46).
10. England (page 47).

Close-ups

1. Windmill (page 55).
2. Cocoa beans (page 53).
3. Asteroids (page 34).
4. Contour lines (page 39).
5. Tsama melons (page 51).
6. Solar panel (page 55).
7. Eskimo clothes (page 50).
8. Merino sheep (page 52).
9. Chinese rice harvester (page 47).
10. City tower block (page 48).

Countries and continents

1. Australia (e).
2. Italy (g).
3. Greece (b).
4. India (c).
5. Japan (d).
6. Canada (f).
7. Norway (h).
8. South America (i).
9. Antarctica (a).
10. Africa (j).

The sky and beyond

1. b) 1969 (page 34).
2. c) a month (page 35).
3. a) the ozone layer (page 56).
4. Mercury (page 34).
5. Hot (page 41).
6. b) a star (page 34).
7. The Universe (page 34).
8. c) plutonium (page 40).
9. Sleet.
10. A hurricane (page 41).

Misfits

1. The Moon is not a planet.
2. Tokyo is a city not a country.
3. The Mediterranean is not an ocean.
4. Lightning is not a wind.
5. Merino are sheep, not people.
6. Wood is not a fossil fuel.
7. Nuclear power is not "free" energy.
8. An axis is not a cloud.
9. Alabama is not a mountain range.
10. Nairobi is a city not a desert.

Silhouettes

1. Chopsticks (page 46).
2. Pineapple (page 53).
3. San bow and arrow (page 51).
4. Snowflake (page 40).
5. Bananas (page 53).
6. Research balloon (page 40).
7. Penguin (page 36).
8. Mbuti hut (page 51).
9. Cod (page 45).
10. Australian farm aircraft (page 52).

True or false?

1. True (page 35).
2. True (page 50).
3. False.
4. False.
5. True (page 52).
6. False.
7. False.
8. True (page 35).
9. True (page 55).
10. False.

Place index

Below is a list of some of the places you can read about in Part Two and where to look them up.

The photos on page 46 are reproduced by kind permission of the Hutchison Library.

Part Three

SCIENCE QUIZBOOK

Paul Dowswell and Marit Claridge

Edited by Judy Tatchell and Lisa Miles

Designed by Ruth Russell and Fiona Brown

Illustrated by Chris Lyon and Chris Shields

Additional text by Carol Varley

Consultants: Peter McKerchar, Geoffrey
Puplett, John and Margaret Rostron

Contents

About Part Three

Part Three of the book is an introduction to scientific ideas.
It looks at what things are made of and how they work –
from plants and animals, to racing cars and video cameras. It
also explains natural forces and effects, such as gravity,
electricity, sound and light.

How to do the quizzes

Throughout the book there are quiz questions to answer as
you go along, printed in italic type, *like this.* Some of the
questions rely on your general knowledge, others have clues
elsewhere on the page. Keep a note of your answers and
check them against the answers on pages 92-95.

The Science Megaquiz

On pages 90-91 is the Science Megaquiz – a
set of ten quick quizzes to test you on your
general knowledge and what you
have read about in Part Three.

Exploring space

The whole of space and everything in it is known as the Universe. Scientists do not know how large the Universe is, but the part they do know about contains millions of groups of stars, called galaxies. Each galaxy is in turn made up of millions of stars.

Where is the Earth?

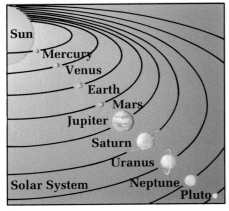

Sun
Mercury
Venus
Earth
Mars
Jupiter
Saturn
Uranus
Solar System
Neptune
Pluto

The Earth is one of nine planets which circle around a central star, the Sun. The Sun and its planets are called a solar system. The Sun is a star in the galaxy called the Milky Way.

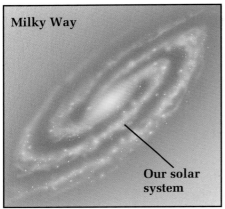

Milky Way

Our solar system

As far as we know, the Earth is the only planet that provides the air, water and warmth that living things need. It is just the right distance away from the Sun for water to exist as a liquid, rather than gas or ice. Earth's atmosphere also protects it from getting too hot or too cold.

1. Venus, Neptune and Mars are named after: a) Roman gods; b) astronomers; c) Egyptian pharaohs.

2. Are Sirius, Betelgeuse and Alpha Centauri stars or planets?

How old is the Universe?

Most scientists believe that the Universe began about 15 thousand million years ago. An enormous explosion, called the Big Bang, created an immensely hot, dense fireball. Everything in the Universe came from this fireball. The force of this explosion was so great that stars and galaxies are still being blasted away from each other, and the Universe is still expanding.

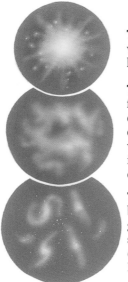

The fireball was made of hydrogen gas.

The gas formed a dense cloud of particles which broke into separate clouds.

These clouds became galaxies of stars, like our own Milky Way.

How do we know what is in space?

Scientists use a variety of telescopes to see what is out in space. For example, optical telescopes use lenses to magnify light. These telescopes were first used about 400 years ago and enabled astronomers to get a closer look at the night sky. Today, photographic film and electronic sensors can record faint images that the eye cannot see.

Stars and planets give off other rays besides the light we can see. Telescopes can now detect radio waves, ultra-violet and X-ray signals from stars which are so distant they cannot be seen by even the most powerful optical telescopes.

3. Radio waves from stars contain: a) blips, bleeps and hisses; b) alien traffic reports; c) light music.

4. Einstein was the first scientist to use a telescope. True or false?

Why is the Sun hot?

The Sun is an immense ball of burning hydrogen gas. It releases huge amounts of energy in a similar way to a nuclear bomb, in the form of heat and light. The Sun is so big, it is taking millions of years to burn.

The temperature at the surface is about 6,000°C (11,000°F).

Sun

The middle of the Sun is 2,500 times hotter than the surface.

7. One day the Sun will go out. True or false?

8. Is it safe to look directly at the Sun?

9. Which one of these would you find in space: a) a purple pixie; b) a white dwarf; c) a green gremlin?

This radio telescope picks up radio waves from stars which cannot be seen by optical telescopes.

5. You can see X-rays and ultra-violet rays. True or false?

6. A group of stars is called: a) a compound; b) a collection; c) a constellation.

How does a rocket fly?

Rockets need an immense amount of energy to blast themselves out of the Earth's atmosphere. They burn fuel, which creates hot gas which escapes through exhaust nozzles. This produces a force like air rushing out of the end of a balloon, which pushes the rocket forwards.

The space shuttle uses two sets of rockets to blast it into space. Once in space, launch rockets and the main fuel tank fall back to Earth.

The shuttle can launch satellites in space, or carry out scientific experiments. It glides back to Earth and lands like an aircraft.

10. The first spacecraft to land men on the Moon was called: a) Sputnik; b) Apollo 11; c) Starship Enterprise.

11. Dogs have been up in space. True or false?

What is a satellite?

A satellite is anything that orbits around a planet. The Moon is a satellite, and so is a spacecraft. Man-made satellites have many uses. Weather satellites take pictures of cloud formations which can be used to predict the weather. Astronomy satellites send back information on stars and planets. Communication satellites send telephone conversations and television transmissions around the world.

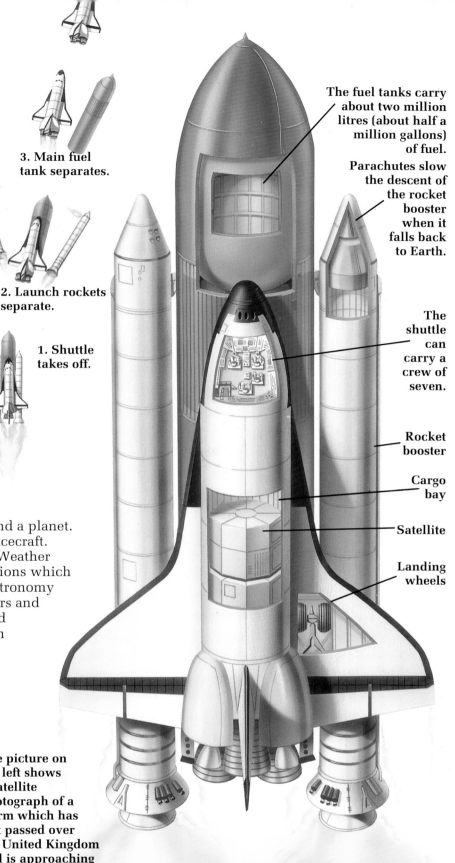

3. Main fuel tank separates.

2. Launch rockets separate.

1. Shuttle takes off.

The fuel tanks carry about two million litres (about half a million gallons) of fuel.

Parachutes slow the descent of the rocket booster when it falls back to Earth.

The shuttle can carry a crew of seven.

Rocket booster

Cargo bay

Satellite

Landing wheels

The picture on the left shows a satellite photograph of a storm which has just passed over the United Kingdom and is approaching Scandinavia.

12. Sailors use satellites to navigate around the oceans. True or false?

13. The word "satellite" comes from a Latin word for: a) attendant; b) star; c) spacecraft.

14. Which country was the first to launch a satellite?

15. Yuri Gagarin was the first man: a) on the Moon; b) to go into space; c) to drive his spaceship into a satellite.

Did you know?

When astronomers look at stars, they are seeing many of them as they were thousands or millions of years ago. Some of these stars may even no longer exist. Starlight takes this long to reach Earth because distances in space are so huge.

What are things made of ?

Everything in the world, from mountains and oceans, to air and animals, is made of chemicals.

What are chemicals?

All chemicals are made up of minute particles called atoms. The simplest chemicals are made of only one kind of atom and are called elements. Chemicals made up of two or more elements are called compounds. There are around one hundred elements, and over ten million compounds. New compounds are being discovered all the time.

Glass is a compound made of the elements silicon, sodium and oxygen.

Water is a compound made of the elements hydrogen and oxygen.

Copper, which is used in electrical wiring, is an element.

The mercury in a thermometer is an element.

Gold is an element.

Helium is an element. It makes balloons float up in the air.

Sand is a compound made of the elements silicon and oxygen.

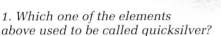

1. Which one of the elements above used to be called quicksilver?

Although food, wood and plastic are very different, most contain the same three elements: hydrogen, carbon and oxygen. What makes them different is the way their atoms have joined together to form larger particles, called molecules, and how these molecules have arranged themselves.

2. Diamonds and coal are both made from the same element. True or false?

3. Which of these is sand not used for: a) making glass; b) putting out fires; c) seasoning food?

What makes something a solid, a liquid or a gas?

Atoms and the molecules they form are always moving, even in things that look still. Whether something is a solid, liquid or gas depends on how much these molecules are moving.

When water is solid ice, the water molecules are packed together evenly. These molecules are moving, but they are only vibrating.

Ice

When water is liquid, the molecules are close together, but are able to slip past each other. Liquids flow because the molecules can move around and change places with each other.

Water

How small is an atom?

Atoms are so small that if you magnified an atom to the size of a table tennis ball, the ball magnified by the same amount would be the size of the Earth.

Atom

Table tennis ball

Earth

4. Where in the world is water always ice?

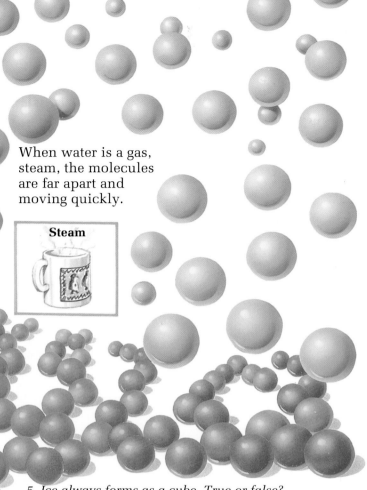

When water is a gas, steam, the molecules are far apart and moving quickly.

Steam

5. *Ice always forms as a cube. True or false?*

6. *Can iron be turned into a liquid?*

7. *Gas squashed into a smaller space is called:*
a) commendable; b) contaminated; c) compressed.

Did you know?

Ancient Greeks guessed that everything was made of atoms two and a half thousand years ago. The word "atom" comes from the Greek word *atomos* which means "uncuttable".

Is anything smaller than an atom?

Atoms are made of even smaller particles called protons, neutrons and electrons.

Protons and neutrons are found in the middle, or nucleus, of an atom.

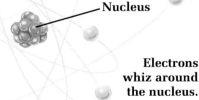

—Nucleus

Electrons whiz around the nucleus.

- Proton
- Neutron
- Electron

Elements such as gold and mercury are different from one another because their atoms have a different number of electrons and protons.

8. *Electrons carry: a) specks of dust; b) an electrical charge; c) water molecules.*

What is nuclear energy?

Nuclear energy (also called atomic energy) is stored in the nucleus in the middle of an atom. This energy can be released in the form of heat, in two ways. Large atoms can be split in two, or small atoms can be joined to other small atoms. Nuclear energy can be used to make electricity and very powerful weapons.

Nuclear power stations produce energy by heating steam which drives turbines to make electricity.

Heat is produced by nuclear energy.

Turbines make electricity here.

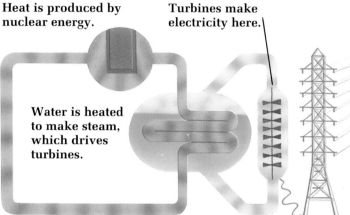

Water is heated to make steam, which drives turbines.

Nuclear bombs produce huge amounts of heat and are tremendously destructive. Some are so powerful that just one could destroy an entire city.

9. *Which of these metals is used to make nuclear energy: a) uranium; b) iron; c) copper?*

10. *Nuclear bombs have only been used against one country. Do you know which one?*

Can you see atoms?

It is possible to see atoms with a scanning electron microscope. This can magnify up to around 50 million times by passing a stream of electrons through an object, which then strike a screen. A computer turns the pattern the electrons make into a picture, in which individual atoms are depicted.

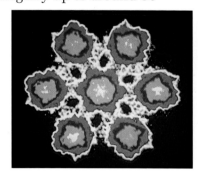

11. *A microscope which uses lenses to magnify is called an: a) oracle; b) electrical; c) optical microscope.*

12. *All nuclear energy is man-made. True or false?*

13. *Are smells solids, liquids or gases?*

14. *Which squashed gas do divers, astronauts and firemen carry in tanks, to enable them to breathe?*

15. *Unravel each of these words to make the names of three elements: dogl, propec, geynox.*

Using materials

The earth and sea are full of useful substances which are called raw materials. Raw materials are the basic ingredients for anything that people make.

What are raw materials?

Raw materials are natural materials. Most look different from the products they are used to make. Metals, for example, come from rocks called ores. This diagram shows some raw materials and their products.

1. Can you match these raw materials with their products?

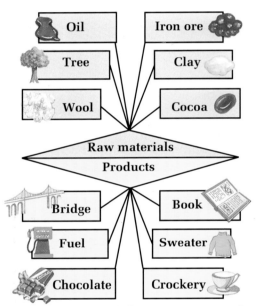

2. Which one of these is a man-made material: a) wool; b) copper; c) nylon?

How are new materials made from raw materials?

Some raw materials, such as wood, can be used as they are. Others, such as metal ores, contain useful chemicals which have to be extracted before they can be used. This can be done with heat, or by combining the raw material with other chemicals.

Ores generally produce only one product: the metal inside them. Oil, called crude oil in its natural state, is more complex. It contains thousands of chemicals which can be turned into millions of products.

How are new materials made from oil?

The thousands of chemicals in oil can be separated, or refined, by a process called fractional distillation. Many of the products of distillation, such as diesel oil, can be used as they are, but many others need further refining. This diagram shows how a distillation tower works.

3. Which area is famous for producing crude oil: a) Texas, USA; b) the North Pole; c) Paris, France?

4. Does cooking oil come from crude oil?

1. Crude oil is heated to a very high temperature, and most of it enters the distillation tower as a gas.

4. The chemicals obtained from crude oil can be used to make many things, such as medicines, detergents, waxes, plastics and fuel.

3. Chemicals in the gas cool to a liquid at different temperatures. They are collected at different levels in the tower.

2. As the gas rises, it cools.

How are materials used?

When designers create a product, they specify the most suitable materials for the job. For example, in motor racing, materials are chosen to keep the driver safe and also to help the car perform well. This picture shows how some of these materials are used in the car and clothing of a top racing driver. Many of the materials come from metal ores and crude oil, but plant and animal materials are also used.

The car body is made of a mixture, or composite, of man-made materials known as plastics. One of these plastics is called Kevlar*, which comes from the chemicals in crude oil. Kevlar gives the car strength. It is a very useful material because not only is it strong and rigid, it is also very light. It has many other uses, such as in the manufacture of bulletproof vests and the bodies of boats and aircraft.

5. Why is it important that the car is light in weight?

Seat

Steering wheel

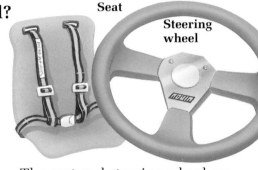

The seat and steering wheel are covered in suede, a velvety kind of leather. Suede helps the driver grip.

The tyres are mainly made of rubber, which grips the track well. Layers of steel and fabric give strength and flexibility.

■ Rubber

□ Steel

▨ Fabric

6. What kind of raw material is rubber made from?

How is metal taken from ores?

There are about 80 known metals. A few, such as gold, exist on their own, but most are found within ores, which are mined.

Metals are extracted from their ore by heating them with other materials. The atoms in these substances are rearranged to make new substances. This process is called a chemical reaction.

The diagram shows how iron is extracted from iron ore by a process called smelting.

10. More than three-quarters of elements are metals. True or false?

11. This type of furnace is called an: a) open; b) closed; c) blast furnace.

12. Some metals explode if they are dropped in water. True or false?

Iron ore, coke (a form of coal) and limestone are heated at very high temperatures in a furnace.

Iron ore breaks down, producing iron.

Air blown in here makes the coke burn fiercely.

Limestone combines with other substances in the ore, making waste material called slag.

Iron, now a liquid, sinks to the bottom where it is removed.

The driver's suit and gloves are made from another oil product: a light, fire-resistant material called Nomex*. Fire-fighters and astronauts also wear Nomex suits.

7. Why is the driver's suit fire-resistant?

8. Can crude oil be used directly in cars as fuel?

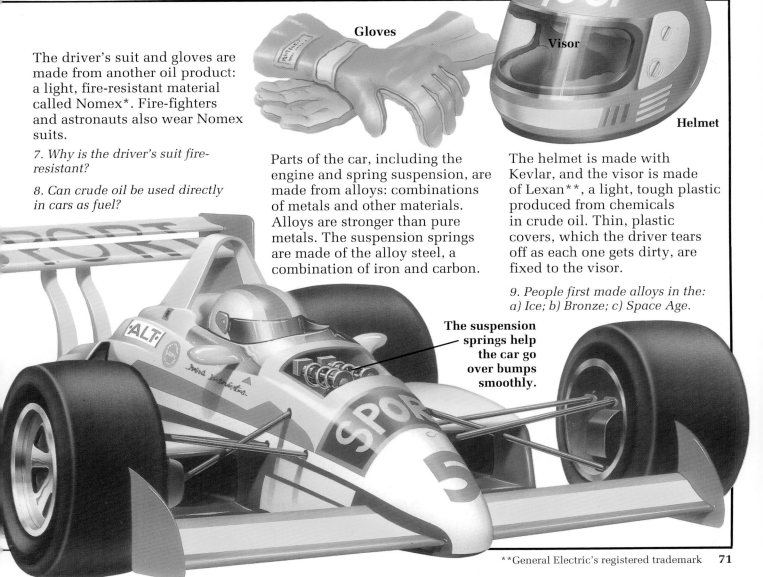

Gloves

Visor

Helmet

Parts of the car, including the engine and spring suspension, are made from alloys: combinations of metals and other materials. Alloys are stronger than pure metals. The suspension springs are made of the alloy steel, a combination of iron and carbon.

The helmet is made with Kevlar, and the visor is made of Lexan**, a light, tough plastic produced from chemicals in crude oil. Thin, plastic covers, which the driver tears off as each one gets dirty, are fixed to the visor.

9. People first made alloys in the: a) Ice; b) Bronze; c) Space Age.

The suspension springs help the car go over bumps smoothly.

Moving, flying and floating

Deep in space, a moving object will carry on at the same speed, in the same direction endlessly. This does not happen on Earth. Forces act on everything, making them speed up, slow down, change direction and even change shape.

What is a force?

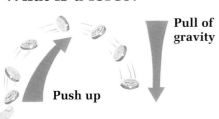

Pull of gravity

Push up

Everything on Earth has forces acting on it. There are two main types of force: a push and a pull. If you flip a coin into the air, your hand pushes the coin up. The coin is pulled down by a force called gravity.

What is gravity?

Gravity pulls all objects towards one another. However, it is a weak force. Only huge objects, such as planets, have a strong enough gravity to pull things to them.

Gravity pulls objects down.

Force of ground pushes up.

Gravity pulls everything towards the middle of the Earth. Things are not sucked in because the ground pushes up against them. Gravity, like all forces, has an opposite force working against it.

1. Astronauts on the way to the Moon go most of the way with their rocket engines switched off. True or false?

What makes things heavy or light?

How heavy something is depends on how big it is, how heavy its atoms are, and how closely these atoms are packed together. A steel ball weighs more than an apple of the same size because its atoms are heavier: it is said to have a greater density. It feels heavier because gravity pulls harder on denser materials.

2. Is stone more dense than chocolate?

3. Steel is made from copper and lead. True or false?

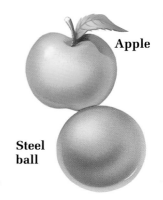

Apple

Steel ball

How do forces work?

This picture shows how forces act on a bike when you are riding along. The different forces affect how the bike moves and how fast it is able to go.

1. The force of the Earth's gravity pulls the bike down against the road.

2. The ground pushes in the opposite direction against the wheels of the bike.

3. As you turn the pedals, the wheels are pushed around. The wheels push the bike forwards.

4. Air pushes in the opposite direction to your body and the bike, as you ride along.

4. In a race, why do cyclists crouch down low over the handlebars?

5. Which type of bike is made for two riders: a) a tandem; b) a unicycle; c) a tricycle?

What makes things slow down?

Objects pushing against each other, such as a wheel pushing against the ground, create a force called friction. Friction slows moving objects down. It also produces heat. This is why bike wheels feel hot when you have been riding. Some of the bike's energy is turned into heat instead of moving the wheels, which slows the bike down.

Brakes work using friction. When you work the brakes on a bike, the brake blocks are pulled against the wheel rims. Friction acts between them, bringing the bike to a halt.

6. Would you feel more friction on ice or on gravel?

7. You can get a friction burn from: a) a candle flame; b) boiling water; c) sliding down a rope.

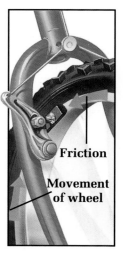

Friction

Movement of wheel

How do planes fly?

Planes need tremendous power to lift them into the air. Their engines give them the power to accelerate forwards, while the shape of their body and wings helps them to lift upwards.

Gravity pulls everything downwards. However, planes stay in the sky because of the way that air pushes on them. Air presses on objects from all sides, and slow-moving air pushes harder than fast-moving air.

Planes' wings are shaped to make the air under the wings travel slower than the air going over the wings. When a plane reaches a certain speed, the slower air beneath the wings pushes harder than the air going over them, forcing the plane into the sky. This force is called lift.

8. Most birds have hollow bones. True or false?

9. The first people to fly used aircraft which were driven by: a) paddles; b) propellers; c) rockets.

10. Do all aircraft have wings?

11. Some aircraft can fly without engines. True or false?

The engines push the plane forwards.

Air flow

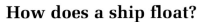

Cross-section of wing

The top of the wing is curved, so air flowing over it travels farther and faster, to catch up with the air flowing underneath.

Air going under the wing travels less distance than air going over it, so it travels more slowly.

Push down

Cross-section of wing

Push up

Faster-moving air pushes down with less force.

Slower-moving air pushes up with more force.

How does a ship float?

Some materials, such as polystyrene and paper, float because they are less dense than water. Other materials, such as metal, sink because they are more dense than water. The force of gravity pulling on them is greater than the force of water pushing up against them.

Even so, steel ships with heavy loads can float. There are two reasons why. Ships' bodies, or hulls, push a lot of water down beneath them. This is called displacement. The water then pushes back up against the ship, holding it up. This upward force of the water is called upthrust.

The ship and cargo push down.

The water pushes up.

12. Would an empty ship sit higher or lower in the sea?

13. Does cork sink or float in water?

14. A submarine sinks by: a) rolling over; b) pointing its nose down; c) filling tanks with water.

The hull is wide, so that it pushes a lot of water down.

Also, ships are not solid. They have air spaces inside them, such as storage holds. Air makes the ship less dense, so that it pushes down with less force. If the force of the ship pushing down is equal to the upthrust of the water, the ship will float.

Did you know?

Over 300 years ago, in the 1660s, the scientist Isaac Newton was the first person to realize how gravity worked. One story says that the idea first came to him when he saw an apple fall from a tree and hit the ground.

15. Isaac Newton was also well known for: a) painting portraits; b) studying mathematics; c) writing romantic novels.

Making things work

In order for something to grow, move, light up, or do any sort of work at all, it needs energy. Without energy, there would be no life.

What is energy?

There are many different forms of energy. Some are shown below. Energy does not always stay in the same form, but can change from one form, such as chemical energy, to another, such as heat energy.

Heat energy

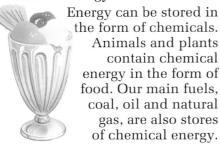

Something hot has more energy than something cold because its atoms are moving around faster. Heat energy can spread from one place to another.

Light energy

Light is a form of energy that moves very fast, in straight lines. Nothing travels faster than light. It is usually given out by things that are very hot.

The hot filament of a light bulb gives out light energy.

Chemical energy

Energy can be stored in the form of chemicals. Animals and plants contain chemical energy in the form of food. Our main fuels, coal, oil and natural gas, are also stores of chemical energy.

Sound energy

Sound energy travels in waves, called sound waves. Sound waves move through the air, making it vibrate. When the sound waves reach your ears you hear them as sounds.

Potential energy

Potential energy is the stored energy an object has because of its position. A spring that is squeezed or stretched has potential energy. Energy is released when the spring is let go.

Nuclear energy

Nuclear energy is stored in the nucleus (middle) of atoms. Nuclear power stations use this to produce electricity. The light and heat given out by the Sun are produced by nuclear energy.

Electrical energy

Electrical energy travels through electric wires by jumping from atom to atom. It can be turned into many other forms of energy such as sound and light.

1. Which sort of energy does a piece of stretched elastic have?

2. Hot water has more energy than steam. True or false?

Kinetic energy

Kinetic energy is the energy in movement. Everything that moves has kinetic energy. The faster it moves and the heavier it is, the more kinetic energy it has.

3. Can you name two forms of energy that you would find in lightning?

4. The first nuclear power station opened in: a) 1601; b) 1956; c) 1990.

5. Can sound energy travel through walls?

Where does energy come from?

Almost all of the energy on Earth comes from the Sun. The Sun's heat warms the land, sea and air. It also causes the winds, waves and ocean currents, which all have kinetic energy. The energy in food also comes directly from the Sun, as shown in the picture.

Plants use sunlight to make their food, which they store as chemical energy in their stems and leaves.

The energy in meat comes from the plants which were eaten by the animal.

Coal, oil and natural gas have formed over millions of years from plant and animal remains. Their energy comes from the chemical energy stored in plants and animals.

6. Manure can be used as a source of energy. True or false?

7. Oil, coal and natural gas are called: a) solid fuels; b) fossil fuels; c) solar fuels.

8. Without the Sun, there would be no rain. True or false?

Three main sources of energy do not come directly from the Sun's heat and light. These are radioactive materials such as uranium, which are used to make nuclear power; the heat deep within the Earth; and tidal energy, which is caused by the pull of the Sun and Moon on the Earth's oceans.

9. Uranium is a type of: a) metal; b) plastic; c) salt.

Where does energy go?

When energy is used, it changes into another form of energy. Energy never goes away and new energy is never made. Even energy that seems to fade to nothing, such as the sound of your voice, is not lost: it just spreads out further and further as tiny vibrations.

Fireworks are stores of chemical energy. When they explode, the chemical energy is suddenly turned into sound, light, heat and kinetic energy.

When a cat pounces, the chemical energy stored within its body is turned into kinetic energy. When animals move, their muscles also produce heat energy.

Light energy

Heat energy

Sound energy

Kinetic energy

Chemical energy

A cat stores chemical energy from its food.

Chemical energy is turned into kinetic energy and heat.

Did you know?

Around 70% of the energy in fuels is lost when they are used to produce electricity. This is because some energy escapes as heat each time energy changes form. At a power station, energy has to change three times, from fuel to heat, to movement and then to electricity. Heat escapes at each stage.

10. What sorts of energy does a burning candle produce?

11. Which form of energy cannot travel through space: a) heat; b) light; c) sound?

12. Most light bulbs lose 95% of their energy as heat. True or false?

How is food turned into energy?

When you eat, food is broken down, or digested, in your stomach and intestines. It is then absorbed into your blood, which is pumped around your body to your muscles.

In your muscles, energy is released from food by a process like very slow burning, called respiration. Respiration, like burning, needs oxygen. This is why you breathe.

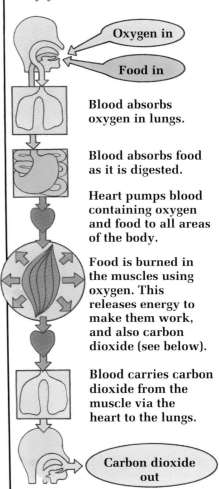

Oxygen in

Food in

Blood absorbs oxygen in lungs.

Blood absorbs food as it is digested.

Heart pumps blood containing oxygen and food to all areas of the body.

Food is burned in the muscles using oxygen. This releases energy to make them work, and also carbon dioxide (see below).

Blood carries carbon dioxide from the muscle via the heart to the lungs.

Carbon dioxide out

When fuel burns, it produces a gas called carbon dioxide. Your blood carries the carbon dioxide produced in your muscles back to your heart, which pumps it to your lungs so you can breathe it out.

13. Energy in food is measured in: a) calories; b) watts; c) grams.

14. Who has more stored energy, a fat person or a thin person?

15. Do you use energy when you are asleep?

Electricity and magnetism

Electricity and magnetism are forms of energy, like sound and light. They have an effect on each other that can be put to many uses, from driving an electric motor to powering a computer.

What is electricity?

Electricity is made from electrons: the particles that make up the outside of an atom (see page 69).

In some materials, the electrons can move easily from atom to atom. This flow of electrons is called electricity. It occurs naturally, and it can also be man-made.

Materials that electrons can pass through easily, such as metals, are called conductors. Copper is used in electrical wiring because it is a good conductor. Materials which electrons cannot pass through, such as plastic, are called insulators.

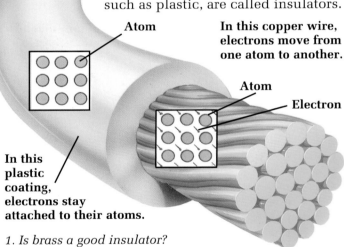

Atom

In this copper wire, electrons move from one atom to another.

Atom

Electron

In this plastic coating, electrons stay attached to their atoms.

1. Is brass a good insulator?

Did you know?

Electricity produces heat and fires can start if electrical wiring overheats. Fire-fighters use foam instead of water to put out electrical fires. This is because water conducts electricity and could give the fire-fighters electric shocks.

What causes lightning?

Lightning is caused by static electricity. This is the same kind of electricity as man-made electricity but it is made in a different way. It happens naturally when two materials rub against each other.

3. Thunder is the noise made when lightning hits the ground. True or false?

4. Does lightning hit the highest or lowest point on the ground beneath it?

Lightning occurs when water and air particles in a cloud rub against each other. An electrical force, or charge, builds up and jumps to the Earth, or another cloud, in a huge flash.

Cloud

Water rubs against air.

Lightning

5. Which one of the following can be caused by static electricity: a) hair standing up on end; b) fireworks; c) torrential rain?

If you walk on a nylon carpet and drag your feet, electrons jump from the carpet to your feet. This causes an electrical charge to build up on your body. When you touch a metal object, the static electricity jumps over to it, giving you a tiny electric shock.

Nylon carpet

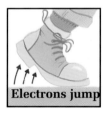
Electrons jump

Electric shock

6. Lightning never strikes in the same place twice. True or false?

7. Tiny electric shocks keep you alive. True or false?

8. Which of these would help prevent electric shocks: a) rubber boots; b) steel helmet; c) cotton socks?

9. Why is it unsafe to use an electrical appliance when your hands are wet?

How does electricity get to your home?

Electrons do not move along a wire by themselves, they are pushed along by a force. Power stations create this force, which is measured in volts.

Heat from a nuclear reaction, for example, turns water to steam. The steam drives a turbine which spins a magnet in a coil of wire.

2. Are all turbines powered by steam?

This causes an electric current to flow in the coil. This device, called a generator, sends electricity from the power station along a wire cable.

Power station

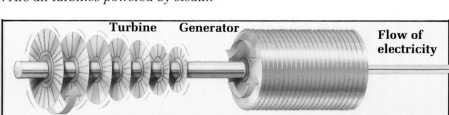
Turbine   Generator

Flow of electricity

How do magnets work?

In a magnet, there are millions of particles which all have a tiny magnetic force. These particles line up to point the same way, making a force strong enough to pull or push certain metals within the magnet's range, or field.

Only a few metals, such as iron, have magnetic particles. In iron, these particles can be lined up easily to make a magnet. If you hit it with a hammer, the particles no longer line up and the iron loses its magnetic force: it becomes demagnetized.

10. Can magnets pick up wood?

11. Is the Earth magnetic?

12. Does glue work by magnetism?

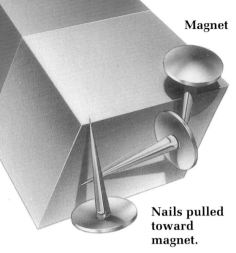

Magnet

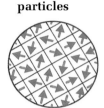

Particles in an iron magnet.

Demagnetized particles

Nails pulled toward magnet.

How does a junk-yard magnet work?

Powerful magnets, which can be switched on and off, are used to move heavy pieces of metal around junk yards. These magnets, called electromagnets, work because an electric current flowing along a wire creates a magnetic field. This effect is called electromagnetism. It is used to work many machines in factories and homes.

An electromagnet is made by coiling electrical wire around a bar of easily magnetized metal, such as iron. When the current is switched on, the magnetism of the metal bar and the wire coil combine.

So, when the operator of a junk-yard magnet wants to pick up metal, the magnet is switched on. The operator can then move the metal by swinging the giant magnet. When the operator wants to drop the metal, the current is switched off.

Electrical wire coiled around magnet.

13. Electrical power is measured in:
a) Whys; b) Sparks;
c) Watts.

How does an electric motor work?

If a coil of wire is put inside a magnetic field and the current switched on, the coil is attracted by the magnetic field around it, which makes it spin. The spin of the wire coil can drive a machine. This device is called an electric motor. Electric motors are used in many machines such as an electric fan, or a food blender.

Magnet

Spindle turns blades.

Wire coil

Blades turn, circulating air in the room.

14. Which one of these electric devices uses an electric motor:
a) kettle; b) light bulb; c) doorbell;
d) washing machine?

15. Electric motors were invented in: a) 1421;
b) 1621; c) 1821.

At home, electricity is fed into a meter which records how much is used. It also flows through a fuse, a narrow wire which melts if the current is too strong.

The wires and machines that electricity flows through are called a circuit. All parts of a circuit must connect for electricity to flow.

Switches control electricity in the circuit. Switching on or off completes or breaks the circuit, working a radio, for example.

Meter

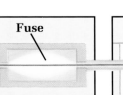

Fuse

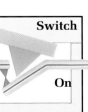

Switch

On

Off

Sound and music

Sound is a kind of energy which travels through air, water and solid objects such as walls and the ground. Most types of sound contain only a small amount of energy.

How are sounds made?

Sounds happen when the tiny particles that make up the air are made to move back and forth very quickly. This movement is called vibration.

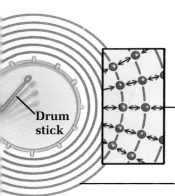

When a drum is hit, the skin vibrates and bumps into air particles.

Air particles bump into the ones next to them.

Sound travels as waves of vibrating air.

Drum stick

The waves travel in an expanding circle. Strong vibrations make loud noises and gentle ones make quiet noises.

1. Which has more energy, the sound of a handclap or a clap of thunder?

2. The loudness of a sound is measured in: a) handbels; b) loudbels; c) decibels.

3. Can sound travel around corners?

What makes sounds different?

When air particles vibrate quickly, the sound waves travel close together. You hear them as a high-pitched sound, such as a bird's chirrup.

If air particles vibrate slowly, the sound waves are further apart. You hear them as a low-pitched sound, such as the chugging of a truck. The speed of vibration is called frequency.

What is an echo?

When sound waves hit a solid surface, such as a cliff, some travel through it. Others bounce back, like waves in the sea bouncing back off the cliff.

Sound waves travel back through the air towards the source of the original sound. You then hear the sound again, as an echo. Short, loud noises make the best echoes.

Fishing boats find shoals of fish by sending high-pitched sounds down into the sea. The sounds echo back off the fish, and a computer on board interprets the echoes, locating the fish.

7. Can children hear higher frequencies than adults?

8. Would you hear an echo better on a windy day or a calm day?

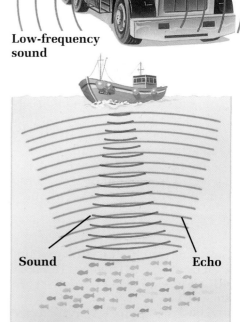

High-frequency sound

Low-frequency sound

Sound   Echo

9. Some sounds are so loud they are able to travel around the world. True or false?

10. Locating objects by listening to echoes of high-frequency sound is called: a) radar; b) sonar; c) laser.

How do you hear?

Your ears pick up vibrations in the air, and turn them into electrical signals that your brain can understand.

The outside flap is called the pinna. It helps to funnel the vibrations toward the eardrum.

The eardrum vibrates when sounds hit it.

4. The bones in the middle ear are called the nut, bolt and screw. True or false?

Three tiny bones pick up the vibrations. These bones carry the vibrations to the inner ear.

The vibrations go into a spiral tube full of liquid, called the cochlea. Nerves change vibrations into electrical signals and carry them to your brain.

Nerves

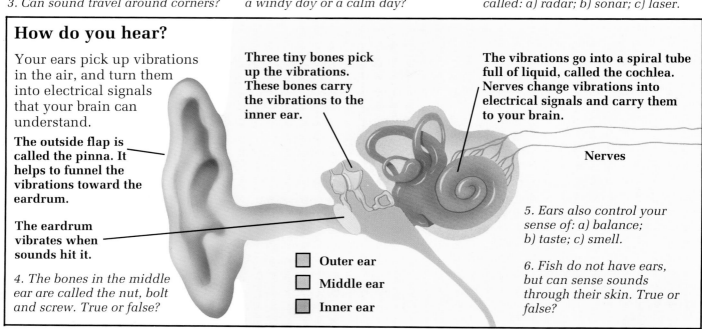

☐ Outer ear
☐ Middle ear
☐ Inner ear

5. Ears also control your sense of: a) balance; b) taste; c) smell.

6. Fish do not have ears, but can sense sounds through their skin. True or false?

What sounds do animals hear?

Many large animals, such as elephants, can hear lower sounds than people, but not the high sounds that we do. Many small animals, such as shrews and bats, can hear and make higher sounds than people. Bats listen to the echoes of the sounds they make, to find insects to eat.

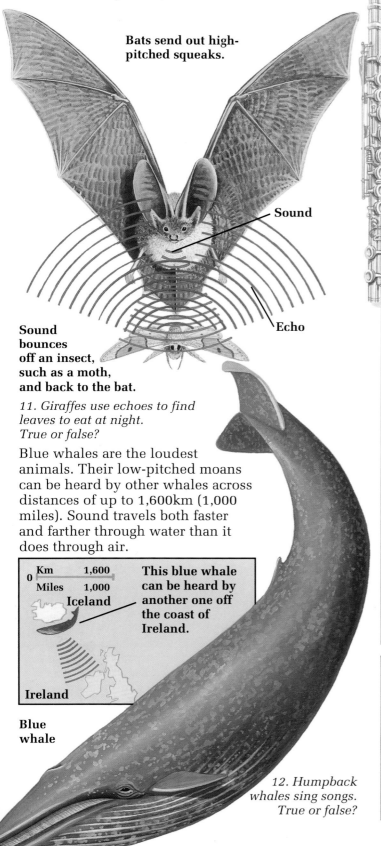

Bats send out high-pitched squeaks.

Sound

Echo

Sound bounces off an insect, such as a moth, and back to the bat.

11. Giraffes use echoes to find leaves to eat at night. True or false?

Blue whales are the loudest animals. Their low-pitched moans can be heard by other whales across distances of up to 1,600km (1,000 miles). Sound travels both faster and farther through water than it does through air.

0	Km	1,600
	Miles	1,000

Iceland

This blue whale can be heard by another one off the coast of Ireland.

Ireland

Blue whale

12. Humpback whales sing songs. True or false?

What makes instruments sound different?

Musical instruments sound different because they make vibrations in different ways. Their shape, the materials they are made of, and how they are played, affect the way that they vibrate. This gives each instrument its own range of notes and its own distinctive tone.

Musical notes all have a similar pattern. They begin, build up to full volume and then fade away. The time that each stage takes depends on the instrument and the way the player controls the note. The graph below shows an example of the shape of a flute note.

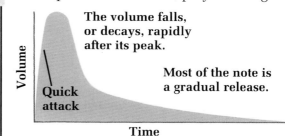

Volume

The length of time the note stays at its loudest is called the sustain.

The start of the note is called the attack.

The fade of the note is called the release.

Time

Flute

Wind instruments, such as the flute, have a fairly quick attack and release. The note sustains for as long as the player blows. The graph below shows the shape of another note, played on a guitar.

Volume

The volume falls, or decays, rapidly after its peak.

Most of the note is a gradual release.

Quick attack

Time

Instruments that are plucked, such as the guitar, have a quick attack and no sustain. There is a long release as the string gradually stops vibrating.

13. Drums, cymbals and xylophones are all: a) percussion instruments; b) percolated instruments; c) polystyrene instruments.

14. Unravel each of these words to make the names of four instruments: angor, batu, napio, tirgua.

Guitar

Did you know?

There are no sounds in space. This is because there is no air for sound waves to travel through. Without air, water or solid particles to vibrate, there is no noise. In space, astronauts talk to each other by radio.

15. Any place, such as outer space, where there is no air is called: a) air-tight; b) arid; c) a vacuum.

Light and colour

Light is a form of energy, which enables us to see the things around us. It is released by sources of heat, such as the Sun, a light bulb or a candle.

Light is made up of seven different colours – red, orange, yellow, green, blue, indigo and violet. These colours normally merge together, so that you cannot see them separately.

What is a rainbow?

Light travels in waves and the wavelengths of the seven colours are all slightly different. A rainbow appears when the colours are split apart.

Light waves are so small that around 40 thousand of them would fit in this wavelength here.

Wavelength

If light enters a transparent substance (such as glass or water) directly, it travels straight through. However, if it enters at an angle, it bends. This is called refraction. At some angles, the seven colours all bend in a slightly different direction, so you can see them all. This is called dispersion.

You can see this effect if you shine light through a triangular glass block, called a prism. The prism is shaped to refract and disperse light.

Rainbows happen when the Sun shines when it is raining, or just after a shower. Sunlight travels through the raindrops and is refracted and dispersed.

Each colour travels in a slightly different direction.

Prism

Light

Red
Orange
Yellow
Green
Blue
Indigo
Violet

How do you see colour?

When light waves hit objects, they bounce back. This is called reflection. Objects appear to be different colours because they reflect some of the colours in light and absorb others. When light shines on an object, the reflected colours bounce back into your eyes.

This T-shirt is black because it absorbs all the colours in light. It reflects hardly any light.

This plant appears green because it only reflects green light and no other colours.

This rabbit appears white because it reflects all the colours in white light equally well.

4. All animals see in black and white. True or false?
5. Some animals make light. True or false?
6. What colours does snow reflect?

What makes the sky blue?

When sunlight hits the Earth's atmosphere, it begins to break up and blue light is scattered all over the sky. This happens because the upper atmosphere contains gas and dust particles which are about the same size as the wavelength of blue light. This causes blue light to bounce off them.

The atmosphere gets thicker the nearer it is to the Earth's surface, and as light travels through it, more light is scattered. Light with shorter wavelengths, like blue and violet are scattered most.

At sunset or sunrise, sunlight travels through much more of the atmosphere before it reaches you. Most of its colours are scattered by the time it reaches the lower atmosphere. Only reds and oranges are left.

At midday, blue light is scattered over the sky.

7. The sea is blue because: a) it contains blue seaweed; b) squid squirt blue dye; c) it reflects the sky.

8. Can light travel through space?

At sunset, only red and orange light can be seen.

1. If red and yellow are mixed together, do they make: a) blue; b) green; c) orange?

2. Another name for the colours of the rainbow is: a) a spatula; b) a spectrum; c) a sporran.

3. Can light travel around corners?

How does a mirror work?

Light waves reflect in a similar way to a ball bouncing. For example, when a tennis ball hits a smooth clay court, it bounces evenly, leaving the surface of the court at the same angle at which it arrived. Light behaves like this when it hits a mirror. It travels through a smooth, glass layer and then bounces off a shiny, metal coating. Light waves all bounce back evenly, staying in the same order, which enables you to see a reflection.

If you play tennis on an uneven surface such as grass, balls hitting different bumps will bounce at different angles. Light behaves like this when it hits a dull, rough surface, such as wood. Light rays scatter in all directions.

9. Ancient Egyptians used mirrors. True or false?

10. Can you see a reflection in polished wood?

The ball bounces back at the same angle that it hits the clay.

Light remains in same order.

The ball bounces back at a different angle than at which it hits the grass.

Light is scattered.

How do you see?

You see objects because light bounces off them and reflects into your eyes. This picture shows how what you see is turned into an image that your brain can recognize. Light enters through the pupil, a black hole at the front of the eye. The coloured area around the pupil, the iris, prevents harmful light rays from entering the eye. Light then passes through a transparent, rubbery disc, called a lens.

The lens helps you see more clearly, or focus, by bending light, so that it hits the back of the eye, which is called the retina. The lens turns what you see upside down. The retina is made up of millions of tiny cells which are called rods and cones. Rods are sensitive to dim light. Cones are sensitive to bright light and colour. There are over 130 million rods and cones in an eye. When light falls on them electrical messages are passed to the optic nerve.

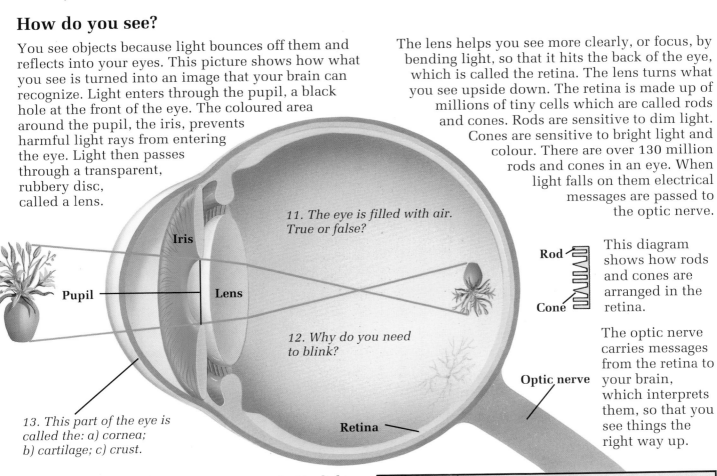

Iris

Pupil

Lens

11. The eye is filled with air. True or false?

12. Why do you need to blink?

Rod

Cone

This diagram shows how rods and cones are arranged in the retina.

Optic nerve

Retina

The optic nerve carries messages from the retina to your brain, which interprets them, so that you see things the right way up.

13. This part of the eye is called the: a) cornea; b) cartilage; c) crust.

In bright light, the iris closes up to protect your eyes.

In dim light, the iris opens up to let more light in, so you can see better.

Did you know?

Light travels quicker than anything in the Universe. Its speed is around 300,000km (186,000 miles) per second. This means that it takes eight minutes to travel the 150 million km (93 million miles) from the Sun to Earth.

15. Which travels faster, thunder or lightning?

14. Which two of these animals can see well in the dark: a) dogs; b) cats; c) owls; d) sheep; e) ducks?

Living things

There is life in almost every part of the world. The sky, sea, soil and surface of the Earth are full of plants and animals.

What makes something a living thing?

Living things have particular features which non-living things lack. For instance, they can react to their surroundings, they need energy to live and can reproduce. Below you can see the qualities which separate living things from non-living things.

Leaf cells

All living things are made up of tiny units, called cells.

All living things need oxygen, which they get from air or water.

The bodies of living things produce waste, which they need to get rid of.

All animals can move part of their bodies. Flowers can open and close petals.

Almost all living things grow. Growth occurs when cells divide.

All living things reproduce so that new ones live on when they die.

All living things need food to give them energy to breed, move or grow.

All living things are aware of their surroundings and react to them.

1. Which one of the following do plants not do: a) reproduce; b) make food; c) think; d) move?

2. An erupting volcano is a living thing. True or false?

What is the difference between an animal and a plant?

Here is how plants and animals differ.

Food

The main difference between plants and animals is the way in which they get their food.

Animals eat plants or other animals, or both. The food is broken down in their bodies and gives them energy. This breakdown of food is called digestion.

3. This animal is a: a) sloth; b) orang-utan; c) lemur.

Plants take carbon dioxide from the air, water and minerals from the soil, and energy from the Sun to make their own food. The process is called photosynthesis.

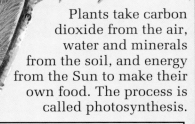

Leaves take in carbon dioxide from the air.

The Sun's energy turns carbon dioxide and water into simple sugars.

Cells

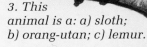

The cells in animals' bodies have soft walls.

Animal cell

Plant cells have thick, tough walls.

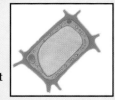

Plant cell

Movement

Most animals can move their bodies around. They are more sensitive than plants and can react quickly to change.

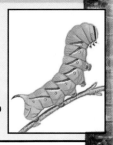

Most plants can only respond slowly to changes. Some turn to follow the Sun around the sky, for example.

4. Is a stick insect a plant or an animal?

5. Some plants can eat animals. True or false?

6. Do you know what the yellow flowered plants above are called?

7. Plants always grow away from the Sun. True or false?

What are you made of?

Your body is made of millions of cells, which can reproduce, grow and feed. Cells contain a lot of water; in fact, two-thirds of your body is made of water. The body organs are all made of different kinds of cells. Each has a particular job to do.

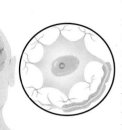

The brain is made of nerve cells. Nerve cells elsewhere in your body send messages to your brain, which tells your body how to react.

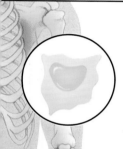

Bone cells make a hard skeleton, which gives your body shape.

8. Which of these is not a bone: a) femur; b) pelvis; c) pancreas?

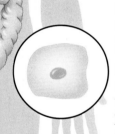

Some cells are only found in one part of the body. The stomach and intestines have digestive cells which produce juices to break down, or digest, food.

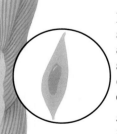

Muscle cells squeeze tight and then relax so you can move different parts of your body.

9. Is your brain a muscle?

Did you know?

The stomach produces strong digestive juices. It is lined with mucus, a sticky substance, which protects it from being eaten away by its own juices.

Where do you come from?

All human beings, and most other animals, begin as just two cells, one from the mother (the egg cell), and one from the father (the sperm cell). These two cells join together to make one cell. This cell then divides into two and each of those cells divides again. This process continues and the number of cells increases. As the baby grows within the mother's womb, specialized cells begin to form the baby's body organs.

After a baby has been born, it continues to grow. Growing bodies need a lot of a certain substance made by the cells, called protein. When you eat food rich in protein, such as cheese, the body absorbs it and the cells use it to make their own protein.

10. In the womb, a baby is attached to its mother by the: a) umbilical cord; b) major chord; c) spinal cord.

11. Which is bigger, an egg cell or a sperm cell?

Why do you stop growing?

Your body grows longer and larger as the bones of your skeleton grow. A group of cells near the brain, called the pituitary gland, produce chemicals which control how much you grow. When the pituitary gland stops making these chemicals, you stop growing.

Growth occurs in three main spurts: in the first two years, between five and seven, and between twelve and eighteen.

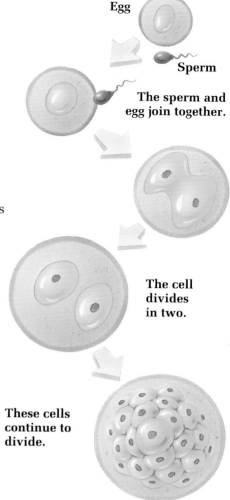

Egg

Sperm

The sperm and egg join together.

The cell divides in two.

These cells continue to divide.

12. Which one of these types of food is essential for growth: a) fat; b) sugar; c) protein?

13. You are taller first thing in the morning than last thing at night. True or false?

14. Human skeletons have over 200 bones. True or false?

15. Which one of the following never stops growing while you are alive: a) nails; b) teeth; c) feet?

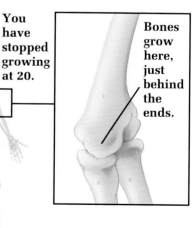

Growth is rapid during early teen age.

Seven year old

At the age of one you are over a third of your adult height.

You have stopped growing at 20.

Bones grow here, just behind the ends.

Evolution

When living things reproduce, their offspring look similar to them. However, living things can change their appearance if their environment changes. For example, if it gradually gets colder, over many generations, a species of animal may grow a thicker and thicker coat. This change is called evolution. Over millions of years, these changes can make a new plant or animal which may be quite different from its ancestor.

1. Cats have evolved from dogs. True or false?

How does evolution work?

Evolution depends on a process called natural selection, which works like this. All animals and plants within one species are slightly different. Some of these differences enable some of the species to survive better than others. For example, a deer that can outrun predators successfully will be more likely to survive to reproduce. Its running abilities may be passed on to, or inherited by, its offspring.

Evolution has produced countless ways of coping with the hazards of life on Earth. For example, the horse chestnut has evolved a spiky covering for its seeds.

The spikes protect the seed when it falls from the tree.

2. Are horse chestnut seeds edible?

3. Would animals with short life-spans and many offspring evolve quicker than those with long life-spans and one or two offspring?

How quick is evolution?

Evolution is usually very slow, but in some cases one type of animal can change very quickly rather than over thousands or millions of years. For example, over the last two hundred years peppered moths have evolved by changing colour, to fit into areas of Europe which have a lot of heavy industry.

Most peppered moths used to have pale wings. They rested on pale tree trunks where they were well hidden. About 1% of them had dark wings. These were easily spotted by birds, and were usually eaten.

About 200 years ago, coal-powered factories were built in western Europe. Smoke from factory steam engines began to blacken tree trunks with soot. The pale moths then became easier to spot.

The few dark moths survived as they were not seen by the birds. They then produced more dark-winged offspring. Now most peppered moths in industrial areas have dark wings.

4. Do moths usually come out during the day or the night?

Why do some animals become extinct?

Some living things are not able to evolve when their environment changes, so they die out. Large, hairy, elephant-like animals called mammoths probably became extinct because the Earth's climate became more extreme. It became too hot in summer and too cold in winter. Also, human hunters had reduced their numbers. Sabre-toothed tigers became extinct because their huge fangs were only suitable for hunting large animals, such as mammoths. They were not able to hunt the smaller animals that remained, so they died out.

5. Sabre-toothed kittens were the first household pets. True or false?

6. Which of these is not extinct: a) Stegosaurus; b) armadillo; c) giant sloth?

7. Apart from its teeth, in what other major way does this tiger look different from a present day tiger?

How do we know humans have evolved?

Most scientists think that humans have evolved from tree-living animals similar to apes and monkeys. There is evidence in our bodies that supports this view, and suggests that we used to live on a vegetarian diet of fruit, roots and stems.

At the base of the spine there is a set of bones called the coccyx. This is all that remains of what used to be a tail.

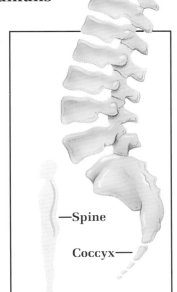

Spine

Coccyx

Most of your body hair is downy, but it used to be much thicker. Each hair has a muscle to make it stand up if you are cold. On hairy mammals this traps air which keeps them warm.

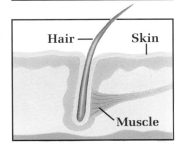

Hair — Skin

Muscle

Many adults still have large back teeth called wisdom teeth. These are no longer necessary, but were originally needed to chew the tough vegetables our ancestors used to eat.

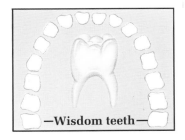

—Wisdom teeth—

The appendix is a small tube attached to the intestine. Your distant ancestors needed it to help digest their vegetable diet. It is no longer needed and is slowly getting smaller.

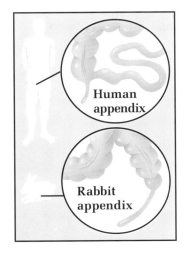

Human appendix

Rabbit appendix

Plant-eating animals, such as rabbits, have a particularly well-developed appendix.

8. Are wisdom teeth only found in intelligent people?

9. People have eyebrows to: a) keep sweat out of their eyes; b) trap insects; c) keep their eyes warm.

10. Most scientists think that the first humans lived in: a) Antarctica; b) Africa; c) Argentina.

Can people control evolution?

People have been controlling animal evolution for over 10,000 years. For example, most breeds of dog today probably evolved from the wolves which used to gather around early human settlements. Gradually, the wolves that came to live with humans evolved into a separate species, dogs. Humans began to breed them for particular tasks. This is called selective breeding. There are now over 150 breeds of dog.

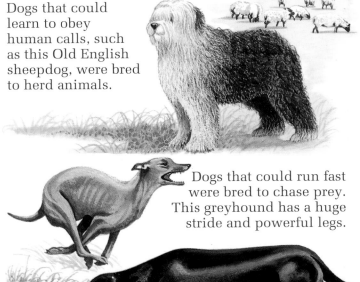

Dogs that could learn to obey human calls, such as this Old English sheepdog, were bred to herd animals.

Dogs that could run fast were bred to chase prey. This greyhound has a huge stride and powerful legs.

Dogs with a good sense of smell were bred to track down prey. This smooth-haired dachshund can burrow into rabbit warrens.

Natural selection and evolution are usually very slow. Selective breeding is much faster.

11. Dogs that are from one particular breed are called: a) pedigree dogs; b) pedestal dogs; c) perennial dogs.

12. Which of these dogs looks most like a wolf: a) boxer; b) terrier; c) husky?

13. Are lions the product of selective breeding?

14. Which animal is a cross between a donkey and a horse?

What is genetic engineering?

In the 1970s, scientists discovered how to change the character of a living thing by altering its genes. This is called genetic engineering. Genes, a biological recipe contained in every cell, also determine the size and appearance of a living thing. Genetic engineering can be used to breed plants and animals that grow bigger, or are more resistant to disease.

15. Genetic engineering is a branch of which science: a) botany; b) bionics; c) biotechnology?

The balance of nature

Everything in nature is linked together in a delicate balance. When a plant or animal dies, it becomes food for other living things, so nothing is wasted. People can disturb this balance by taking too much from nature for food and industry, and by polluting their environment.

1. The study of living things in their environment is called economics. True or false?

2. Protecting the environment is called: a) conurbation; b) conservation; c) contamination.

How does the Sun provide energy?

Plants need energy from the Sun in order to make their food, in a process called photosynthesis.* Plants provide energy for the animals which eat them. These animals are then eaten by other animals. This transfer of energy from the Sun through plants to animals is called a food chain. A typical food chain is shown here.

3. Do hawks hunt by day or by night?

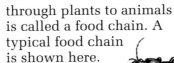

Beetle eats plant.   **Thrush eats beetle.**   **Hawk eats thrush.**

What is a food web?

Most animals eat a variety of food, and what they eat affects the other plants and animals in their environment. Scientists call this feeding relationship a food web. Here is the kind of food web you would find in a forest environment. In any food web there are millions of plant-eating animals at the bottom of the web, but only a few animals at the top.

4. Which has more choice of food, the owl or the thrush?

5. Which animal does the rabbit need to watch out for?

6. All large animals are carnivores. True or false?

7. Are humans carnivores, herbivores or omnivores?

8. Would there be more hawks or more caterpillars in a forest food web?

9. Which of these is a real beetle:
a) Boiling beetle;
b) Boring beetle;
c) Bouzouki beetle?

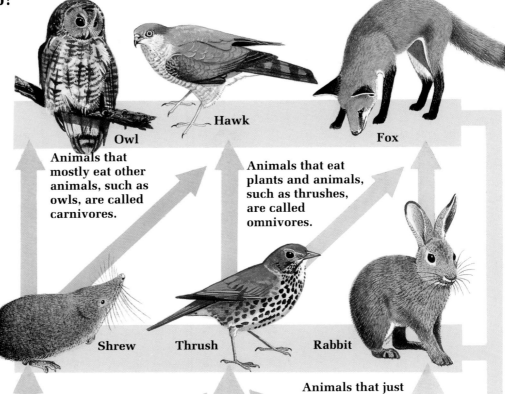

Owl   **Hawk**   **Fox**

Animals that mostly eat other animals, such as owls, are called carnivores.

Animals that eat plants and animals, such as thrushes, are called omnivores.

Shrew   **Thrush**   **Rabbit**

Animals that just eat plants, such as rabbits, are called herbivores.

Beetle   **Caterpillar**   **Berry**

Dead plants and animals add goodness to the soil.

Can food webs be damaged?

Because living things in a food web feed on each other, poisoning or removing one plant or animal will affect many others. Here are three ways in which food webs can be damaged.

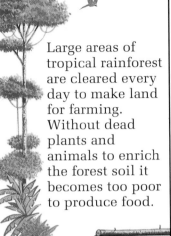

Large areas of tropical rainforest are cleared every day to make land for farming. Without dead plants and animals to enrich the forest soil it becomes too poor to produce food.

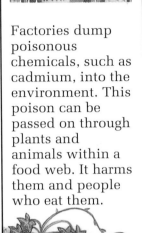

Factories dump poisonous chemicals, such as cadmium, into the environment. This poison can be passed on through plants and animals within a food web. It harms them and people who eat them.

If a type of animal disappears from an area, the animals that eat it are affected. For example, many sea birds have far less food because the sand eels they eat have been caught and turned into farm animal food.

How can you protect your environment?

See if you can reuse items you might usually throw away. Much household waste can also be taken to recycling points if you collect it separately.

Paper can be used to make new paper, cardboard and tissue. It can also be used for insulation.

Bottles can be cleaned and used again. Glass can be melted down and made into new bottles.

Many metal goods, such as drink cans, can be recycled.

Plastic bags can be reused several times. However, most plastics cannot be recycled.

Rotting vegetables and fruit make a substance called compost, which contains a lot of goodness. It can be dug into your garden.

Rags can be used by industry to make items such as roof felt or furniture stuffing.

What happens to the waste that people produce?

The recycling that occurs in nature does not exist in most human societies. Waste from homes and factories cannot be absorbed back into the environment.

Most waste from homes and shops is buried in the ground. Soil keeps it in place, keeps out scavengers, and stops the smell.

10. Sites where waste is buried are called: a) landfills; b) subways; c) grottoes.

Nuclear power stations make waste which remains dangerous for centuries. The waste is set in concrete and stored underground or dumped in the sea.

11. Which Ukrainian nuclear power station caused widespread pollution when it exploded in 1986?

Waste from factories is often poisonous. Some factories dispose of their waste carefully, but many others pollute the air, land and water in their environment.

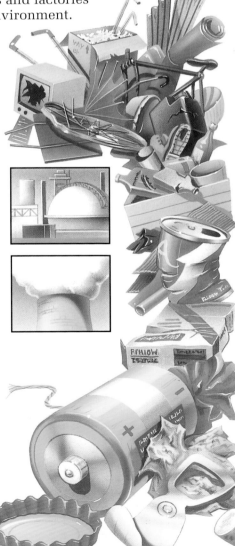

Did you know?
Pollution is not a new problem. In 1306 King Edward I of England complained of the "unbearable stench" caused by burning coal in London, and prohibited its use.

12. Can iron be recycled?

13. Compost heaps take about: a) a week; b) a month; c) six months to rot.

14. Materials that rot are called: a) biographical; b) biodegradable; c) diabolical.

15. The average North American home throws away over a tonne (ton) of waste every year. True or false?

Science and technology

Using scientific ideas in a practical way is called technology. Scientists develop new technology to sell products and to improve your lifestyle. Here are some examples of where technology has been used to create new electrical equipment and new products to help protect the environment.

How do compact discs store music?

When music is recorded for a compact disc (CD), a computer measures the sound wave 40,000 times per second. These measurements are converted into a number system called binary code. In this system, all numbers are represented by a combination of the digits zero and one.

A computer measures the height and shape of the wave, as shown by the red arrows. These measurements describe the wave's shape.

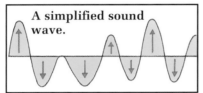

A simplified sound wave.

Inside the computer, binary numbers are represented by patterns of electrical pulses: a pulse stands for the digit one, and no pulse stands for the digit zero. This way of coding information as a pattern of pulses is called digital coding. Recording music in this way is very accurate, giving excellent sound quality on the CD.

The digital code is cut into the shiny surface of the CD in a sequence of pits and flat areas, representing zeros and ones. In the CD player, an extremely strong beam of light, called a laser, is shone on the disc as it spins. When light hits a flat area, it is reflected. When it hits a pit, it is not reflected.

The CD player interprets these reflections as a series of on and off signals, which make up the digital code of the recorded sound. The code is then converted back by a reverse process into the sound waves of the original piece of music.

1. CDs are coated with a protective layer of: a) paper; b) plastic; c) marble.

2. Is music the only kind of information that can be stored on CD?

The CD surface has a sequence of millions of pits and flat areas, representing a digital code. Pits are read as zero. Flat areas are read as one.

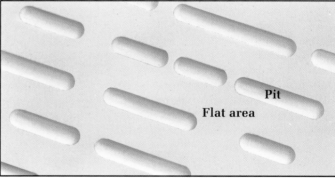

Pit
Flat area

3. The picture above has been magnified around: a) 8 times; b) 80 times; c) 8,000 times.

4. CDs wear out if they are played several times a day. True or false?

Did you know?

Unlike daylight, laser light is made up of only one wavelength. Its waves do not scatter, but travel together in one direction. This makes it so strong that some lasers can cut through metal. Lasers were invented in 1960, but for years no one knew what to do with them. They now have many uses, such as in eye surgery, where they are used to make fine, precise cuts.

Laser beam

5. Lasers are used in supermarkets. True or false?

6. Can lasers measure distances?

7. Laser light can be brighter than the Sun. True or false?

Can car pollution be reduced?

Car exhaust fumes contain poisonous chemicals which cause air pollution. To reduce this, all new cars that use unleaded fuel can be fitted with a machine called a catalytic converter, which cleans exhaust gases. As exhaust gases flow through the converter, they pass over a surface covered with metal atoms. These make the chemicals in the gas react to make less harmful gases.

EXHAUST FUMES IN	EXHAUST FUMES OUT
Carbon monoxide	Carbon dioxide
Nitrogen oxides	Nitrogen
Hydrocarbons	Water

Catalytic converter: palladium, platinum and rhodium atoms.

8. How many new cars in the USA are fitted with catalytic converters: a) none; b) half; c) all of them?

9. Can exhaust fumes cause acid rain?

10. Breathing carbon monoxide makes your hair turn white. True or false?

How can light bulbs save energy?

When the metal wire in a light bulb glows, it produces heat as well as light. Producing this heat wastes electrical energy.

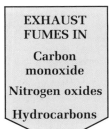

Energy efficient light bulbs

An energy efficient bulb makes light with chemicals instead of heat. Inside the bulb is a folded fluorescent tube. When electricity passes through it, chemicals glow, giving off light.

11. Energy efficient light bulbs last: a) 8; b) 30; c) 150 times as long as ordinary bulbs.

12. Energy efficient bulbs can only light up in the dark. True or false?

How does a camcorder work?

A camcorder is a mini combination of two machines – a TV camera and a video recorder. It works by using lenses to create an image on a tiny light-sensitive electronic component called a charge-coupled device (CCD).

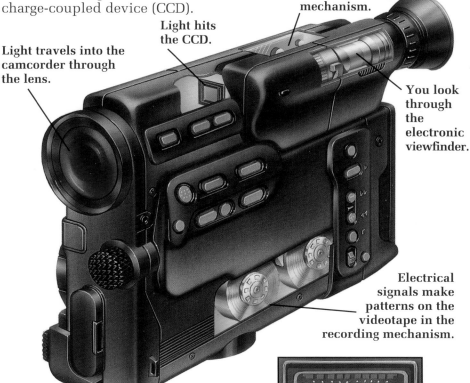

Light hits the CCD.

Light travels into the camcorder through the lens.

Electronic circuits send electrical signals to the recording mechanism.

You look through the electronic viewfinder.

Electrical signals make patterns on the videotape in the recording mechanism.

13. What does camcorder stand for?

The CCD is divided into a grid of tiny squares, called pixels, which are coated with a light-sensitive chemical. When light hits the CCD, it generates an electrical signal, which corresponds to the amount of light hitting it. Bright light produces a strong signal and dim light produces a weak signal.

These electrical signals travel to the recording mechanism. Here, the electrical signals create a magnetic field* which makes a pattern on magnetic particles on the surface of a plastic videotape.

The patterns on the tape store the picture information represented by the electrical signals. The sound is recorded on a separate area of the videotape. The tape can then be played back through the camcorder itself or through a video recorder.

Charge-coupled device (CCD) magnified 1.85 times.

Cutaway of video cassette, to show tape inside.

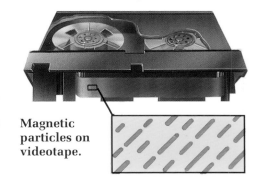

Magnetic particles on videotape.

14. There are about 400,000 pixels on the CCD. True or false?

15. What is a palmcorder?

See pages 76-77 for more about electricity and magnetism. **89**

Science Megaquiz

These ten quizzes test you on what you have read in Part Three of this book, and also on your general knowledge of science.

You can write your answers on a piece of paper and then check on page 96 to see how many you got right.

Misfits

In each set of three below, there is one misfit. Can you spot which it is?

1.	2.	3.	4.	5.	6.	7.	8.	9.	10.
pupil iris pinna	kinetic original chemical	gravity friction density	violet brown indigo	light bulb turbine generator	growth feeding magnetism	cat greyhound mammoth	proton electron siphon	egg baby sperm	flute xylophone drum

Inventions and discoveries

Can you match these inventions and discoveries to their dates?

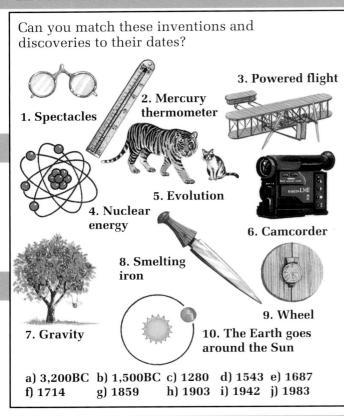

1. Spectacles
2. Mercury thermometer
3. Powered flight
4. Nuclear energy
5. Evolution
6. Camcorder
7. Gravity
8. Smelting iron
9. Wheel
10. The Earth goes around the Sun

a) 3,200BC   b) 1,500BC   c) 1280   d) 1543   e) 1687
f) 1714   g) 1859   h) 1903   i) 1942   j) 1983

Talking science

Each of these sentences is missing a word. The missing words are highlighted in the box below. Can you match the words and sentences?

1. At ....., the sky may appear orange and red.
2. Rotting fruit and vegetables can be used to make.....
3. Gold, silicon and oxygen are all ......
4. The Earth is surrounded by its own magnetic ....., with a north and a south pole.
5. A ..... splits light into the different colours of the rainbow.
6. All animals and plants in an environment are linked to each other by a ..... web.
7. ..... is the force which pulls you to the ground.
8. Our solar system is part of a ..... called the Milky Way.
9. Acid rain causes ..... in many places, including lakes, forests and cities.
10. Plastic is a good ..... of electricity.

food	prism	compost

sunset	field	galaxy	insulator

gravity	elements	pollution

Materials

1. Which material is the best conductor of electricity: a) air; b) wood; c) metal?
2. Name one harmful substance that may be found in car exhaust fumes.
3. Which raw material is different from the others: a) ore; b) coal; c) trees; d) clay?
4. Is water a compound or an element?
5. Where does suede come from?
6. In the past, what precious metal did alchemists try to make?
7. Which gas is the Sun made out of?
8. The cells of living things contain which material: a) oil; b) water; c) blood?
9. Which metal is used in electrical wiring?
10. Which of these raw materials is not used to make energy: a) cocoa; b) coal; c) clay; d) oil?

Close-ups

These are all close-ups of pictures in Part Three. Can you recognize what they are?

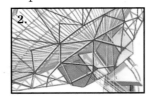

Animals and plants

Which of these living things...

1. ...do thrushes eat?
2. ...is the loudest animal in the world?
3. ...reflects all the colours in sunlight?
4. ...comes from a horse chestnut tree?
5. ...uses echoes to find insects to eat?
6. ...is extinct?
7. ...was bred to herd animals?
8. ...is the nearest animal relative to a chimpanzee and a gorilla?
9. ...eats sand eels?
10. ...lives in a warren?

True or false?

1. When you look at the stars you are looking back in time.
2. Green plants scare caterpillars away.
3. All metals are magnetic.
4. Daylight is a mixture of colours.
5. Two-thirds of your body is water.
6. Stomach cells have teeth.
7. Tiny particles exist which are smaller than an atom.
8. Telephones are connected by cables containing bundles of string.
9. Foxes are herbivores.
10. Sound travels in waves.

Silhouettes

All these silhouettes are things that appear in Part Three. How many can you recognize?

Body bits

Which part or parts of your body...

1. ...carries oxygen around your body?
2. ...do you no longer need to digest food?
3. ...produces chemicals which control how much you grow?
4. ...carries signals from your eye to your brain?
5. ...covers your whole body?
6. ...enables you to move by squeezing tight and relaxing?
7. ...gives your body its shape?
8. ...opens or closes, to let more or less light into your eye when it is bright or dark?
9. ...is all that is left of a tail?
10. ...directs sounds into your eardrum?

What do you know?

1. By what process do plants make food?
2. What kind of electricity is lightning?
3. What does CD stand for?
4. Is it possible to see atoms?
5. How many millions of years ago did the Big Bang happen: a) 15 thousand; b) fifty; c) five?
6. What are rocks which contain metals called?
7. What force, apart from electricity, makes an electric motor work?
8. Which material is not made from oil: a) polythene; b) silk; c) acrylic; d) nylon?
9. What sort of light could cut through metal?
10. Are animals or plants at the bottom of a food web?

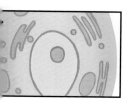  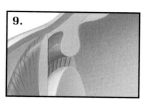  

Quiz answers

The answers to the 12 quizzes from *Exploring space* to *Science and technology* are on the next four pages. Give yourself one point for every right answer. The chart below helps you to find out how well you have done.

0-5	Read through the answers, then try the quiz again. See how many answers you can remember this time.
6-10	Quite good. Think more carefully about the questions and you might get more right.
11-14	Good score. If you get this score on most of the quizzes, you have done very well.
15	Excellent. If you do this well in more than half of the quizzes, you are a science genius!

Your score overall

You can find out your average score over all 12 quizzes like this:

1. Add up your scores on all 12 quizzes.
2. Divide this total by 12. This is your average score. How well did you do?

General knowledge

All the answers to general knowledge questions are marked ★. These questions are probably the hardest in the quizzes. Add up how many of them you got right across all 12 quizzes. There are 50 of them in total. If you got over 30 right, your science general knowledge is good.

Exploring space

1. a) Venus, Neptune and Mars are named after Roman gods.
★ 2. Sirius, Betelgeuse and Alpha Centauri are stars.
3. a) Radio waves from stars contain blips, bleeps and hisses.
4. False. Telescopes were first used around 1600, by scientists such as Galileo.

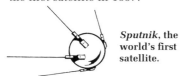
Galileo used a telescope to help him draw pictures of the Moon.

5. False. X-rays and ultra-violet rays are invisible.
6. c) A group of stars is called a constellation.
7. True. Scientists believe that in 5,000 million years time, the Sun will use up all its fuel and stop shining.
★ 8. No. It is not safe because the Sun is too bright and may hurt your eyes.
9. b) You would find a white dwarf in space. When the fuel in a star is used up, it shrinks and becomes a very dense, planet-like mass, called a white dwarf.
10. b) Apollo 11 landed the first men on the Moon in 1969.
11. True. Dogs were sent up into space on experimental space flights.
12. True. Many ships carry equipment that uses information from satellites to tell them exactly where they are.
13. a) The word "satellite" comes from the Latin word for attendant.
★14. The former Soviet Union launched the first satellite in 1957.

Sputnik, the world's first satellite.

15. b) Yuri Gagarin was the first man to go into space, in April 1961.

What are things made of?

★ 1. Mercury used to be called quicksilver. It is a silvery metal, but it is a liquid at room temperature.
2. True. Diamonds and coal are both made from carbon atoms. The carbon atoms fit together in different ways.

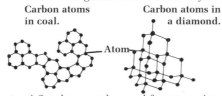
Carbon atoms in coal. **Carbon atoms in a diamond.** — Atom

3. c) Sand cannot be used for seasoning food.
★ 4. Water is always ice at the North and South Poles, where the temperature never rises above freezing point.
5. False. Ice forms in many shapes.
★ 6. Yes. Iron is a metal which can be turned into a liquid by heating it.
7. c) When gas is squashed into a smaller space it is called compressed.
8. b) Electrons carry an electrical charge. A flow of electrons is called electricity.
9. a) Power stations use the element uranium to make nuclear energy.
★10. Japan. The USA dropped two nuclear bombs there in 1945.
11. c) A microscope which uses lenses to magnify an object is called an optical microscope.

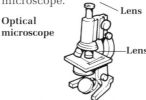
Optical microscope — Lens — Lens

12. False. Light and heat from stars is released by nuclear energy.
★13. Smells are gases. Smells spread because gas molecules move easily.
★14. Divers, astronauts and fire fighters carry compressed oxygen in tanks.
15. The three elements are gold, copper and oxygen.

Using materials

★ 1. Oil and fuel; iron ore and bridge; tree and book; clay and crockery; wool and sweater; cocoa and chocolate. Score a point if you got them all right.
2. c) Nylon is a man-made material.
3. a) Texas, USA is famous for crude oil.

USA — Texas

★ 4. No. Cooking oil comes from vegetables.
★ 5. The racing car needs to be light in weight to help it travel faster.
★ 6. Rubber comes from latex – the sap of a rubber tree. Score a point if you guessed it was a plant or a tree.

The trunk of the tree is cut. **Latex flows out.**

★ 7. The suit has to be fire-resistant to protect the driver if the car crashes, and oil and fuel catch fire.
8. No. Crude oil cannot be used in cars as fuel. It has to be refined first.
9. b) People first made alloys in the Bronze Age. Bronze is an alloy of the metals copper and tin.
10. True. More than three-quarters of all elements are metals.
11. c) This is called a blast furnace. Air is blasted, or blown, into it.
12. True. Many metals react, or change, if they come into contact with air or water. Some metals, such as sodium or potassium, may even explode. For this reason, they are stored in oil.
13. c) The purity of gold is measured in carats. A carat is the amount of pure gold mixed with other metals in an object. 24 carat gold is pure gold.
14. False.
15. a) A thin sheet of gold is called gold leaf. It can be used to cover cheaper metals.

Moving, flying and floating

1. True. Friction does not act in space, and the weak gravity between the Earth and Moon has very little effect on a fast moving spaceship.

★ 2. Yes. Stone is more dense than chocolate. The material in it is packed closer together.

3. False. Steel is made from iron and carbon. Over 90% of metal produced is either iron or steel.

★ 4. Cyclists crouch low so that air flows over them smoothly, enabling them to go faster.

5. a) A tandem is a bike for two riders.

Tandem

★ 6. You feel more friction on gravel. Ice has a very smooth surface, so things slide over it, rather than grip it.

7. c) Sliding down a rope might give you a friction burn.

8. True. Most birds have hollow bones to make them lighter. This makes it easier for them to take off and fly.

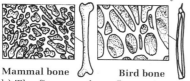

Mammal bone   **Bird bone**

9. b) The first people to fly used aircraft driven by propellers.

★ 10. No. Helicopters have blades. These lift the aircraft into the air directly, making a wing unnecessary.

Rotor blades

Helicopter

11. True. Gliders fly without engines. They are made with light materials, and glide in patches of warm air.

12. An empty ship would sit higher in the sea. A heavy cargo pushes the ship's hull farther down against the upthrust of the water underneath it.

★ 13. Cork floats. It is less dense than water.

14. c) A submarine dives by filling compartments, called ballast tanks, with water. This makes it heavier than water so it sinks. It surfaces by filling these tanks with a supply of compressed air.

Submarine on surface.

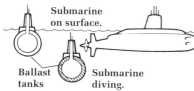

Ballast tanks   **Submarine diving.**

15. b) Isaac Newton was well known for studying mathematics.

Making things work

1. A piece of stretched elastic has potential energy, which will be released when the elastic is let go.

Potential energy   **Kinetic energy**

2. False. Steam has more energy than hot water, because it is hotter and its molecules are moving faster.

★ 3. You would find the following forms of energy in lightning: heat, light, electrical and kinetic. Score a point if you got two or more.

4. b) The first nuclear power station opened in 1956.

5. Yes. Sound can travel through walls.

6. True. Animal manure can be used to produce energy. When it rots it gives off a gas called methane, or biogas. Millions of people in China already use this gas as a fuel.

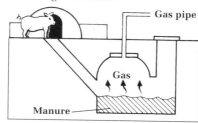

Gas pipe

Gas

Manure

7. b) Oil, coal and natural gas are called fossil fuels.

8. True. The Sun evaporates water from the Earth's surface. The water then condenses to form clouds and falls as rain. This cycle of water would not be possible without heat from the Sun.

9. a) Uranium is a type of metal.

★ 10. A burning candle produces heat and light energy.

11. c) Sound cannot travel through space because there are no air particles to pass on sound waves.

12. True. Most energy produced by a light bulb is heat.

13. a) Energy in food is measured in Calories.

This cake has 300 Calories.   **This celery has 8 Calories.**

14. A fat person has more stored energy than a thin person. If you eat more food than your body uses for energy, the extra is stored in your body as fat.

★ 15. Yes. Even when you are asleep, your body still uses energy.

You digest food.   **Your heart beats**

You breathe.

Electricity and magnetism

1. No. Brass, like all metals, is a conductor of electricity.

★ 2. No. Some turbines are turned by running water, for example in hydroelectric power stations. The wind can also work turbines.

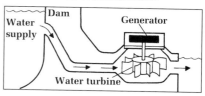

Water supply   **Dam**   **Generator**

Water turbine

3. False. Thunder is caused by lightning heating up the air it passes through. The air expands rapidly, creating a bang.

★ 4. Lightning always hits the highest point on the ground beneath it. This is why tall buildings have lightning rods to draw the lightning to them, rather than the building they are on.

5. a) Hair standing on end can be caused by static electricity.

6. False. There is nothing to stop lightning from striking the same place, such as a lightning rod, twice.

7. True. Your heart makes tiny electric shocks to keep it beating. These shocks can be measured by a machine called an electrocardiograph.

Electrocardiographs record your heartbeat in a pattern like this.

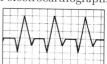

8. a) Rubber boots. Rubber is a very good insulator. If you were to touch a live electric wire while wearing rubber boots, the rubber would prevent the electricity from flowing through you and reaching the ground.

★ 9. It is unsafe because water could seep into the appliance and conduct electricity to your body. This could give you a dangerous electric shock.

★ 10. No. Wood is not a magnetic material.

★ 11. Yes. The Earth has a metal core, which has a magnetic field. This makes the magnetic material in a compass needle point north.

The magnetic field of Earth.   **North**

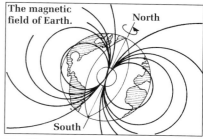

South

12. No. Glue picks up material because it is sticky. It has no magnetic quality.

13. c) Watts are units of electrical power.

14. d) A washing machine uses an electric motor.

★ 15. c) The electric motor was invented in England, in 1821, by Michael Faraday.

Sound and music

1. A clap of thunder is louder than a handclap, so it has more energy.
2. c) The loudness of sound is measured in decibels (or dB).
★ 3. Yes. Sound travels around corners. Sound waves spread out as they go through gaps or around obstacles.
4. False. The bones in the middle ear are called the hammer, anvil and stirrup.

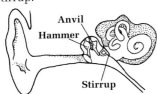

Anvil
Hammer
Stirrup

5. a) Balance. Inside your ear are three semi-circular tubes. These contain liquid which flows against tiny hair cells when you move. These cells send signals to your brain telling you which way you have moved.
6. True. Fish pick up sound vibrations with a tube-like organ called the lateral line, which runs along their bodies.

Lateral line

★ 7. Yes. Children can hear higher frequencies than adults.
★ 8. You would hear an echo better on a calm day. On a windy day, returning sound waves would be scattered.
9. False. However, some sounds can travel a very long way, especially in water. Underwater loudspeakers can make sounds in the Antarctic, that scientists can detect in the Arctic.

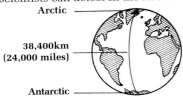

Arctic

38,400km
(24,000 miles)

Antarctic

10. b) Locating objects by listening to high frequency echoes is called sonar. It stands for SOund, NAvigation and Ranging.
11. False.
12. True. The sound humpback whales make has specific notes and patterns which they repeat, like a bird's song.
13. a) Drums, cymbals and xylophones are all percussion instruments. This type of instrument is struck to make sounds.
14. Angor, batu, napio and tirgua can be unscrambled to make these instruments.

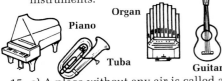

Organ
Piano
Tuba
Guitar

15. c) A place without any air is called a vacuum.

Light and colour

1. c) Red and yellow make orange.
2. b) Another name for the colours of the rainbow is a spectrum.
3. No. Light travels in straight lines. Light can only go around a corner if it is reflected off a surface.

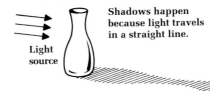

Light source

Shadows happen because light travels in a straight line.

4. False. Most animals have colour vision, but some, such as dogs, can only see in black and white.
5. True. Fireflies and some sea animals make light with chemicals produced inside them. They make light to attract a mate or to lure food.

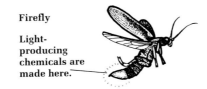

Firefly

Light-producing chemicals are made here.

6. Snow reflects all the colours in white light equally well.
7. c) The sea is blue because it reflects the sky, which is also blue.
★ 8. Yes. Light can travel through space. If it could not, we would have no sunlight on Earth.
9. True. Ancient Egyptians made mirrors from polished bronze metal.

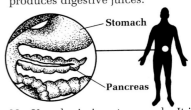

Egyptian mirror

★ 10. Yes. Polished wood is fairly smooth. Some light is reflected evenly off this smooth surface, so you see a reflection.
11. False. The eye is filled with fluid. This helps bend light towards the retina.

This part of the eye is filled with a watery fluid.

Eye

This part of the eye is filled with a jelly-like fluid.

★ 12. You need to blink in order to clean the surface of the eye.
13. a) This part of the eye is called the cornea. Along with the lens and eye fluids, it focuses light on the retina.
14. b) Cats and c) owls can see well in the dark. They hunt at night because there is less competition for food.
★ 15. Lightning travels faster than thunder. Thunder and lightning happen at the same time, but lightning reaches you first because light travels faster than sound.

Living things

1. c) Plants do not think. However, some can react very quickly. For example, when you touch a mimosa plant, its leaves collapse. This may shake off insects that are trying to eat it.
2. False. An erupting volcano is no more alive than the wind and the rain.
3. b) This animal is an orang-utan.
★ 4. A stick insect is an animal. It looks like a twig.

Stick insect

5. True. There are several plants, such as the venus flytrap, which catch and eat insects and other small animals.

The venus flytrap

★ 6. These plants are called sunflowers.
7. False. Plants grow towards sunlight to absorb as much energy as possible.
8. c) The pancreas is not a bone. It is a group of cells, called a gland, which produces digestive juices.

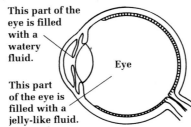

Stomach

Pancreas

★ 9. No. Your brain is not a muscle. It is an organ. An organ is a specific part of the body, such as the heart or the liver, which does a particular job.
10. a) In the womb, a baby is attached to the mother by the umbilical cord, which suppplies it with food and oxygen.

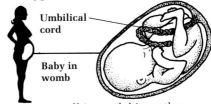

Umbilical cord

Baby in womb

11. An egg cell is much bigger than a sperm cell.
12. c) Protein, found in meat, cheese and fish, is essential for growth.
13. True. When you get up in the morning, you are at full height. During the day, gravity presses down on you and closes the tiny gaps between your joints. By the evening you are a little shorter.
14. True. There are 206 bones in your body, including 32 in each arm and 31 in each leg.
15. a) Your nails never stop growing while you are alive.

Evolution

1. False. Scientists think that domestic cats have evolved from wild cats, possibly from Africa.
★ 2. No. You should not eat horse chestnut seeds, but you can bake and eat the seeds of sweet chestnut trees.

Horse   Sweet
chestnut   chestnut

3. Yes. Animals with short life-spans and many offspring evolve quicker, because any change in their appearance or the way they act will be passed on to their own offspring much quicker.
★ 4. Moths usually come out at night.
5. False.
6. b) The armadillo is not extinct. Armadillos are found in North and South America, and have thick bony plates around their bodies to protect them from predators.

Armadillo

★ 7. Present day tigers have stripes to help them blend in with the light and shade of the forests they inhabit.

Modern tiger   Sabre-tooth tiger

8. No. Wisdom teeth are found in all sorts of people.
9. a) Eyebrows help to keep sweat from the brow out of the eyes.
10. b) Most scientists think the first humans lived in Africa.
11. a) Pedigree dogs. A dog must have ancestors of the same breed for three generations (back to its great grandparents), to be a pedigree dog.
12. c) The husky is most like a wolf.

Husky   Wolf

13. No. Lions are the product of natural selection in the wild. They are too fierce and dangerous to be of any practical use to humans.
★ 14. The mule is a cross between a donkey and a horse. Mules are strong animals, but they cannot usually have their own offspring.
15. c) Genetic engineering is a branch of biotechnology.

The balance of nature

1. False. The study of living things in the environment is called ecology.
2. b) Protecting the environment is called conservation.
★ 3. Hawks hunt by day, when they make the best use of their sharp eyesight.

Sparrowhawks hide in trees and ambush their prey.

4. The thrush has more choice of food than the owl. It is an omnivore, eating both plants and animals.
5. In this particular food web, rabbits need to watch out for foxes.
6. False. Many large animals, such as elephants and horses, are herbivores.
★ 7. Humans are omnivores.
8. There would be more caterpillars than hawks in a forest food web. For a food web to feed all its animals, there have to be more animals at the lower end to provide food for those at the top.
9. b) The boring beetle is a real beetle.

Boring beetles burrow into trees.

10. a) Sites where waste is buried are called landfills.
★ 11. Chernobyl power station caused much pollution when it exploded in 1986. Large parts of the former Soviet Union and Northern Europe were affected.

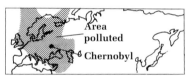

Area polluted

Chernobyl

★ 12. Yes. Almost half the iron used to make steel is recycled. Recycling iron is cheaper, and uses less energy than making new iron from iron ore.
13. c) Compost heaps take around six months to rot.
14. b) Materials that rot are called biodegradable, which means they can be broken down by bacteria. Materials made from living things are able to rot, but metals, glass and most plastics do not rot.

Biodegradable

Cauliflower Newspaper

Cotton T-shirt

Non-biodegradable

Plastic bottle

Glass jar   Batteries

15. True. In 1990, Americans threw away nearly 2kg (4lbs) of waste a day.

Science and technology

1. b) CDs are coated with a protective layer of transparent plastic.
★ 2. No. Written information and pictures can also be stored on CD.
3. c) The picture has been magnified around 8,000 times.
4. False. CDs are very hard-wearing. It is unlikely that they will wear out. Unlike records and tapes which rub against another hard surface, the CD surface is only touched by light.
5. True. Lasers are used to read bar codes. The reflections of the laser beam form a digital code, which registers the price of goods.

Bar code

White reflects light.   Black does not reflect light.

9 7 7 0 7 4 6 0 1 1 2 7 4

★ 6. Yes. Laser light travels in a straight line and is used to measure distances.

Lasers have measured the distance between the Earth and the Moon.

Moon   Earth

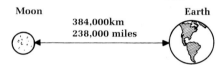

384,000km
238,000 miles

7. True. Some lasers are brighter than the Sun. Scientists are trying to find a way to use bright lasers to generate nuclear power.
8. c) All new cars in the USA are fitted with catalytic converters.
★ 9. Yes. Exhaust fumes are acidic. They dissolve in moisture in the air, which then falls as acid rain.

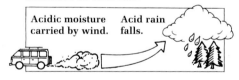

Acidic moisture carried by wind.   Acid rain falls.

10. False. Breathing carbon monoxide will not make your hair go white, but it is poisonous. If you breathe a great deal of it, it can kill you.
11. a) Energy efficient light bulbs last 8 times longer than ordinary bulbs.
12. False. Energy efficient light bulbs work as long as there is an electricity supply.
13. Camcorder stands for CAMera and reCORDER.
14. True. There are about 400,000 pixels on a CCD.
★ 15. A palmcorder is a very small, modern camcorder, named because it can be held in one hand. The lightest ones weigh around 800g (1lb 12oz).

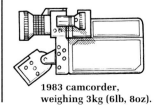

1993 palmcorder.

1983 camcorder, weighing 3kg (6lb, 8oz).

Science Megaquiz answers

There are 100 possible points in the whole Science Megaquiz. Score a point for each correct answer. If you score over 50 you have done well. Over 75 is excellent. You can find out more about some of the answers on the page listed after it.

Misfits

1. The pinna is not part of the eye.
2. Original is not a type of energy.
3. Density is not a force.
4. Brown is not a colour of the rainbow.
5. A lightbulb does not make electricity.
6. Magnetism is not a feature of all living things.
7. The mammoth is extinct.
8. A siphon is not part of an atom.
9. A baby is not a cell.
10. Flutes are not percussion instruments.

Inventions and discoveries

1. Spectacles (c).
2. Mercury thermometer (f).
3. Powered flight (h).
4. Nuclear energy (i).
5. Evolution (g).
6. Camcorder (j).
7. Gravity (e).
8. Smelting iron (b).
9. Wheel (a).
10. The Earth goes around the Sun (d).

Talking science

1. Sunset (page 80).
2. Compost (page 87).
3. Elements (page 68).
4. Field (page 77).
5. Prism (page 80).
6. Food (page 86).
7. Gravity (page 72).
8. Galaxy (page 66).
9. Pollution (page 89).
10. Insulator (page 76).

Materials

1. c) metal (page 76).
2. Hydrocarbons/nitrogen/carbon monoxide (page 89).
3. c) trees (pages 70-71).
4. A compound (page 68).
5. Animal skin (page 70).
6. Gold (page 71).
7. Hydrogen (page 66).
8. b) water (page 83).
9. Copper (page 76).
10. c) clay (page 74-75).

Close-ups

1. Owl (page 86).
2. Radio telescope (page 66).
3. Suspension springs (page 71).
4. Peppered moth (page 84).
5. Camcorder (page 89).
6. Cell (page 82).
7. Atoms (page 68).
8. Cow (page 74).
9. Eye (page 81).
10. Compact disc (page 88).

Animals and plants

1. (d) berries.
2. (c) blue whale.
3. (a) white cat.
4. (g) horse chestnut seed.
5. (b) bat.
6. (e) sabre-toothed tiger.
7. (i) old English sheepdog.
8. (j) orang-utan.
9. (h) puffin.
10. (f) rabbit.

True or false?

1. True (page 67).
2. False.
3. False.
4. True (page 80).
5. True (page 83).
6. False.
7. True (page 69).
8. False.
9. False.
10. True (page 78).

Silhouettes

1. Hawk (page 86).
2. Spring (page 74).
3. Ship (page 73).
4. Coccyx (page 85).
5. Balloon (page 68).
6. Wisdom tooth (page 85).
7. Guitar (page 79).
8. Nerve cell (page 83).
9. Atom (page 69).
10. Caterpillar (page 82).

Body bits

1. Blood (page 75).
2. Appendix (page 85).
3. Pituitary gland (page 83).
4. Optic nerve (page 81).
5. Skin.
6. Muscles (page 83).
7. Skeleton (page 83).
8. Iris (page 81).
9. Coccyx (page 85).
10. Pinna (page 78).

What do you know?

1. Photosynthesis (page 82).
2. Static electricity (page 76).
3. Compact disc (page 88).
4. Yes, with an electron microscope.
5. a) 15 thousand (page 66).
6. Ores (page 70).
7. Magnetism (page 77).
8. b) silk (page 70).
9. Laser light (page 88).
10. Plants (page 86).

Scientists and inventors

Below are some scientists and inventors who contributed to ideas and inventions in Part Three of this book.

Carothers, Wallace 1896-1937
American chemist who discovered nylon (pages 70-71), which was the first man-made fibre to be widely used.

Dalton, John 1766-1844
English self-taught chemist who carried out important research into the existence of atoms (pages 68-69).

Darwin, Charles 1809-1882
English naturalist, who proposed the natural selection theory of evolution (pages 84-85).

Dunlop, John 1840-1921
Scottish veterinary surgeon who invented the first air-filled tyre, called the pneumatic tyre (page 70).

Einstein, Albert 1879-1955
German physicist who made many important discoveries concerning nuclear energy (page 69) and light (pages 80-81).

Faraday, Michael 1791-1867
English scientist who invented the electric motor (page 77).

Franklin, Benjamin 1706-1790
American scientist and politician who showed that lightning is a form of electricity. He also invented the lightning rod (page 76).

Galilei, Galileo 1564-1642
Italian physicist who was one of the first people to use a telescope to study the solar system (page 66).

Goddard, Robert 1882-1945
American physicist who was a leading figure in the development of the space rocket (page 67). He launched the first liquid-fuelled rocket in 1926.

Lemaitre, Georges 1894-1966
Belgian astronomer who first suggested the Big Bang theory (page 66).

Mendel, Gregor 1822-1884
Austrian monk who discovered that living things pass on characteristics to their offspring (page 84).

Newton, Isaac 1642-1727
English mathematician and physicist who proved light was a mixture of colours (pages 80-81) and proposed theories on gravity and motion (pages 72-73).

Watt, James 1736-1819
Scottish engineer who developed the steam engine. The Watt, a unit of electrical power (page 77), is named after him.

The publishers would like to thank the following for the use of their photographs and reference material in this section of the book: NRSC LTD/Science Photo Library (page 67, left); Dr Mitsuo Ohtsuki/Science Photo Library (page 69, bottom right); Canon (UK) Ltd (page 89, top).

Part Four

HISTORY QUIZBOOK

Alastair Smith

Edited by Judy Tatchell

Designed by
Nigel Reece and Richard Johnson

Illustrated by
Jonathon Heap and Peter Dennis

Additional illustration by
Kuo Kang Chen, Guy Smith and Steve Lings

Consultant: Julie Penn

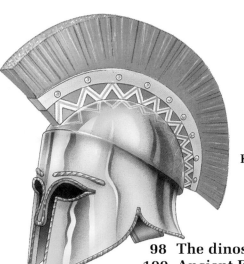

Contents

About Part Four

Part Four of the book covers 12 topics from history. The topics range from **The dinosaur age** to **The twentieth century** and each one takes up two pages. There is lots to read about all these topics, with quiz questions to answer as you go along.

How to do the quizzes

Within each of the two-page topic sections there are 15 quiz questions for you to answer. These questions are printed in italic type, *like this*. Some of the quiz questions rely on general knowledge. Others ask you to guess whether a statement is true or false, or to choose between several possible answers. You will be able to answer some questions if you study the pictures on the page. Jot your answers on a piece of paper and check them against the correct answers on pages 124-127.

The History Megaquiz

On pages 122-123 is the **History Megaquiz**. This consists of ten quick quizzes which ask questions about things you have read about earlier in Part Four. Again, keep a note of your answers and then check them against the **History Megaquiz answers** on page 128.

The dinosaur age

Millions of years ago, strange reptiles called dinosaurs dominated the Earth. They probably appeared about 210 million years ago and died out about 65 million years ago. Humans did not appear until about two million years ago.

Hundreds of different sorts of dinosaurs developed and then died out. Those on this page lived several million years before those opposite.

1. The word "dinosaur" means: a) terrible lizard; b) massive teeth; c) giant feet.

What was Earth like then?

When dinosaurs were alive, most of the land was fairly warm. There were swamps and oases scattered about. Dinosaurs and other reptiles liked these conditions.

2. Which dinosaur shown on these pages has a name which means Tyrant Lizard King?

3. What do you think this tail was used for?

4. Baby dinosaurs hatched from eggs laid in the sand. True or false?

Were all dinosaurs big?

Not all dinosaurs were big. Some, such as Compsognathus, were no bigger than large turkeys.

Stegosaurus was 7m (23ft) long – but its brain was only as big as a walnut.

Compsognathus

5. Bones preserved in rock are called: a) toggles; b) fossils; c) skulls.

Which was the biggest dinosaur?

The biggest dinosaur was called Brachiosaurus. It ate plants. It was longer than two buses and its footprints would have been big enough for you to sit down in.

6. Brachiosaurus was good at climbing trees. True or false?

Brachiosaurus

7. Nobody knows what colour the dinosaurs were. True or false?

8. Which of these is not a reptile: a) alligator; b) Stegosaurus; c) hippopotamus?

Stegosaurus

How did we get here?

The Earth is about 4,600 million years old. Over time, its environment changes. Some living things adapt to changes. This is called evolution. Others do not adapt so they die out. This panel shows when different living things evolved.

9. Animal life began:
a) in the air;
b) in the sea;
c) on land.

3,000 million years ago.
Bacteria, the first life

1,500 million years ago.
Algae and jellyfish

500 million years ago.
Plants

280 million years ago.
Reptiles

200 million years ago.
Dinosaurs and mammals

Parasaurolophus' head was as long as a man.

10. Could any dinosaurs fly?

11. How many of the animals shown on these two pages still exist?

Which was the fiercest dinosaur?

Tyrannosaurus rex was the largest meat-eater that has ever lived. Its teeth were as long as daggers.

12. A meat-eater is called: a) a carnivore; b) a herbivore.

13. Was Tyrannosaurus rex the biggest dinosaur?

The top of Pachycephalosaurus' head was tougher than a brick. It was useful for butting enemies.

14. The number of different types of dinosaur found so far is about: a) 6; b) 40; c) 800.

15. How many man-eating dinosaurs are shown on these two pages?

Tyrannosaurus rex

The first dinosaur fossil was found over 300 years ago. The finder thought it was a giant's bone.

How is a fossil made?

A dead animal's flesh rots away, leaving only the bony parts.

The bones are buried under mud, sand and rotting plants.

As pressure builds up on top of it, this earthy mixture turns to rock.

Rock

Over millions of years, the bones soak up minerals from the rock around them.

The bones become rock (fossilized). Fossils provide clues to what living things looked like long ago.

Why did the dinosaurs die out?

Nobody is certain why dinosaurs died out. A change in climate is the most likely reason. This would have led to a shortage of food.

This section shows how humans might have evolved from early sorts of ape.

35 million years ago. First apes

14 million years ago. Ramapithecus

5 million years ago. Man-ape

2 million years ago. Handy Man

1.5 million years ago. Upright Man

200 thousand years ago. Neanderthal Man

40 thousand years ago. Modern Man

Ancient Egypt

Thousands of years ago, the Ancient Egyptians built huge tombs, called pyramids, for their dead kings and queens. Some pyramids were taller than a 30-storey tower block.

When a king or queen died, the Egyptians preserved the body. They thought this would mean that the dead person's spirit would live forever. They built a pyramid so that the spirit would always have a house on Earth to return to.

By about 1550BC, the Ancient Egyptians had stopped building pyramids. Instead, they buried royalty in tombs cut out of the rock in a valley called the Valley of the Kings.

1. Is there still a country called Egypt?

2. Most of the pyramids have now sunk into the sand. True or false?

How was the body preserved?

To preserve the body, some organs were removed. The skin, bones and other remains were dried using a salty chemical. This took several weeks. Finally, the body was perfumed and bandaged in cloth. This process is called embalming.

The chief priest, dressed as Anubis, god of the dead, embalmed the body.

3. What kind of animal was the god Anubis?

4. Embalmed bodies are known as:
a) dummies;
b) mummies;
c) tummies.

5. The embalmed bodies of some Ancient Egyptians have lasted until today. True or false?

What was the funeral like?

The coffin was put on to a decorated sledge and dragged to the tomb. The sledge looked like a boat. The Egyptians thought the king would need a boat to cross the imaginary water between Earth and heaven.

Boat-like sledge

King's coffin

Adults wore heavy eye make-up. This protected the eye area from the sun.

How long did it take to build a pyramid?

It took 4,000 workers 20 years to build one of the biggest pyramids. The workers had to spend three months each year working on them.

The Egyptians wanted the pyramids to last forever. Only the best built pyramids are still completely standing today, though.

The Egyptians could have used more machinery but they built the pyramids mostly by hand. The harder the work, the more honour it did to the ruler. The Egyptians thought their kings were half god, half human.

The Egyptians built hundreds of statues like this, called sphinxes. The heads were carved to look like the heads of kings.

Ramps made of rubble and mud spiralled up around the pyramid. Builders dragged the huge stone blocks up these ramps.

7. Where was this stone, called a capstone going to be put?

Pyramids were covered with white limestone.

6. Which of these was not a queen of Egypt: a) Cleopatra; b) Nefertiti; c) Elizabeth I?

Most adults shaved their hair and wore wigs. This was clean and cool.

Many children had shaved heads except for a single lock of hair.

Some girls had hair like dreadlocks.

8. A sphinx has the body of: a) a woman; b) a lion; c) a fish.

The dead king was buried in here.

After the burial this passage was sealed.

Passages

False tombs might have been built to confuse grave robbers.

9. What made the pyramids white?

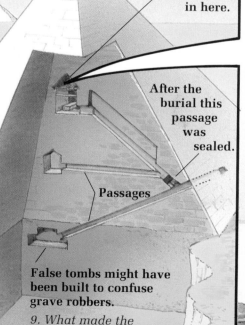

Did you know?

Tutankhamun became king when he was 10 and died aged 18. His tomb in the Valley of the Kings was discovered in 1922. Most other royal tombs had been robbed over the years but his was untouched.

10. What were Egyptian kings called?

11. Was Tutankhamun buried in a pyramid?

Some people believed that Tutankhamun's tomb was protected by a curse. The curse meant that anyone who entered the tomb would die. One of the people who found the tomb died a few weeks later. Some people thought this was due to the curse.

Tutankhamun's coffin was made of solid gold.

Where were other Egyptians buried?

Most people were buried in the sand on the outskirts of town. Embalming was so expensive that only rich people could afford it.

13. Unscramble the name of this Egyptian city: ariCo.

12. What did Egyptian children usually wear in the summer?

What was on the tomb walls?

14. The symbols on the wall are called: a) anagrams; b) anaglypta; c) hieroglyphics.

On the tomb walls were carved rows of pictures and symbols. This was a sort of writing. It told stories of the king's life and explained to his spirit how it should find its way to heaven.

Most of what we know about the Ancient Egyptians was discovered from picture-writing in pyramids and rock-cut tombs.

The coffin had a sculpture of the dead king's face on it.

Food, furniture and embalmed bodies of the king's pets.

15. Which of the symbols on the wall means "to walk"?

Ancient Greece

About 2,500 years ago, Greece was made up of many cities. Each one ruled the countryside around it. What it was like to be alive then depended a lot on where you lived.

A wealthy person in the city of Athens, for instance, would have a comfortable life, with visits to the theatre and parties to go to. A young man in Sparta would be a soldier living in a grim barracks.

1. What is the capital of Greece now, Athens or Sparta?

What were Greek plays like?

You could watch two sorts of play in a Greek theatre. They were called tragedies and comedies. Women were not allowed to act so men had to dress up to play female roles.

Tragedies were about the fates of past Greek heroes and were serious. Actors wore masks to show the age, sex and mood of a character.

Comedies often made fun of politicians and important people.

2. What moods do these masks show?

3. Are Ancient Greek plays still performed today?

4. Greek actors used microphones so they could be heard. True or false?

Who was in charge of Athens?

Athens is famous for its system of government, called democracy. Each citizen could vote on how the city was run. Unfortunately, the Greeks did not allow women or slaves to be citizens, so they did not have a vote.

5. The word "democracy" means:
a) governed by the king; b) governed by the people;
c) governed by women.

Architects ever since have copied the elegant style of Ancient Greek buildings. The style is known as "classical".

A political meeting

6. It was a crime to chop down an olive tree in Athens. True or false?

The ruin of this theatre is still standing in Athens. It held 14,000 people.

Stage area

Who was Homer?

Homer was a Greek poet who might have lived about 800BC. He made up long poems about mythical Greek heroes. Two of his poems, the *Iliad* and the *Odyssey*, have survived until now. The *Iliad* is about the legendary Trojan War.

7. Homer's poems were called:
a) epics; b) topics; c) episodes.

What was the Trojan War about?

A Trojan prince called Paris kidnapped Helen, the beautiful wife of Menelaus. Menelaus and his brother Agamemnon, a Greek king, raised an army and sailed to the city of Troy to fetch her back. There were 1,000 ships in the fleet that carried the army.

8. Greece is part of which continent?

The Greeks besieged Troy for ten years without success. Then Odysseus, a Greek general, had a plan. The Greeks built a huge model horse and led the Trojans to believe it was a gift to the gods. They left the horse outside Troy and pretended to sail away.

Who were the Greek gods?

The Greek gods behaved a bit like humans – they got jealous, argued and played tricks. However, they had magic powers so they could change shape, make things happen and get from one place to another in a flash.

12. Guess which god is which:
a) Poseidon, god of the sea;
b) Aphrodite, goddess of love;
c) Zeus, king of the gods;
d) Athene, goddess of wisdom.

How were children treated in Sparta?

Spartan boys were brought up to be the toughest soldiers in Greece. Girls also trained to be strong so they would have good warrior sons. The Spartans wanted to be able to resist any invasion or slave rebellion.

Boys were sent away to an army training school at the age of seven. They were taught to read and write but learning to use weapons was more important. They also had dancing lessons to make them strong and agile.

There is a story that the boys were underfed and had to steal extra food from local farms. If they were caught they were beaten by teachers – not for stealing, but for getting caught.

13. Before battle, Spartan soldiers put perfume in their hair. True or false?

Did you know?

If the sports festival at Olympia started during a war, fighting was stopped so that soldiers could go and take part.

15. Which modern sports festival is named after the Games at Olympia?

The winners were given these prizes:

Olive wreath

Palm branches

Ribbons

Why were the Greeks keen on sport?

The Greeks were often at war. Fit, strong men made better soldiers so they exercised regularly at sports centres, called *gymnasia*.

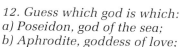

Athletics festivals were held in stadiums like this.

Athletics festivals were held in honour of the gods. The most famous one was held every four years in the city of Olympia. People came from all over Greece to compete.

14. Can you identify these four sports, all played by the Ancient Greeks?

What is Homer's *Odyssey* about?

The Trojans took the horse into the city to please the gods. However, Greek soldiers were hiding inside. That night, they climbed out, and opened the city gates. The Greeks raided the city and won the war.

9. What was the horse made of?

The *Odyssey* is about Odysseus' adventures on his way home after the Trojan War.

He had to outwit the Sirens who lured sailors to their deaths on the rocks by singing beautifully.

Sirens had the faces of beautiful women, with birds' bodies and clawed feet.

10. Odysseus took:
a) one week;
b) two days;
c) ten years to get home.

He had to escape from Circe, a witch who turned men into animals, and kill a terrifying one-eyed monster.

11. A one-eyed monster is called a:
a) cyclone; b) cyclops; c) cygnet.

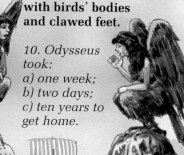

Ancient Rome

Two thousand years ago, Rome was the most important city in Europe. It was the hub of a huge empire which ruled over much of Europe and the Mediterranean lands.

What were Roman baths?

Roman baths were not like modern swimming baths. They had several pools, all at different temperatures. Bathers went from one to another. This left them feeling very clean and refreshed. Men and women went to the baths at different times of day.

1. Unscramble the name of this famous Roman ruler: luiJus Carsae.

A slave working as a hair plucker. It was fashionable to have a smooth, hairless body.

A slave giving a massage.

2. Rome is now the capital of which European country?

Did you know?

To get clean the Romans covered themselves in olive oil, then scraped it off with a scraper, called a *strigilis*. It worked just as well as soap.

3. In some places, people still clean themselves with olive oil. True or false?

4. Some Roman houses had central heating. True or false?

Hot bath

This furnace heated a tank of water. The water was pumped to the hot bath, warm bath and steam room. The furnace was tended by a slave.

Warm bath

What did Romans do for entertainment?

5. Which month is named after Mars, the Roman god of war?

The crowd gave this sign if they wanted the loser to live.

In Rome, fights were put on for the public to watch. These fights were called the Games. The loser was often killed in the fight. If not, the crowd voted whether or not he should be put to death. A brave loser might be allowed to live.

6. Neptune was the Roman god of: a) the Moon; b) the wind; c) the sea.

The fighters were criminals or prisoners of war. They might be forced to fight against wild animals, professional fighters or each other.

7. Which of these was a famous fighter who led a revolt against the Roman government: a) Spartacus; b) Diplodocus; c) Muhammad Ali?

8. Professional fighters were called: a) gladiators; b) exterminators; c) mashpotaters.

9. What sign did people give if they wanted the loser to die?

The biggest Games arena in Rome was the Colosseum. It held 48,000 people. This is what it looks like now.

Where were chariot races held?

Chariot races were held in a massive stadium called the Circus Maximus. It held about 280,000 people. Chariot racers belonged to different teams. Supporters in the crowd wore the colours of the team they wanted to win. There were even supporters' clubs to join.

10. The Circus Maximus was larger than any soccer stadium. True or false?

Chariots were very light so that they would go fast.

Most crashes happened on sharp bends.

In the steam room people sweated a lot. This was like a sauna.

11. What do you think this hooked knife was for?

The horses' reins were tied around the driver. If the chariot crashed, the driver had to free himself as quickly as possible.

Changing room

14. The Romans spoke: a) Latin; b) Greek; c) Turkish.

Food seller with sausages and honey cakes.

Where did slaves come from?

Most slaves were prisoners of war that the Roman army captured on their foreign campaigns. They were brought back to Rome to do the worst jobs in return for their keep.

12. Can you see three different jobs that slaves are doing at the baths?

The cold bath (*frigidarium*) was for cooling off after the hot baths or exercise.

13. What is this building?

15. Roman men wore trousers. True or false?

The Vikings

The Vikings came from the far north of Europe. About 1,200 years ago they began exploring the world in search of riches.

Some Vikings raided towns and villages and stole what they wanted. Others traded peacefully in foreign towns.

1. Can you name any of the countries where the Vikings came from?

2. Where did Vikings keep their shields during voyages?

3. What weapon did the Vikings use most often?

What was a Viking raid like?

Vikings tried to catch their victims by surprise. They did not want to waste their energy on a hard fight.

4. How many Vikings have been killed on this raid?

They took prisoners and killed anyone who got in the way. Important prisoners were held to ransom. Poor prisoners were taken back home to be slaves.

Viking ships were flat-bottomed so that they could be sailed into shallow waters. This made surprise attacks easier.

5. Viking boats were called: a) galleons; b) longships; c) rafts.

Where did Vikings trade?

The Vikings traded mainly with places which they could reach by ship. They founded trading towns all over Europe, such as Dublin in Ireland and Kiev in the Ukraine. Many Vikings settled permanently in trading towns.

9. The name Viking comes from a Viking word meaning: a) King Vic; b) adventurer; c) red beard.

How far did they travel?

Vikings were such good sailors that they even reached North America. They travelled about 11,000km (7,000 miles) there and back. It was 400 years before any other Europeans went there.

10. Which was further away from the Vikings' home, Ireland or North America?

Some traders did not like the Vikings – they thought that the Vikings swore, fought and got drunk too often.

11. In winter, Viking traders made overland journeys on skis. True or false?

Vikings loved Arabian silks and cloths like these.

Treasures from a raid

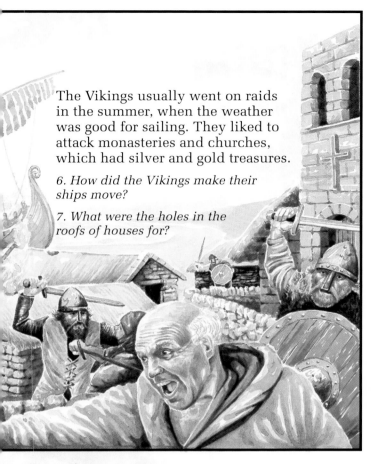

The Vikings usually went on raids in the summer, when the weather was good for sailing. They liked to attack monasteries and churches, which had silver and gold treasures.

6. How did the Vikings make their ships move?

7. What were the holes in the roofs of houses for?

How did the Vikings celebrate?

When they got home, the Vikings held huge feasts that went on for days. Poets called bards told long, exciting stories about famous battles and adventures.

Bard

8. The stories were called: a) sagas; b) lagers; c) lyrics.

Did you know?

Vikings often took their sons with them on trading voyages. That way the boys learned how to be skilful sailors.

Slaves

How were the Vikings buried?

Important warriors were buried or burned in their ships. The Vikings believed that the person's soul sailed to Viking heaven in the ship. There, men fought all day. Every evening there was a huge feast.

12. Viking heaven was called: a) Valhalla; b) Hell; c) Iceland.

Vikings thought that to die of natural causes was boring and cowardly. They called it a "straw death". The best way to die was in battle.

13. Which one of these was not a Viking king: a) Cnut the Great; b) Erik Bloodaxe; c) Herod the Great?

14. Which weekday is named after Thor, the Viking god of thunder?

15. Viking women were called Viqueens. True or false?

The Crusades

The Crusades were wars between groups of Christians and Moslems. They began in 1096 and lasted on and off for the next 200 years. The wars were about who should rule Syria and Palestine (see map on the right).

Why was this area important?

Jerusalem in Palestine was a holy place for Moslems. They believed that their leader, Muhammad, rose to heaven from Jerusalem.

1. Why was there a wall around Jerusalem?

Palestine was important to Christians because Jesus Christ had lived there. Christians called the area the Holy Land. They made journeys, called pilgrimages, to pray there.

2. In which town was Jesus Christ born?

ITALY

GREECE

PALESTINE   SYRIA

Jerusalem

Mediterranean Sea

Moslem soldier

EGYPT   Bethlehem

3. This area of water is called: a) the Caribbean Sea; b) the Red Sea; c) the Blue Sea.

Christian soldier

4. What sort of armour is this Christian soldier wearing?

Why did the Crusades begin?

Before the Crusades, Moslems had ruled Palestine for centuries. The Moslems had let Christian pilgrims visit the area safely.

In 1076, though, another Moslem group called the Seljuk Turks took over Palestine. They killed Christians they found there.

In 1096, the Pope, who was head of the Christian Church, asked Christians to take the Holy Land from the Seljuks. He said that if they did, God would forgive all their sins.

About 50,000 people set off from all over Europe. Whole families joined the Crusade, most of them poor. They thought Palestine was a rich land where they would make a good living. This Crusade was called the People's Crusade.

5. Were children allowed to join the Crusades?

The army travelled over 2,000 miles to the Holy Land, mostly on foot.

Who won the People's Crusade?

Many Crusaders starved or died of disease on the way. The Seljuks killed those who got there.

6. 20,000 people died on the way to the Holy Land. True or false?

Did the Christians ever win?

Three years after the start of the People's Crusade, another army of Crusaders captured the Holy Land. It was difficult for them to keep order, though, because most of the people there were Moslems. Bit by bit, the Moslems won the area back.

7. The Moslems had faster horses than the Crusaders. True or false?

Who led the armies?

The Moslem general who won back most of the Holy Land from the Christians was called Saladin. He was a brilliant general and he was fierce but he treated his enemies fairly.

Richard the Lionheart (King Richard I of England) led a Crusade against Saladin. Although he lost the war, Saladin promised to allow pilgrims to visit Jerusalem. Saladin and Richard respected each other although they were enemies.

8. Saladin's sword was called:
a) a scimitar; b) a scythe; c) a scarab.

9. Moslem soldiers were called:
a) Salads; b) Saracens; c) Aladins.

10. Why was Richard I nicknamed "the Lionheart"?

How did the Crusades change Europe?

Crusaders brought back types of food and other goods that were new to Europe. Some of these are shown in the picture.

11. Which of these did the Crusaders NOT bring back to Europe:
a) oranges; b) pepper; c) potatoes?

Moslem castles were very strong so European castle-builders copied them. (See next page.)

▼

Europeans began to use Moslem-style glass mirrors instead of polished metal ones.

Crusaders took rugs and carpets back to replace straw and rushes in wealthy homes.

Silk

Sugar

Ginger, pepper and cinnamon

Dates

Cloves

Figs

Almonds

Rice

Raisins

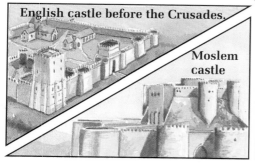

English castle before the Crusades.

Moslem castle

Did you know?

The way numbers are written developed from symbols used by Moslem mathematicians.

12. The numbers on the right were used by Moslem mathematicians. Can you match them to the modern numbers above them?

9 7 4 1

١٣٤٧٩

How big was the Moslem Empire?

This map shows how big the Moslem Empire was during the Crusades.

13. The Moslems ruled parts of three continents. True or false?

Syria and Palestine

Spain

Moslem Empire (in red)

Moslems occupied parts of Spain from the 7th to the 15th century. You can still see Moslem buildings in Spain, such as the Palace of Alhambra in Granada.

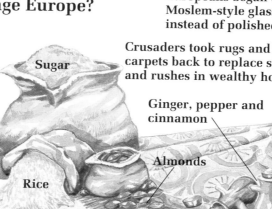

Palace of Alhambra

14. The Palace of Alhambra was built as a new home for the Pope. True or false?

15. The game below was first played in Europe by Moslems. What is it?

A medieval castle

Medieval castles in Europe were the homes of rulers and wealthy landowners. They protected the owner, his subjects and possessions from local bandits or invading armies.

During the 13th century, Crusaders brought back ideas from the Middle East for how to improve European castles. Features marked with a star (★) show some of these ideas.

Where were castles built?

Most castles were built on steep hills or cliffs. This made them difficult to attack. It also gave the defenders a good view of the surrounding area so that they could see approaching enemies.

1. Medieval means: a) dark and eery; b) belonging to the Middle Ages; c) made of stone.

2. Where did the castle defenders get their drinking water from?

Did castles take long to build?

It could take 3,000 builders ten years to build a big castle.

3. Which were stronger – round towers or square ones?

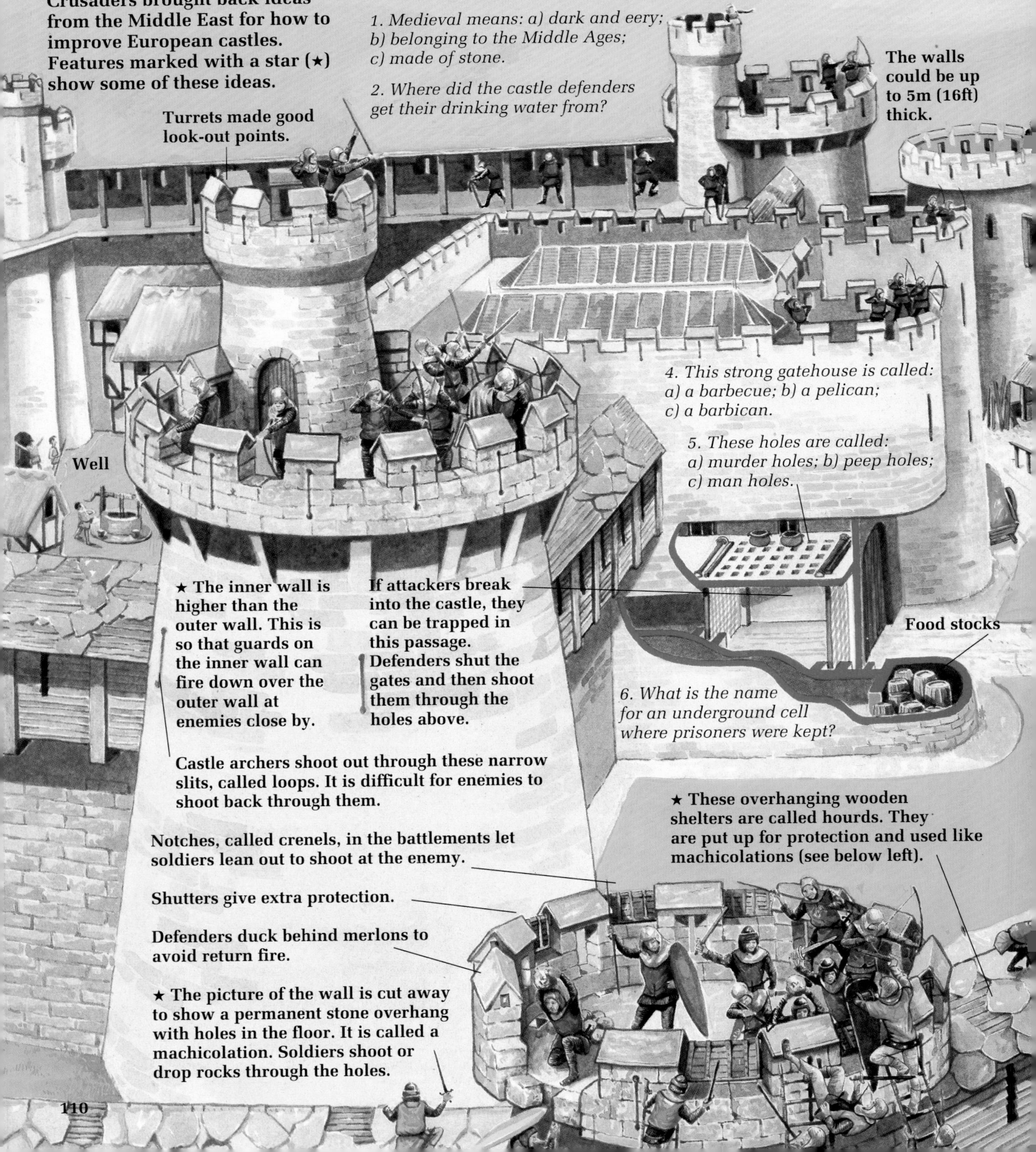

The walls could be up to 5m (16ft) thick.

Turrets made good look-out points.

Well

★ The inner wall is higher than the outer wall. This is so that guards on the inner wall can fire down over the outer wall at enemies close by.

If attackers break into the castle, they can be trapped in this passage. Defenders shut the gates and then shoot them through the holes above.

4. This strong gatehouse is called: a) a barbecue; b) a pelican; c) a barbican.

5. These holes are called: a) murder holes; b) peep holes; c) man holes.

Food stocks

6. What is the name for an underground cell where prisoners were kept?

Castle archers shoot out through these narrow slits, called loops. It is difficult for enemies to shoot back through them.

Notches, called crenels, in the battlements let soldiers lean out to shoot at the enemy.

Shutters give extra protection.

Defenders duck behind merlons to avoid return fire.

★ The picture of the wall is cut away to show a permanent stone overhang with holes in the floor. It is called a machicolation. Soldiers shoot or drop rocks through the holes.

★ These overhanging wooden shelters are called hourds. They are put up for protection and used like machicolations (see below left).

What was a siege?

During a siege, attackers surrounded a castle to stop anyone from entering or leaving it. The people inside could survive for months if they had fresh water and plenty of food stored up.

Attackers hoped that a long siege would cause the people inside to run out of food or get ill. They might just get tired of fighting.

7. The longest siege lasted for six months. True or false?

8. The archers in this picture are using: a) longbows; b) shortbows; c) strongbows.

Did you know?

Once cannons had been invented, castles were no longer so safe. Cannonballs could blast huge holes in the walls. Cannons were invented in the 14th century.

9. The explosive that fired a cannon was: a) dynamite; b) gunpowder.

10. Gunpowder was invented by the Chinese. True or false?

11. Were cannonballs explosive?

What weapons did attackers use?

Attackers used huge catapults, called mangonels and trebuchets. These hurled heavy objects into the castle or at its walls. Sometimes dead and rotting animals were flung into the castle to spread disease.

12. Put these weapons in order of invention: a) mangonel; b) tank; c) spear.

Scaling tower

Mangonel

Trebuchets

13. What is this type of bridge called?

14. What is this siege weapon called?

15. What is this deep channel of water called?

The Aztecs and the Incas

About 500 years ago, much of Central and South America was ruled by two powerful tribes, the Aztecs and the Incas. They worshipped the Sun and had so much gold that they even used it to decorate gardens. Less than 50 years later, though, their empires had disappeared. They had been destroyed by Spanish conquerors who came in search of fabulous wealth.

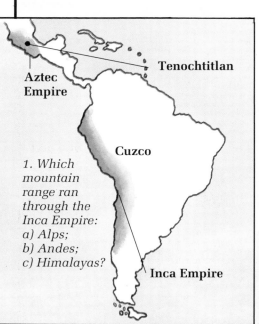

1. Which mountain range ran through the Inca Empire: a) Alps; b) Andes; c) Himalayas?

Aztec Empire

Tenochtitlan

Cuzco

Inca Empire

Who were the Aztecs?

The Aztecs ruled several other tribes in part of what is now Mexico. Their king was called the Great Speaker. He had a deputy called Snake Woman. These two people stood for the man and woman who had created the Earth.

2. The Spanish invaders were called: a) bandits; b) cowboys; c) conquistadores.

Did you know?

The post of Snake Woman was always held by a man. This was because only men were allowed to rule in the Aztec kingdom.

3. The South Americans sometimes ate guinea pigs. True or false?

What did Aztecs wear?

The more important someone was, the grander the clothes they were allowed to wear. It was illegal for a lowly person to copy a powerful person's clothing.

What was the Aztec capital city?

The Aztec capital was called Tenochtitlan. It was built on an island in the middle of a lake. It had a main square with temples and palaces around it.

4. The capital of present-day Mexico is called: a) Tenochtitlan; b) Mexico City; c) Los Angeles.

The Great Temple

Warrior

5. Which of these people did the Aztecs think was the most important: a) warrior; b) farmer; c) weaver?

Where was the Inca kingdom?

The Inca kingdom ran down the west of South America. It was larger than the Aztec Empire. The Inca king, Sapa Inca, lived in Cuzco, the capital city. Most people in the Inca kingdom were farmers or craftspeople.

How did the Incas travel?

Incas travelled on foot. A huge network of tracks criss-crossed the Empire. There were huts called rest houses, a day's walk apart so that travellers had somewhere to spend the night.

12. Incas made clothing out of horsehair. True or false?

Rest house

Bridge made from thick rope.

Runners carried messages from town to town.

Steps were built up steep hills.

There were no horses in America. Incas used these animals to carry heavy loads, instead.

11. What is this animal?

Who did the Aztecs worship?

Aztecs had thousands of gods, from a flower god to a war god. The Aztecs believed that the gods could bring them good or bad luck. They tried to keep the gods happy by giving them gifts.

What happened in the Great Temple?

The Aztecs worshipped their gods in the Great Temple. Often they made a human sacrifice, that is, they killed someone as an offering to a god. Every evening they made a human sacrifice to the Sun god. They hoped this would mean the Sun would rise again the next morning.

6. Aztecs made purple dye out of sea snail slime. True or false?

8. Which Aztec god is this?

Weaver

Farmer

Cocoa beans

7. Which is worth more, the bird or the rug?

What happened in the market?

In the market in the main square, Aztecs swapped one sort of goods for another. They used cocoa beans as small change if one half of the swap was worth more that the other.

9. Swapping goods instead of selling them is called: a) bartering; b) bantering; c) battering.

10. This bird is: a) a toucan; b) an albatross; c) a turkey.

Why did the empires collapse?

Spanish invaders first reached Central and South America early in the 16th century. They had several important advantages over the Aztecs and Incas, as shown below.

Aztecs and Incas had not seen horses before.

Aztecs and Incas always travelled on foot. The Spaniards had horses, so they could travel much faster along the Inca tracks.

13. How did the Spaniards travel to South America?

Aztec and Inca warriors

The Spaniards had guns. Aztecs and Incas only had arrows, knives, spears and clubs.

Spanish weapons

The Aztecs and Incas had no resistance to European diseases brought by the Spaniards.

Aztec and Inca weapons

14. Thousands of Aztecs and Incas died from catching colds. True or false?

Who took over South America?

The Spanish conquerors were the first Europeans to explore South America. Some set up their own kingdoms. Many boundaries of present-day South American countries can be traced back to these Spanish kingdoms.

This map shows the modern countries of Central and South America.

15. Today, most South Americans speak: a) English; b) Spanish; c) Chinese.

Inventions and discoveries

People don't always welcome new inventions and discoveries. Here are some important or useful ones which were unpopular at first.

When did people disagree about trousers?

An American called Amelia Bloomer designed trousers for women in 1853.

In those days, smartly dressed women had to wear bulky dresses. Many people thought that trousers should only be worn by men. It was a hundred years before trousers for women became fashionable.

1. What were the trousers designed by Amelia Bloomer called?

2. What type of hat is the man wearing?

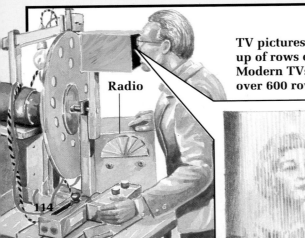

This is what Amelia Bloomer's trousers looked like.

Who was imprisoned for a discovery?

In the 1630s, Galileo, an Italian scientist, wrote a book supporting the discovery that the Earth and the other planets travel around the Sun.

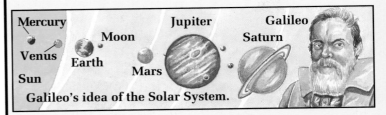

Mercury · Venus · Sun · Earth · Moon · Mars · Jupiter · Saturn · Galileo

Galileo's idea of the Solar System.

This made the leaders of the Catholic Church angry. They believed that the Earth was the middle of the Universe and that the Sun and other planets went around the Earth.

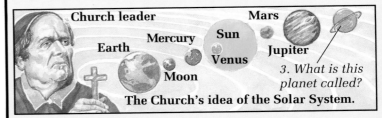

Church leader · Earth · Mercury · Moon · Sun · Venus · Mars · Jupiter · *3. What is this planet called?*

The Church's idea of the Solar System.

Galileo was accused of lying and put on trial. He was forced to plead guilty and was imprisoned in his own home.

4. Was Galileo right or wrong?

5. What are scientists who study the stars called?

Why did steam engines cause riots?

Steam-powered machinery was first used on farms and in factories in the early 19th century. Each machine did the job of several workers, so many lost their jobs. This led to riots. Usually the rioters attacked the steam engine, as shown here.

6. Can you think of another way steam engines were used, apart from on farms and in factories?

7. The invention of steam engines led to a period of great change called: a) the Industrial Revolution; b) the Reformation; c) the Iron Age.

Did you know?

People saw the first TV broadcast via their radios. The radios were fitted with a device to pick up the TV signals. Only a few people saw the first pictures. They showed a person sitting down.

TV pictures are made up of rows of dots. Modern TVs have over 600 rows.

Radio

8. Which came first, cinema or television?

9. The first regular TV broadcasts were made in: a) 1336; b) 1936; c) 1986.

What is this cartoon about?

The cartoon above made fun of a doctor called Edward Jenner, in 1802. He had found a way to prevent people from catching a deadly disease called smallpox. He injected patients with germs from a similar but non-deadly disease called cowpox. People who had been injected did not catch smallpox.

People found this discovery, called inoculation, hard to believe. Nowadays, though, inoculation is used to prevent hundreds of different diseases.

10. Another word for inoculation is:
a) incubation; b) vaccination; c) transfusion.

11. Dairymaids often caught cowpox. True or false?

12. Which of these illnesses cannot be prevented by inoculation: a) flu; b) measles; c) a cold?

Why was Charles Darwin unpopular?

About 130 years ago, the scientist Charles Darwin made himself unpopular because he disagreed with a story from the Bible. The story told how God created the Earth and everything on it in six days.

Darwin said that over thousands of years the Earth's environment changes. Animals and plants have to adapt to survive. Some die out but those that adapt become more efficient. Darwin gave many examples of this process. (See pages 98-99.)

13. Darwin's theory is called:
a) revolution; b) evolution; c) evaluation.

Powerful beak to crush seeds and nuts.

Sharp, strong beak to dig into cacti and chew seeds.

Thin beak to probe for insects and pierce fruit.

One of Darwin's examples came from a study of birds on an island in the Pacific Ocean. He found that similar birds had developed different beaks to eat various types of food.

14. These birds are all types of: a) finch; b) parrot; c) ostrich.

Why was nuclear power unpopular?

Nuclear fuel was first used in power stations in the 1950s. If the fuel leaks, it poisons everything that it touches, even the air. Many people were worried about this and went on demonstrations to protest against nuclear power.

Until the 1950s, most power stations ran on oil or coal. These are safer to use than nuclear fuel but the supply may run out eventually. Also, the smoke from them dissolves in the rain. When the rain falls it damages pastures and forests. This sort of rain is called acid rain.

In 1986, nuclear fuel leaked from a power station at Chernobyl in the Ukraine. The environment for several miles around was ruined. It is still not safe for people to live near Chernobyl, eat food grown there or drink water from the region.

15. Put the following in order of invention:
a) nuclear power; b) steam power; c) electricity.

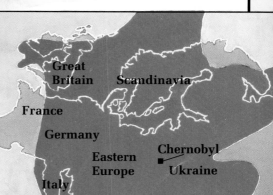

The red area shows how far the wind blew the nuclear pollution. Scientists had to check that the areas were safe for people and animals.

Great Britain · Scandinavia · France · Germany · Eastern Europe · Italy · Chernobyl · Ukraine

The Wild West

There used to be hundreds of American Indian tribes in North America. As European settlers arrived, they began to take over Indian land. By the 19th century, much of the land was being used for huge cattle farms, worked on by cowboys.

1. What were the Indians' tents called?

2. What were the tents made from?

3. What is an American Indian woman called?

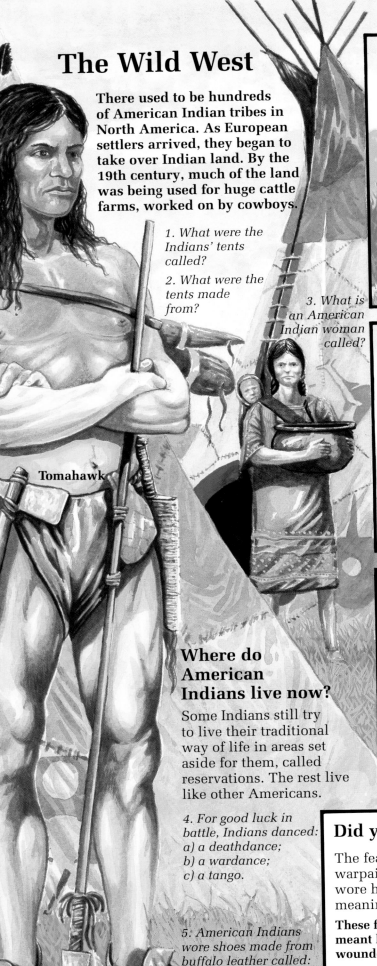

Tomahawk

Where do American Indians live now?

Some Indians still try to live their traditional way of life in areas set aside for them, called reservations. The rest live like other Americans.

4. For good luck in battle, Indians danced:
a) a deathdance;
b) a wardance;
c) a tango.

5. American Indians wore shoes made from buffalo leather called:
a) jerkins;
b) bodkins;
c) moccasins.

How did the Indians live?

Many tribes trailed herds of buffalo all over the prairies. When hunting, Indians often wore the skins of other animals. This disguised them and their scent from the prey.

What did cowboys do?

Cowboys worked on huge cattle farms, called ranches. The biggest cattle herds had over 15,000 cattle. Cowboys used horses to get around the ranches to check the cattle. The horse usually belonged to the ranch owner but the cowboy owned his own saddle. Cowboys spent most of their working life in the saddle.

6. These cattle are:
a) blackhorn cattle;
b) shorthorn cattle;
c) longhorn cattle.

Why did Indians and cowboys fight?

Ranch owners took over land where Indians had lived for centuries. Sometimes, cowboys used force to push the Indians and the buffalo which they hunted off the ranches. The Indians might attack the ranches in revenge.

9. "Smoke sticks" were what Indians called:
a) guns; b) cigars;
c) matches.

Did you know?

The feathers and warpaint that Indians wore had special meanings.

These feathers meant he had been wounded in battle.

This paint meant he would chase intruders away.

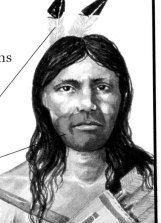

India

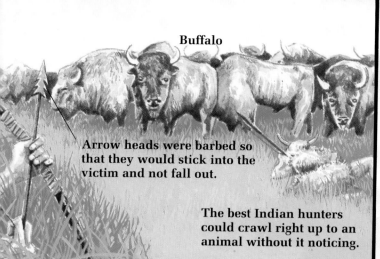

Buffalo

Arrow heads were barbed so that they would stick into the victim and not fall out.

The best Indian hunters could crawl right up to an animal without it noticing.

Who were the cowboys?

Most cowboys were young, unmarried men. They usually slept in dormitories at the ranch. Ten good cowboys could manage a herd of 1,000 cattle.

12. Most cowboys wore hats called: a) stetsons; b) top hats; c) bowlers.

13. Why did cowboys' hats have wide brims?

Bandana

Winchester rifle

Six-shooter

14. Why was the pistol called a six-shooter?

Leather leggings, called chaps, protected trousers and legs from brush and barbed wire.

7. American Indians had no horses before European settlers took them to America. True or false?

8. What is this called?

Why were they called "Red Indians"?

North America
Spain
South America

The explorer Christopher Columbus named the American Indians "Red Indians". 500 years ago, he sailed from Spain to find a sea route to India. Instead, he landed in America. He thought the people he met were Indians, but with skin a redder shade of brown.

10. Which of these is the odd one out: a) Sioux; b) Apache; c) Zulu?

11. Which two of these countries now make up North America: USA, Peru, Canada, Brazil, Chile?

Brand for marking cattle.

15. Why were cattle branded?

Spur

Trains, cars and planes

Before the invention of trains, cars and planes, a journey that now takes hours could take days or even weeks.

People travelled overland either on foot, on horseback or in horsedrawn carriages. Roads were dirt tracks. When they were dry they were hard and bumpy. When they were wet they became deep, sticky bogs.

1. How many different forms of transport can you see on these two pages?

When did the first passenger train run?

The first passenger train service was in Kent in southern England. It opened in 1830 with a journey only 1.6km (1 mile) long. A steam engine, called Invicta, pulled the train at about 20kmph (12mph).

2. The first trains were slower than a galloping horse. True or false?

Most carriages had no roofs.

Invicta

Did you know?

The longest railway line is over 9,000km (5,600 miles) long. It was built between 1891 and 1905 and stretched from the west to the east of the Russian Empire.

3. Does the Russian Empire still exist?

4. The longest railway is called: a) the Great Western Railway; b) the Trans-Siberian Railway; c) the Orient Express.

By 1916 there were over 400,000km (250,000 miles) of railway in the USA.

RUSSIAN EMPIRE

Moscow

Nakhodka

CHINA

What was the first car like?

Early cars still looked similar to horse carriages. Karl Benz made the first car in Germany just over 100 years ago. A fuel engine drove the back wheels. Its top speed was 16kmph (10mph).

5. Can you name a modern car company that uses Benz's name?

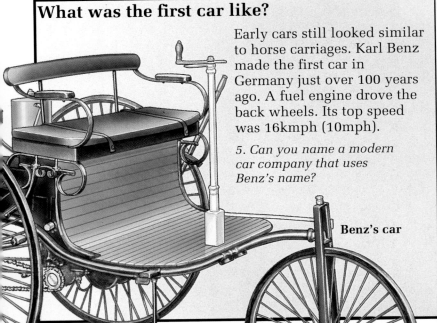

Benz's car

Were cars popular?

At first most people hated cars. They said they were dirty, noisy and a danger to horses and people. For many years after the car's invention only rich people could afford them.

Early car

How long did it take to cross the Atlantic?

Before air travel, a journey between America and Europe took almost a week on the fastest ship. It can now take just three and a quarter hours by jet.

12. Which came first: a) canoe; b) car; c) bicycle?

The Montgolfier brothers' balloon

Who were the first people to fly?

The Montgolfier brothers made a balloon flight in Paris about 200 years ago. The balloon was filled with hot air to make it rise.

Who flew the first plane?

Orville Wright made the first flight in a powered plane in 1903. He flew for 12 seconds and rose about 3m (10ft) into the air.

13. The wings of Wright's plane flapped like a bird's. True or false?

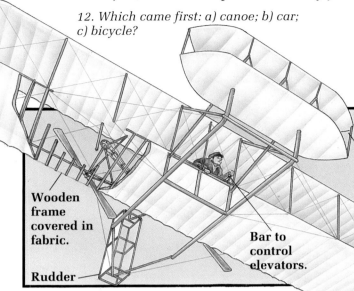

Elevators. These made the plane go up or down.

Wooden frame covered in fabric.

Bar to control elevators.

Rudder

Orville Wright's plane

When were the first passenger flights?

The first passenger air service began in 1910 in Germany. It used airships called Zeppelins. They were filled with a gas that was lighter than air to make them float.

14. No airships ever crashed. True or false?

Zeppelin

Rudders to steer from side to side.

Moveable engines for steering.

Gas was held in bags, called cells.

Walkway for workers.

Workers could climb outside to fix holes while the ship was in flight.

Metal frame

Fabric skin

15. A Zeppelin could carry 5,000 passengers. True or false?

Gondola. Passengers and flight crew travelled in here.

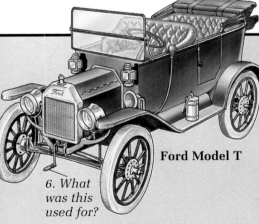

Ford Model T

6. What was this used for?

Henry Ford's company made the first car that ordinary people could afford in 1908. It was called the Model T and Ford made 16 million of them altogether.

7. For many years the Ford Model T was only available in: a) pink; b) black; c) silver.

Ford stopped making the Model T in 1927 but it remained the world's best-selling car until the 1960s. The record was broken by a car made by Volkswagen, shown on the right.

8. What type of Volkswagen is it?

9. Where is its engine?

Early cars had solid rubber tyres. Modern tyres are filled with air for a softer ride and better grip on the road.

10. Air-filled tyres are called: a) pneumatic; b) rheumatic; c) aromatic.

11. Volkswagen means: a) people's car; b) little bug; c) road machine.

The twentieth century

There have probably been more changes since 1900 than during any other century. On these pages you can read about some of the events which have taken place this century.

What was the Russian Revolution about?

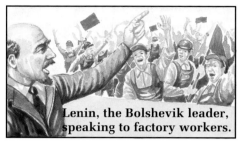
Lenin, the Bolshevik leader, speaking to factory workers.

A factory run by the new government.

Tsar Nicholas II with his family.

Before the Revolution, the emperor of Russia, called the tsar, chose the government from among his noblemen and those he preferred. The leaders of the Revolution, called the Bolsheviks, wanted a government made up of ordinary people. They thought this would be better for most Russians.

The Bolsheviks seized power in 1917. The new government owned and ran every business in the country. They thought that this would benefit everyone. The system was called communism.

1. What did the Bolshevik flag look like?

In 1918, Tsar Nicholas II was shot by Bolshevik supporters. In 1923, the Russian Empire became known as the Union of Soviet Socialist Republics, or USSR. It was the first communist country.

2. The USSR never had a tsar after 1918. True or false?

Who were the Nazis?

The Nazis were a German political party. They governed Germany from 1933 to 1945. They rose to power because they promised to make Germany strong again after years of hardship following World War I.

The man in the photograph (left) was the leader of the Nazi party.

3. What was his name?

4. Was the Nazi symbol: a) a fox; b) a swastika; c) a star?

How did World War II begin?

During the late 1930s, the Nazis began to take over parts of Europe. In 1939, Britain and France declared war on Germany to try to stop them.

Germany continued to invade other countries. In 1941, the USA and USSR joined Britain and France. In 1945, Germany surrendered.

Denmark
Norway
Holland
Belgium
Great Britain
Germany
France

Countries invaded by Germany before World War II.

Countries invaded by Germany in the first year of World War II.

5. Did Germany invade Great Britain?

Poland: invaded in 1939, provoking declaration of war.

Czechoslovakia: invaded in 1938.

Austria: taken over in 1938.

The German army invaded Holland in 1940.

6. Countries that join forces in war are called: a) chums; b) allies; c) troops.

7. How long did World War II last?

Did you know?

The first nuclear weapon was used during World War II. It was a bomb dropped by the USA on Hiroshima in Japan in 1945. Japan was on Germany's side in World War II.

Hiroshima after the bomb.

8. There have been: a) two; b) five; c) 23 World Wars.

120

What was the Cultural Revolution?

Communists took power in China in 1949, after fighting the old government for over 20 years. By the mid-1960s, they felt that people were forgetting the true aims of communism. They started a scheme which was supposed to increase support for Chinese communism. It was called the Cultural Revolution.

An inspector sacks a teacher who criticized communism.

In schools, teachers had to praise Chinese communism to their pupils.

The government banned plays and books that supported life before communism. New books and plays had to praise Chinese communism or say that life had been unfair before it.

9. A war between people of the same country is called: a) a star war; b) a civil war; c) a cold war.

This is a play in support of communism being performed during the Cultural Revolution.

Leaders of the Cultural Revolution sent gangs of young people around China to smash up reminders of the old way of life. The gangs, called the Red Guards, also attacked people who opposed communism.

10. Which was the first country to have a communist government?

Red Guards burning books about life before communism.

The Red Guards killed thousands of people. They were finally banned in 1969.

When were computers invented?

The first computer was built during World War II. It was designed to crack secret codes used by the German and Japanese armies.

The first computer filled a large room because its electronic parts, called components, were so big.

During the 1950s and 1960s, scientists invented smaller and smaller components until thousands could be fitted into a space the size of a fingernail.

Components are held inside here on a slice of glass-like material called silicon.

11. This is called: a) a bug; b) a byte; c) a chip.

12. Silicon is mined from Silicon Valley, California. True or false?

Who made the first space flight?

The first space flight was made by Yuri Gagarin (USSR) in 1962. His flight lasted less than two hours.

Gagarin's spaceship went around the Earth once.

In 1969, people landed on the Moon for the first time.

13. Which country did the first people on the Moon come from?

What were the colonies?

In the first half of the 20th century, most of Africa and India were governed by European countries. The Europeans often took the best land and products for themselves. The countries they ruled were called colonies. People in the colonies wanted to govern themselves. Some colonies had to fight their rulers before they won their independence.

14. Which of these is not an African country: a) Nigeria; b) Argentina; c) Kenya?

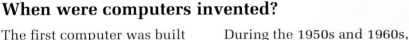

Africa was divided up as follows:

Britain
France
Portugal
Belgium
Spain

Algeria fought its rulers for eight years before it won independence, in 1962.

15. Which country ruled Algeria before it won independence?

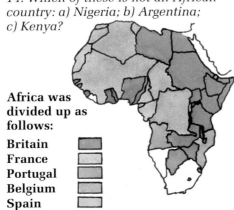

Djibouti was the last African country to gain independence, in 1977.

History Megaquiz

Try these quizzes to see how much you can remember from the rest of Part Four. Write your answers down and then check on page 128 to see how many you got right.

Famous people

Match the descriptions of these ten famous people with their names, listed in the blue box below.

1. A scientist who developed the theory of evolution.
2. An Ancient Egyptian king who died aged 18.
3. A leader of the Moslem army during the Crusades.
4. The title given to the Aztec king.
5. The inventor of the first fuel-driven car.
6. The first person to fly a powered plane.
7. The leader of Germany in the 1930s and 1940s.
8. The scientist who was imprisoned for writing that the Earth travels around the Sun.
9. The last tsar of Russia.
10. The hero of Homer's epic poem, the *Odyssey*.

a) Adolf Hitler
b) Orville Wright
c) Galileo
d) Odysseus
e) Nicholas II
f) Tutankhamun
g) Great Speaker
h) Saladin
i) Karl Benz
j) Charles Darwin

Clothes and fashions

Who wore these costumes and hairstyles?

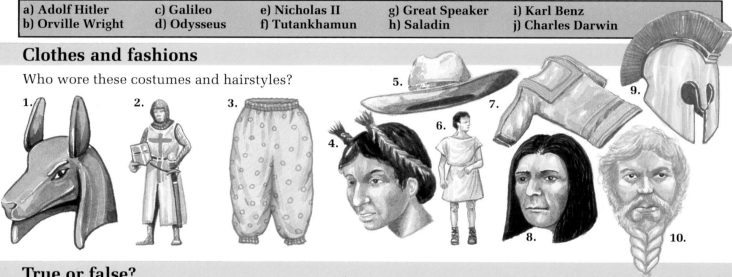

True or false?

1. The Ancient Romans used soap to get clean.
2. Viking warriors were buried or burned in ships.
3. Cowboys rode bicycles around cattle farms.
4. The first computer was smaller than this book.
5. The women's parts in Greek plays were played by men.
6. Dr Edward Jenner found a way to stop people from catching smallpox.
7. The car that the Ford Motor Company first sold in 1908 was called the Model X.
8. During a siege, castle dwellers were allowed out to fetch food and water.
9. Tenochtitlan, the Aztec capital, was built in the middle of a lake.
10. At the Greek sports festival in Olympia, winners received gold medals.

Which came first?

Can you put each set of three people, animals or things in order of appearance or invention?

1. Tyrannosaurus rex; Stegosaurus; jellyfish.
2. Viking; *conquistador*; Bolshevik.
3. Computer; steam engine; horse and cart.
4. Cannon; sword; six-shooter.
5. Tsar Nicholas II; Richard I; Tutankhamun.
6. Inoculation; television; water well.
7. Model T Ford; Viking longship; chariot.
8. Pyramid; Palace of Alhambra; nuclear power station.
9. Amelia Bloomer; Homer; Lenin.
10. USSR; Roman Empire; Inca Empire.

Close-ups

These are all close-ups of parts of pictures in Part Four. Can you recognize what they show?

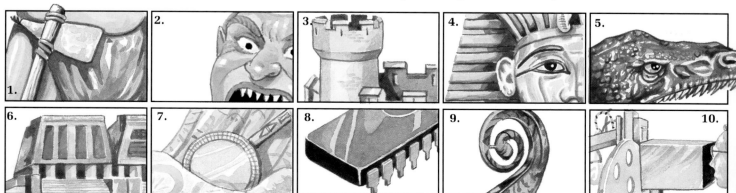

Where in the world?

Can you match the places marked on the map with the descriptions below?

1. Christopher Columbus was trying to sail to this country when he landed in America.
2. The Cultural Revolution took place in this country.
3. There was a nuclear accident here in 1986.
4. *Conquistadores* came from this country.
5. There are hieroglyphics in the tombs here.
6. The Aztecs used to live here.
7. A famous sports festival was held in this city.
8. The Circus Maximus was in this city.
9. The scientist Galileo lived in this country.
10. This country had the first passenger train service.

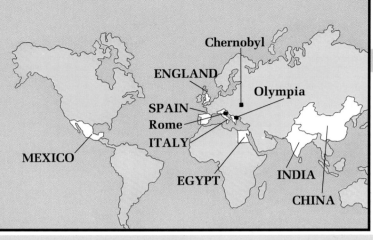

The time line

Can you match these events with the dates on the time line below?

1. Modern man first appears.
2. Homer the poet makes up the *Iliad*.
3. Spanish *conquistadores* attack the Aztecs.
4. Dinosaurs dominate the Earth.
5. Egyptians start building pyramids.
6. Rome is the most powerful city in Europe.
7. Vikings begin exploring the world.
8. The People's Crusade begins.
9. Cannons are invented.
10. The first people land on the Moon.

100 million years ago

About 2,630BC

About 40,000 years ago

About 800BC   About 750AD   About 1400   1521
            0AD   1096   1969

What do you know?

1. Most Ancient Egyptians were not buried in pyramids. Where were they buried?
2. What lived on Earth until 65 million years ago?
3. Can you name a group of people who were not allowed to vote in Ancient Athens?
4. What was the name given to Viking story tellers?
5. Which company made the best-selling car ever?
6. Tsar is a Russian word. What does it mean?
7. What weapon gave European invaders a big advantage over the Aztecs and Incas?
8. Were the first TV pictures in colour or black and white?
9. Where might you find a loop, a crenel and a merlon?
10. When hunting, what did American Indians often wear to disguise themselves?

Silhouettes

All these silhouettes are of things that appear in Part Four. How many can you recognize?

What else do you know?

1. Which was the biggest dinosaur?
2. What country did the first man in space come from?
3. Besides comedies, what sort of plays could you watch in a Greek theatre?
4. What was in the Montgolfier brothers' balloon to make it rise?
5. On the tracks which crossed the Inca Empire, how long did it usually take travellers to walk from one rest house to another?
6. What did the Ancient Romans watch at the Colosseum?
7. What new type of fuel was used in power stations in the 1950s?
8. Did the Ancient Romans know how to make hot water?
9. Who led the Christian army against Saladin during the Crusades?
10. What was the name given to the huge cattle farms where cowboys worked?

Quiz answers

The answers to the 12 quizzes from *The dinosaur age* to *The twentieth century* are on the next four pages. Give yourself one point for every answer you get right. The chart below helps you to find out how well you have done in each quiz.

0-5	Read through the answers, then try the quiz again. See how many answers you can remember second time around.	11-14	Good score. If you get this score on most of the quizzes, you can be very pleased with yourself.
6-10	Quite good. Think carefully about the questions and you might get more answers right.	15	Excellent. If you do this well in more than half the quizzes, you are a history genius!

Your score overall

You can find out your average score over all 12 quizzes like this:

1. Add up your scores on all 12 quizzes.
2. Divide this total by 12. This is your average score. How well did you do?

General knowledge

All the answers to general knowledge questions are marked ★. These questions are probably the hardest in the quizzes. Add up how many of them you got right across all 12 quizzes. There are 50 of them in total. If you got over 30 right, your general knowledge is good.

The dinosaur age

1. a) Dinosaur means "terrible lizard".
2. The name Tyrannosaurus rex means "Tyrant Lizard King".
3. Stegosaurus used its tail as a weapon.
4. True. Dinosaurs laid tough, leathery eggs in the sand.
5. b) Bones preserved in rock are called fossils.
6. False. Brachiosaurus was too big to climb trees.
7. True. No one knows what colour dinosaurs were as no skins remain.
★ 8. c) A hippopotamus is a mammal.
9. b) Animal life evolved from bacteria in the sea.
10. No. No dinosaurs could fly. However, flying reptiles such as pterodactyls lived during the dinosaur age.

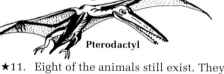
Pterodactyl

★11. Eight of the animals still exist. They are: crocodile, frog, snake, tortoise, ape, human, jellyfish and shrew. Only score a point if you spotted them all. If you spotted the shrew but did not get its name right, score a point anyway, since it is difficult to identify.
★12. a) A meat-eater is a carnivore. A herbivore eats plants. Animals that eat meat and plants are omnivores.
13. No. The biggest dinosaur found so far is Brachiosaurus. These pictures show how big it was compared to T. rex.

14. c) About 800 different kinds of dinosaur have been found so far.
15. None. Man did not exist.

Ancient Egypt

★ 1. There is still a country called Egypt. It has been called Egypt for nearly 5,000 years.

2. False. All the ancient pyramids still exist, although poorly built ones have partly collapsed.
3. Anubis was a type of dog called a jackal. (Score a point if you guessed dog.)
4. b) Embalmed bodies are known as mummies.
5. True. You can see mummies in some history museums.
6. c) Elizabeth I was not a queen of Egypt. She was Queen of England from 1558 to 1603.
7. The pointed capstone went at the top of the pyramid.
8. b) A sphynx has a lion's body.
9. The pyramids were covered with white limestone (see page 100).
★10. Egyptian kings were called pharoahs.

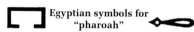
Egyptian symbols for "pharoah"

★11. No. Tutankhamun's tomb was cut into the rock. When Tutankhamun reigned, the pyramids were already historic monuments over 1,200 years old.
12. Egyptian children did not usually wear any clothes at all during the summer (see picture on page 101).
★13. Cairo. This is the capital city of Egypt.
★14. c) The symbols on the wall were called hieroglyphics.
15. The symbol on the right means "to walk".

Ancient Greece

★ 1. Athens is the present capital of Greece (see map below).
2. On page 102, the mask on the left shows happiness and the other mask shows anger. (Score a point if you guessed other similar feelings.)

Mask of a tragic heroine

3. Yes. Translations of some Ancient Greek plays are still performed.
4. False. The Greeks built open-air theatres in hillside hollows so that actors' voices would be heard right at the back.
5. b) Democracy means "governed by the people".
6. True. Olives were valuable. They were crushed to make olive oil, which was sold to foreign traders.
7. a) Homer's poems were called epics.
★ 8. Greece is part of Europe.
★ 9. The model horse was made of wood.
10. c) Odysseus took ten years to return home to Troy. This map shows where Troy probably was.

11. b) Another name for a one-eyed monster is a cyclops.
12. From left to right the gods are: a) Poseidon; d) Athene; b) Aphrodite; c) Zeus.
13. True. This is one luxury that the Spartans allowed themselves.
14. From left to right the sports are: discus throwing, wrestling, relay racing, javelin throwing.
15. The Olympic Games are named after the sports festival at Olympia.

Ancient Rome

★ 1. Julius Caesar. He ruled Rome from 49BC until 44BC, when he was murdered by his rivals.

★ 2. Rome is now the capital of Italy (see map below).

The Roman Empire is shaded in grey.

GREECE
Rome
ITALY

3. True. In some hot countries where there is not much water, people use olive oil to clean themselves.

4. True. Wealthy Romans had a form of central heating called a hypocaust in their homes. Hot air flowed under the floors and up the walls through channels built of hollow tiles.

5. The month of March is named after the Roman god Mars.

★ 6. c) Neptune was the Roman god of the sea.

7. a) Spartacus was a professional fighter who organized a revolt against the Roman government in 73BC. He was defeated in 71BC.

8. a) The fighters were called gladiators.

9. If spectators wanted a fighter to die, they gave a thumbs-down sign. If they wanted a fighter to live, they gave a thumbs-up sign.

Live   Die

10. True. The largest soccer stadium in the world, the Maracana Stadium in Brazil, holds 205,000 people.

Circus Maximus

Maracana Stadium

11. The driver used his knife to cut himself free if there was a crash.

12. At the baths, there are slaves giving a massage, plucking hair and tending the furnace. (Only score a point if you noticed all three.)

13. The building is the toilet block.

★14. a) The Ancient Romans spoke Latin.

15. False. Roman men wore tunics or togas. Togas were for formal wear. They were very heavy. Tunics were much lighter and more comfortable. Togas were made out of a piece of cloth 5m (15ft) in diameter.

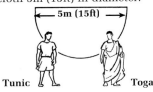

|← 5m (15ft) →|

Tunic   Toga

The Vikings

★ 1. The Vikings came from the lands which are now the countries Denmark, Norway and Sweden. This area is now called Scandinavia. Score a point if you got any of these.

Sweden
Norway
Denmark

2. Vikings fastened their shields to the sides of their ships during voyages (see picture on page 107).

3. Vikings used swords most often. They even gave their swords names, such as Fierce One and Leg Biter.

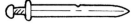 Viking sword

4. One Viking has been killed.

5. b) Viking boats were called longships.

6. Vikings could make their ships move in two ways. When it was windy they used a sail. When it was calm they rowed the ship. Score a point if you got either of these.

Sail for windy weather.   Oars used in calm weather.

★ 7. The hole in the roof let smoke from a fire inside the house escape.

8. a) Viking stories were called sagas. A saga might last as long as a feature film does today.

9. b) The name Viking comes from the Viking word for adventurer.

★10. North America was further from the Vikings' home than Ireland.

11. True. The Vikings used skis and skates made of smoothed bone for winter trading journeys.

Viking skate

12. a) Viking heaven was called Valhalla. It meant "palace of the killed".

13. c) Herod the Great was a ruler of Palestine who died in 4BC.

14. Thursday is named after Thor, the Viking god of thunder. The other weekdays are named after the following:

Sunday: the Sun
Monday: the Moon
Tuesday: Tyr, Viking god of law
Wednesday: Odin, Viking god of war
Friday: Frigg, Viking goddess of love
Saturday: Saturn, Roman god of farming

15. False. There is no special name for Viking women.

The Crusades

1. The wall around Jerusalem was there to protect the city. (Score a point if you got the general idea.)

★ 2. Jesus Christ was born in Bethlehem.

★ 3. b) This area of water is called the Red Sea.

★ 4. This soldier is wearing a type of meshed metal armour called chain-mail.

5. Yes, whole families joined the Crusades. One Crusade, called the Children's Crusade, which set off in 1212, consisted of thousands of children. Most starved to death or were sold as slaves before they reached Palestine.

6. True. Most of the People's Crusaders died from disease or lack of food.

7. True. Moslems rode small Arab horses which could dart around the battlefield. The Crusaders' horses were heavier and slower. They had to carry a knight in full armour.

Arab horse   **Crusader's horse**

8. a) Saladin's sword was called a scimitar. The Crusaders' swords, called broadswords, were heavier.

Scimitar 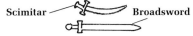 **Broadsword**

9. b) Moslem soldiers were called Saracens.

★10. Richard I was called "the Lionheart" because of his courage. Lions are supposed to be brave animals.

11. c) The Crusaders did not take potatoes back to Europe. These were first taken to Europe from America about 300 years after the Crusades.

12. The numbers as they appear from left to right are 1,4,7 and 9. Here is the whole set of numbers used by Moslem mathematicians, from 0 to 9.

0 1 2 3 4 5 6 7 8 9

13. True. The Moslems ruled lands in Africa, Asia and Europe.

14. False. The Palace of Alhambra was built for Granada's Moslem kings.

★15. The game is chess. The Moslems learned chess when they invaded India in the 11th and 12th centuries. It became popular all over the Moslem Empire.

Moslem chess pieces

King   Knight

A medieval castle

1. b) Medieval means belonging to the Middle Ages. This period lasted from the 5th to the 15th century.
2. The defenders got drinking water from a well. Its position in the picture on page 110 is shown here.

3. Round towers were stronger than square ones because rocks glanced off their surface and did less damage.
4. c) The fortified gatehouse is called a barbican.
5. a) The holes are called murder holes. If attackers went under the murder holes, the defenders fired at them through the holes or poured boiling liquid down onto them.
H 6. An underground cell for prisoners is called a dungeon.
7. False. Some castle sieges lasted up to a year. A besieged city could last out even longer. For example, the siege of Acre in Palestine in 1189 lasted for two years.
8. a) The archers are using longbows.

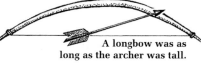

A longbow was as long as the archer was tall.

9. b) The explosive that fired a cannon was gunpowder. Dynamite was not invented until 1865.
10. True. The Chinese invented gunpowder about 1,200 years ago.
11. No, cannonballs did not explode.
H12. The order of invention is: c) spear, a) mangonel, b) tank. Spears have been used for thousands of years. An early type of mangonel was built by the Ancient Greeks. Tanks were first used in 1916, during World War I.
H13. This type of bridge is called a drawbridge. It could be drawn up to make the castle harder to reach.

Drawbridge down   Drawbridge up

H14. The weapon is called a battering ram. The attackers used it to break down the castle gates.
H15. The channel of water is called a moat. Early castles were often built on a man-made mound of earth. The earth was dug from a circular trench which was usually filled with water to make a moat.

The Aztecs and the Incas

H 1. b) The Andes ran through the Inca Empire. The Alps are in Europe and the Himalayas are in Asia.
2. c) The Spanish invaders were called *conquistadores*, which is the Spanish word for "conquerors".
3. True. Incas bred guinea pigs to eat during religious festivals.
4. b) The capital of Mexico is Mexico City. It is the world's biggest city. Part of it covers the site of the old city of Tenochtitlan.

This Aztec building was found when a railway tunnel was dug in Mexico city.

5. a) The Aztecs thought the warrior was the most important. You can tell this because his clothes are finer than the farmer's or the weaver's.
6. True. They also made a red dye, called cochineal, out of beetles, and green dye out of tree bark.
7. The rug is worth more than the bird. This is why the bird-seller is offering cocoa beans as part of the deal.
8. The picture shows the Aztec god of war. He is carrying weapons.
9. a) Swapping goods instead of selling them is called bartering. The picture below shows some examples of what cocoa beans were worth.

Cocoa beans
Feather coat, worth 10,000 cocoa beans.
Canoe, worth 100 cocoa beans.

10. c) The bird is a turkey. Until the 1500s, turkeys were only found in America. They were taken to Europe by the Spanish.
H11. It is a llama. Llamas came from the area now called Peru.

Peru
SOUTH AMERICA
Inca llama brooch

12. False. There were no horses in America until they were brought by the Spaniards.
13. The Spaniards sailed to South America. They crossd the Atlantic Ocean in ships called galleons.
14. True. Colds and other European illnesses such as measles were deadly to the Aztecs and Incas.
15. b) Today, most South Americans speak Spanish.

Inventions and discoveries

1. The trousers were called bloomers, after Amelia Bloomer.
H 2. The man is wearing a top hat.
3. Saturn. (It is labelled in the picture above on page 114.)
H 4. Galileo was right. Galileo developed the telescope, with which he was able to watch the planets.

Galileo was the first to see the planet Saturn, in 1610.

Galileo's telescope

5. Scientists who study stars and planets are called astronomers.
H 6. Steam engines pulled trains and powered ships and early types of car. They were also used to power machinery in mines. Score a point if you got any of these.

A steamship made in 1850.

H 7. a) The period of change following the invention of the steam engine is called the Industrial Revolution.
8. Cinema came before television. The first cinema showing was made in Paris in 1895, by Auguste and Louis Lumière.
9. b) The first regular TV broadcasts were made in 1936. The first colour broadcast was in 1953.
10. b) Inoculations are also called vaccinations. This comes from the Latin word *vacca*, meaning "cow".
11. True. Dairymaids often caught cowpox from the cows they milked. Jenner noticed that those who had caught cowpox rarely got smallpox.
12. c) A cold cannot be prevented by inoculation. Here are some more diseases, though, which can: polio, chicken pox, whooping cough, typhoid and cholera.
13. b) Darwin's theory was called evolution (see page 115).
14. a) The birds are all types of finch.
H15. The correct order of invention is: b) steam power; c) electricity; a) nuclear power. The first steam engine was made in about 1700. Electric power was first produced by a battery made in 1800. Nuclear power was first demonstrated in 1942.

The first electric battery looked like this.

The Wild West

★ 1. The Indian tent on page 116 is a teepee. Score a point if you said teepee or wigwam, though, as many Indians lived in wigwams. A wigwam (shown below) was often covered with leaves and branches.

Wigwam

2. The tents were made from buffalo hides. Score a point if you said leather or animal skins.

★ 3. An American Indian woman is called a squaw.

4. b) For good luck in battle, Indians danced a wardance.

5. c) American Indians wore moccasins on their feet.

6. c) The cattle are longhorn cattle.

7. True. Horses were taken to America by Spanish conquerors about 500 years ago. American Indians tamed and rode the horses that escaped from the Spaniards.

★ 8. It is a lasso or lariat. This is a rope with a loop tied with a sliding knot.

If the loop is tugged, the knot tightens.   **Sliding knot**

9. a) The Indians called guns "smoke sticks".

★10. c) They are all members of American Indian tribes except a Zulu, who is a South African tribesperson.

★11. Canada and the USA make up North America. Score a point if you got them both. The other countries are in South America.

Alaska is part of the USA. **Canada** **USA** **NORTH AMERICA**

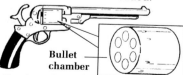

12. a) Most cowboys wore stetsons.

13. Cowboys' hats had wide brims to keep the sun out of their eyes.

14. The pistol was called a six-shooter because it fired six shots before it had to be reloaded.

Bullet chamber

★15. Cowboys branded cattle so that they knew who the cattle belonged to. If branded cattle were stolen, people could identify them.

Trains, cars and planes

1. There are seven different forms of transport on pages 118-119: horse and carriage, train, horseback, car, balloon, plane and airship. Only score a point if you spotted all seven.

2. True. A galloping horse can travel at 45kmph (28mph). The first trains went at about 20kmph (12mph).

3. No. The Russian Empire collapsed in 1923 (see page 118).

★ 4. b) The longest railway is the Trans-Siberian Railway. The area it crosses (shown on the map on page 118) is called Siberia.

★ 5. A modern car company that uses Karl Benz's name is Mercedes-Benz. A car made by Mercedes-Benz has this badge.

6. The handle, called a crank, was turned to start the engine. The first car that had a starter motor was made by Cadillac in 1912.

1912 Cadillac

7. b) For several years the Ford Model T was only available in black. For speed, Ford used quick-drying paint, which, until 1923, was only made in black.

★ 8. The car is a Beetle, or Bug.

★ 9. The engine of a Volkswagen Beetle is at the back of the car.

10. a) Air-filled tyres are called pneumatic tyres. The word comes from the Greek word *pneuma*, meaning "breath".

11. a) Volkswagen means "people's car" in German.

12. a) The canoe came first. This was probably the earliest form of transport. The bicycle was invented in 1839.

13. False. However, the earliest designs for aircraft, such as those by Leonardo da Vinci (1452-1519), included flapping wings.

Leonardo da Vinci's design for a man-powered aircraft.

14. False. Airships crashed quite often.

15. False. Although Zeppelins were huge, most of the space was filled with gas. Passengers sat in the gondola (see picture on page 119). Even large Zeppelins could carry only 50 or so people.

The twentieth century

1. The Bolshevik flag was red. You can see one in the first picture on page 120. The communist government later put a hammer and sickle on the flag. These represented the tools used by industrial workers and rural peasants.

2. True. Nicholas II was the last tsar.

★ 3. The Nazi leader was Adolf Hitler. He became *Führer* (leader) of Germany in 1933. He killed himself in 1945 when the Nazis lost World War II.

★ 4. b) The Nazi symbol was a swastika.

Swastika

5. No. The German army did not invade Great Britain.

6. b) Countries that join forces are called allies.

7. World War II lasted six years, from 1939-1945. More than 50 million people died during it. That is about as many people as live in Australia, Canada and Holland put together.

8. a) There have been two World Wars. World War I lasted from 1914-1918.

9. b) A war between people of the same country is called a civil war.

★10. The USSR was the first country to have a communist government. Score a point if you guessed USSR, Russia or the Russian Empire.

11. c) It is called a chip.

12. False. Silicon Valley has this name because so much computer industry is based there.

★13. The first people on the Moon came from the USA. Between 1969 and 1972, six US missions explored the Moon. The last two took vehicles, called lunar rovers, with them. The lunar rovers are still on the Moon.

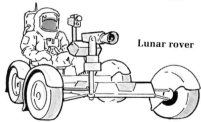

Lunar rover

★14. b) Argentina is a country in South America. Nigeria is in west Africa and Kenya is in east Africa.

15. Algeria was ruled by France before it won independence in 1962.

History Megaquiz answers

There are 100 possible points in the History Megaquiz. If you score over 50 you have done well. Over 75 is an excellent score. You can find out more about each answer on the page listed after it.

Famous people

1. j) Charles Darwin (page 115).
2. f) Tutankhamun (page 101).
3. h) Saladin (page 109).
4. g) Great Speaker (page 112).
5. i) Karl Benz (page 118).
6. b) Orville Wright (page 119).
7. a) Adolf Hitler (page 120).
8. c) Galileo (page 114).
9. e) Nicholas II (page 120).
10. d) Odysseus (pages 102 and 103).

Clothes and fashion

1. Anubis or Egyptian priest (page 100).
2. Crusader (pages 108 and 109).
3. Amelia Bloomer (page 114).
4. Aztec (page 113).
5. Cowboy (pages 116 and 117).
6. Roman (pages 104 and 105).
7. American Indian (page 116).
8. Egyptian (page 100).
9. Greek or Spartan soldier (page 103).
10. Viking (pages 106 and 107).

True or false?

1. False (page 104).
2. True (page 107).
3. False (page 116).
4. False (page 121).
5. True (page 102).
6. True (page 115).
7. False (page 119).
8. False (page 111).
9. True (page 112).
10. False (page 103).

Which came first?

1. Jellyfish; Stegosaurus; T. rex.
2. Viking; *conquistador*; Bolshevik.
3. Horse and cart; steam engine; computer.
4. Sword; cannon; six-shooter.
5. Tutankhamun; Richard I; Nicholas II.
6. Water well; inoculation; television.
7. Chariot; Viking longship; Model T Ford.
8. Pyramid; Palace of Alhambra; nuclear power station.
9. Homer; Amelia Bloomer; Lenin.
10. Roman Empire; Inca Empire; USSR.

Close-ups

1. Tomahawk (page 116).
2. Greek actor's mask (page 102).
3. Castle (page 110).
4. Tutankhamun's mask (page 101).
5. Tyrannosaurus rex (page 99).
6. Aztec Great Temple (page 113).
7. Mirror (page 109).
8. Computer chip (page 121).
9. Viking longship (page 107).
10. Early television (page 114).

Where in the world?

1. India (page 117).
2. China (page 121).
3. Chernobyl (page 115).
4. Spain (page 113).
5. Egypt (page 101).
6. Mexico (page 112).
7. Olympia (page 103).
8. Rome (page 105).
9. Italy (page 114).
10. England (page 118).

The time line

1. About 40,000 years ago (page 99).
2. About 800BC (page 102).
3. 1521 (page 113).
4. 100 million years ago (page 98).
5. About 2,630BC (pages 100 and 101).
6. 0AD (page 104).
7. About 750AD (pages 106 and 107).
8. 1096 (page 108).
9. About 1400 (page 111).
10. 1969 (page 121).

What do you know?

1. In the sand (page 101).
2. Dinosaurs (page 98).
3. Women or slaves. Score a point for either (page 102).
4. Bards (page 107).
5. Volkswagen (page 119).
6. Emperor (page 120).
7. The gun (page 113).
8. Black and white (page 114).
9. A castle (page 110).
10. Animal skins (page 116).

Silhouettes

1. Dinosaur or Parasaurolophus (page 99).
2. Power station (page 115).
3. Greek athlete (page 103).
4. Teepee or wigwam (page 116).
5. Benz's car or early car (page 118).
6. Finch or bird (page 115).
7. Mangonel (page 111).
8. Roman chariot (page 105).
9. Pyramids (pages 100 and 101).
10. Invicta or steam engine (page 118).

What else do you know?

1. Brachiosaurus (page 98).
2. USSR (page 121).
3. Tragedies (page 102).
4. Hot air (page 119).
5. One day (page 112).
6. Fights, or the Games (pages 104 and 105).
7. Nuclear fuel (page 115).
8. Yes (page 104).
9. Richard I or "the Lionheart" (page 109).
10. Ranches (pages 116).

General index

First published in 1993 by Usborne Publishing Ltd, Usborne House, 83-85 Saffron Hill, London, EC1 8RT London.
Printed in Hong Kong / China.
This edition published by in 1998 by Tiger Books International PLC, Twickenham.
ISBN 1-85501-981-7